A ROOT OF JESSE

Besides my arm being broken, it was dislocated; eleven teeth were completely uprooted; my left shoulder was out of joint; part of the right cheekbone was broken off, and pus flowed from it for three months. My mouth was so badly frazzled I could not even drink a cup of tea. We wired to Rajahmundry and Brother W. rushed to the scene the following day. On Monday morning a Hindu came and insisted on seeing me, though I was in no mood to receive visitors. He persisted and finally I agreed to let him come in. He said, "Sir, I brought you part of your mouth which I found on the bridge," and produced a plate with two teeth affixed. He of course had never seen such a contrivance.

You may wonder what I'm doing in Rajahmundry. Well, I'm visiting with my wife's father and mother! Charley was best man and Frank gave the bride away. So I'm a poor henpecked man now. I've got me a wife, finally. I'll send you some snapshots in the near future, also an official announcement at the same time. Love to all.

Camels! Disdainful, arrogant camels, thirty-two of them, carrying beds, rugs, tent equipment, children, pots and pans, even chickens—everything for their people. The women all dressed like Bedouins, in draped black. The children and men leading the camels, or watching that the goats, cows, and calves keep to the path, are dressed in beautifully-folded, filthy padded coats or quilts. Wooly camels—some very dark—led along in "chains," by ropes tied to their nose pegs.

The news of President Roosevelt's death on April 14th, 1945, shared front page space in the Tribune *with a report that Clipper Smith finished second in the Petaluma marathon and that the city of Healdsburg had hired a dog catcher and opened the first dog pound in its history. Nearly 400 people attended the plaza memorial service for the president, and that same night the Cub Scouts celebrated their first anniversary at the Healdsburg Elementary School Auditorium.*

The Korean War began to claim local boys' lives. Some of my classmates began to be killed in action and were tallied up in the Tribune. *The transfer student to whom I lost the student body presidency was killed when his bomber was shot down. Bubby, who upset Bruce Holbrook in the boxing show, died at the Cho Sin reservoir. Rita Rose's brother was blinded by mortar fire. Before the year was out, Gil, Bobby, and Tiger Pat would all be in the Army.*

Jesse and Mother on their wedding day, Rajahmundry, 1936

A ROOT OF JESSE

David E. Manley

Strawberry Hill Press

Strawberry Hill Press
3848 S.E. Division Street
Portland, Oregon 97202-1641

Cover design by Ku, Fu-sheng
Cover artwork by Brian M. Bowe
Book design & typesetting by Brian M. Bowe

Manufactured in the United States of America

Library of Congress Cataloging-in-Publication Data

Manley, David E., 1934–
  A Root of Jesse/David E. Manley
    p.   cm.
  ISBN 0-89407-090-8 : $14.95
  1. Manley, David E., 1934– —Childhood and youth. 2. Actors—United States—Biography. 3. Newspaper editors—United States—Biography. I. Title.
PN2287.M29A3 1997
792' .028'092—dc20
[B]   93-26072
                                                CIP

For my Shirley
Night and day, you are the one

Acknowledgments

For their contributions to this book, I am grateful to the Healdsburg Museum and Historical Society, my sister Margaret Kressler, my aunt Theodora Neudoerffer, my cousins Mary Stewart and Chellie Rowland, my father's "chums" Ev Leger Jensen, Bernard Hansard, and Ralph Hoberg. Linfield (formerly McMinnville) College and Wittenberg University provided records of my parents' student years. Anne Marie Murphy, librarian at the Cloverdale, California, public library was especially helpful in providing me with resource material. Jim and Karen Apland provided friendship and faith in this book when it was most needed. Floriani Productions allowed us to use their computer equipment.

Finally, I want to thank my two adult daughters, Julie and Jocelyn, who were ever in my thoughts as this book was being written.

One

THE STUMPS OF A MOUNTAIN RANGE that was once as high as the Himalayas form a great, jagged plateau in southern India. This plateau is ringed with peaks and, except for canyon-cuts and river gorges, it drops steeply away in granite cliffs to the sea or to narrow coastal plains. In 1934, some of the densest jungles in the world encircled the plateau like a moat.

One of the twelve great rivers of India, the Godavari, flows eastward through the wild ridges of this plateau, and, gathering momentum, drops rapidly through the jungle to the crescent of the eastern plain. As the river broadens on its sweep to the Bay of Bengal it becomes vast until, sixty miles inland, it fractures into a fertile delta—a great expanse of rice fields dotted with villages.

At the delta-head in Rajahmundry my maternal grandfather, the Reverend Ernest Neudoerffer, presided over his Lutheran mission and seminary. Here the dun and dusty plains seemed to stretch to infinity. During April, May, and June, the heat on the plains was nearly unbearable, especially since there was no electricity for fans. In the afternoons, a hot wind carried dust up into the air, and vultures that looked as large as pterodactyls to me soared on upward wind-drafts. Whirling dust storms often turned the sky a brassy color.

Then the rains would come in July, often with violent squalls or a tropical cyclone. Rainy days were mixed with heavy, humid days, and the plowing and sowing of paddies would begin. But cyclones in late summer and autumn months, blowing in from the Bay of Bengal, often caused terrible havoc in the densely populated delta lands.

During the rainy season, the Godavari River ran two miles wide as it thundered past my grandfather's mission. It used to frighten me so that I would call for my mother in the night when we stayed there. The delta became a sheet of water, with only village sites, canal banks, and road and field boundaries visible above it. Later in the year, as the rice grew higher, the dividing boundaries were hidden and the whole delta looked like a single rice field. Only the sails of boats, like fins of cruising sharks gliding through the main canals, broke the sea of green crop.

On the other side of the great plateau, in a southwestern pocket, lie the Nilgiri hills. These hills derive their name from the Hindustani words *nila*, "blue," and *giri*, "mountain." Towering above all other mountains south of the Himalayas, their summits are always masked by light-blue clouds; because of this they were named *Nilgiri*, "blue mountains."

When I was a boy, a dense jungle, infested with panthers and snakes, stretched out on every side of the hills as if to guard their every entrance. The interior landscape was broken into ridges, hills, and valleys at altitudes of five to seven thousand feet, while the highest peak, Mt. Doda Betta, was covered in clouds nine thousand feet above sea level. Here, with temperatures of 38° to 68° in cold weather and 55° to 75° in the summer, a privileged few could escape the heat of the plains.

Half the Nilgiri area is forested, but much of it is rolling green pasture land interspersed with small forests (*sholas*). In the *sholas* grow rhododendron, tree-orchids, blackberries, the Nilgiri lily, and the alpine wild strawberry. In a small village in this mountain paradise, my grandfather Neudoerffer owned a summer home that he named "The Roses."

These two villages, one on the plains and one in the mountains, were as dramatically different from each other as the Indian and American cultures would seem to me.

The missionary roots ran deep on both sides of my family. My father's parents, Will and Alice Manley, were the first Baptist missionary team from Kansas. They were sent to India in 1879. The American Baptist Mission had been ready to abandon their work in India when Will and Alice were posted there, and they are credited in Baptist history for reviving the Christian effort. Will was eventually rewarded with the pulpit of the largest church in Madras, where he served for over ten years until 1916 when it was "physically impossible for him to continue." They retired to America where Jesse's brother Bill looked after them until Will died in 1919 and Alice in 1926 from "rigors of life in India," according to the Baptist *Missionary Review*.

Life was rigorous for missionaries in India. They did not usually have the British government's recognition or support, and among the Indian people they were treated as the lowest class of Hindu—the Untouchable. Since they were Untouchables, they were easy prey for robbers when they traveled the unpopulated wilds. There is a story of my grandmother Alice's bravery on one such occasion. Before leaving on a tour, Will and Alice were warned that thieves on the roads were robbing travelers with impunity. They nevertheless set off in a bullock cart and sang hymns, so it is said. The cart lost a wheel in a remote area, and as Will was repairing it, three men—with oily hair and beards and dressed in rags—emerged from the woods and approached the cart stealthily. Evidently these robbers had never seen Europeans before because they hesitated at first, thinking my fair-skinned grandmother to be a goddess. But they soon gathered courage and began to walk boldly toward her. Alice evidently knew the local dialect well enough to comprehend that they were intent on robbing her of two large trunks full of clothing and goods for the poor, and she quickly ordered them to stop their approach or she would "bring fire down upon them." This halted their advance momentarily, and she was able to fish a large wooden matchstick out of her bag. Then they came on, and when the robbers grew "so close that I could smell their foul breath," she lit the match on the wooden cart and jammed the flaming stick into their beards—one by one. Evidently Will hastily fixed the cart during this scene, and as the robbers rolled in the dirt trying to douse the flames, Will and Alice fled in the cart. Alice told this story herself, and no one in our family doubted it. Alice Manley was not known to be a braggart nor frivolous with her words.

While Will and Alice's service in India brought tributes from the Baptist Mission, it created painful schisms within the Manley clan. Seven sons and three daughters (one daughter died in India) were produced by Will and Alice while they were abroad, and all the children were given away to be raised by Kansas Baptists or sent to orphanages while they were in their infancy.

Remarkably, most of the Manley boys forgave Will and Alice for sending them so young to America. Though almost all missionaries sent their children to stateside boarding schools sooner or later, the Manley boys were children when they were shipped to America to earn their keep on farms. It amounted to indentured labor.

My maternal grandfather, Ernest Neudoerffer, was posted to India in 1900. Turn-of-the-century missionaries are often ridiculed as having been effete and naive, among other things, but no one would have dared to ridicule my grandfather Neudoerffer on those grounds. He considered himself God's warrior. His favorite hymns were battle hymns: "Onward Christian Soldiers," "A Mighty Fortress Is Our God," "The Son of God Goes Forth to War." Unlike modern evangelists, Grandfather Neudoerffer and Grandfather Manley believed that when men or women pledged their lives to Christ, they were bound to give up all their worldly goods, take up the cross, and follow Him. If it led to martyrdom, so much the better. This made both my grandfathers very brave men, for they were completely unafraid of wounds or even of death. Were wounds not battle scars? I once asked Grandfather Neudoerffer if he really believed that faith could move mountains. "Wasn't that a slight exaggeration?" I asked. "Absolutely not," he said. It only served to show how little faith men really had.

I see my grandfather Neudoerffer now as clearly as if I were still looking up at him as a small boy, so deeply are his physical attributes and personality etched in my mind. His stocky, stolid build is dressed in ministerial black, thick gray hair surrounds his dark slab of a face, and he seldom smiles. In my memory he will always be standing before his stone house on the plains. The house and the man look as if they had been quarried together. I think of him as a thundering Old Testament prophet—full of force and power. And yet he could be tender too. He lost two wives to India, and when my mother's mother died, he wrote on March 15, 1915:

I do not seem to live in this world as I used to—the fact is, if it were not for our precious children, and for the great and holy work to which I believe the Lord has called me, which I also believe I have not yet completed, I should feel like asking the Lord to take me too.

Like Will Manley, Ernest Neudoerffer went to the most savage outposts with a fervor and determination to save souls that now almost defy understanding. He set out to do physical as well as spiritual battle with his mortal enemy, the devil. He faithfully kept a journal and in 1900, before being assigned to India, he wrote:

This finally meant that I should choose between India, China, and Madagascar. It may seem childish when I say that Madagascar appealed to me for one special reason—there was opportunity to suffer martyrdom! I had seen pictures of how cruelly the natives put missionaries to death. They would tie a rope around the neck, hang them over a precipice, and cut the rope, thus sending them to a terrible death. Such was my youthful aspiration!

Unlike many missionaries who fancied themselves scholarly theologians, Christian anthropologists, intellectual preachers, or Oriental students, he learned the common native Telegu and Tamil dialects fluently and disdained the aristocratic Urdu language. His quarrels with the missionary board began immediately after his arrival. "You are nothing less than a rebel, Neudoerffer," the director told him angrily, and Grandfather was dispatched as far away from the Rajahmundry headquarters as possible.

He was first sent, in November of 1900, to Tadepallegudem in the sweltering delta country. There, Grandfather could barely communicate with the outside world from his isolated station:

When I moved to Tadepallegudem there was a very nasty Brahmin postmaster in charge. He would not allow any Untouchable, including Christians, to come near him. He made them stand ten feet away. Anything a fellow wanted he got thrown at him, and he in turn threw money to the postmaster on his verandah. One day he came over to see me. He stood on the road calling me, not venturing to come in. I stayed in the doorway of my bungalow and would not go out. Thus we shouted at each other, doing our business.

Grandfather's first district had sixteen congregations in villages scattered throughout the delta, and he often walked thirty miles to get from one village to another when the canals were flooded or too dry to be navigable.

In his journal, he refers to himself as a "rough-neck, fearless even about tramping around in the dark." He writes that he went in many directions to visit congregations. In most of those places he slept under mango trees. Some, being tiger-infested, the people made large bonfires all around the place "where we roosted for the night to keep away the bloodthirsty animals."

In 1908 Grandfather Neudoerffer was recalled to mission headquarters in Rajahmundry by the same director who had banished him. In Grandfather's opinion, this director came to India only because he was "overcome by a pious streak." The director had said, in his original message to the missionaries, "I decide to accept the call to go to Rajahmundry, even if the pangs of hell overcome me." Grandfather Neudoerffer's journal notes that "subsequent stories will reveal that others suffered more pangs of hell than our director ever suffered." Apparently, however, my grandfather's hard work in the delta impressed the director—or maybe the director himself had had enough of India. In any case, the director departed India leaving his fields to my grandfather.

In 1908, at about the same time he took over the director's fields, Grandfather married the woman who would be my mother's mother. Julia Van de Veer was a beautiful and brilliant woman, but delicate:

I took leave of bachelordom and took unto myself a wife, the mission doctor, Dr. Van de Veer. Gradually I came to the conclusion that a missionary should be married for two good reasons: for his own sake and for the sake of the work. Two make a stronger team than just one person.

This applies to unmarried ladies who, in my humble opinion, should always move and work in pairs. The marriage day was a joyous one for the whole district. Since my new wife was a medical person, she would be able to help the sick and distressed. Work seemed so much easier now, and why not?

Grandfather was delighted when, in June of 1910, he inherited a houseboat for traveling the canals of the delta. His tramping days were over. The boat was named "The Dove of Peace," but was so frail and delicate that Grandfather called it "The Piece of Dove." The hull was made of iron and was built in the front yard of the bungalow. "It took fifty coolies to lug the hull to the harbor," grandfather wrote. More coolies constructed a *topee*, or sun helmet, for the boat "that made it look like Noah's Ark." The crude superstructure made the houseboat so top-heavy that two iron tubs had to be riveted on each side of it right underneath the kitchen. The tubs made the boat canal-worthy enough so that Grandfather could now tour his district in relative comfort.

My mother Ernestine was born in 1910 and, Theodora, her sister, was added to the family in 1912. Grandfather still did not have a bungalow to house his family in because the Lutheran mission board took two years to approve his plans.

Though my grandfather made light of it, he was always in danger because of quarreling sects and because of the caste system. Untouchables were always needed to perform coolie labor for the *ryots*, as landowners were called. When Untouchables became Christians, they were not always available for work, and the *ryots* and Hindus blamed the missionaries. Grandfather noted in his journal that:

One evening I was sitting on the verandah reading, when my friend the sub-inspector of police called. He said, "There is a rumor that you are taking one of the students to Tadepallegudem and from there by train to Ellore to make him a Christian. [By this he meant baptism.] Do not go. The people have arranged to waylay you at three different villages along the twenty-eight miles route to the station. We have a report that they not only want to steal the boy from you, but kill you too. They are armed with sticks and knives." Next morning I heard that these rowdies had waited most of the night for me.

By this time, my grandfather was accustomed to ambushes by Hindus, Moslems, and plain robbers. In order to avoid them and to travel quickly by land, he obtained a motorcycle. It was one of the first in India, and he was the first missionary to own one. I loved Grandfather Neudoerffer's motorcycle stories. In America, when we talked about our roots, other boys often made fun of my missionary upbringing. When they did, I told them about young Ernest and his death-defying motorcycle rides. One Sunday, his motorcycle almost killed him:

One Sunday morning I motorbiked to two villages for services. It was a hot day in May, 1914. On my return, as I was nearing the bridge crossing the canal at Bhimavaram, something happened—I do not know what. I think that in changing gears the clutch slipped into high, rushed like mad up the grade, and dashed into the stone wall of the bridge. The consequence was that I was thrown off my cycle to a distance of twenty feet, unconscious and a mess. Some Hindu cartman picked me up, loaded me onto his cart, and took me to the local doctor, a friend of mine. He did the best he could and put my broken right arm into a cast. That much done I was taken for another ride to my bungalow, dragged upstairs, and placed on my bed. Gradually, after about four hours, I became conscious and discovered that I was back home.

Besides my arm being broken, it was dislocated; eleven teeth were completely uprooted; my left shoulder was out of joint; part of the right cheekbone was broken off, and pus flowed from it for three months. My mouth was so badly frazzled I could not even drink a cup of tea. We wired to Rajahmundry and Brother W. rushed to the scene the following day. On Monday morning a Hindu came and insisted on seeing me, though I was in no mood to receive visitors. He persisted and finally I agreed to let him come in. He said, "Sir, I brought you part of your mouth which I found on the bridge," and produced a plate with two teeth affixed. He of course had never seen such a contrivance.

This was another one of those mercies of God I experienced which raised me from death to life to use me for further service. To this day I bear the marks of this adventure. My motorbike was a complete wreck. Ten days after my mishap I traveled to Tadepallegudem by oxcart and from there took the train to Rajahmundry to attend a meeting of the Council.

Shortly after this 1914 entry, my grandmother Julia died and Grandfather's journal becomes less precise. Also, World War I touched India in 1914 and, in spite of his own sorrow, Grandfather volunteered to help fellow German missionaries who were being interned because of the war. Grandfather himself never spoke of this, but Mother told me about it during World War II. I was disappointed because none of my family were or ever had been soldiers, and Mother pointed out that courage is not confined to the battlefield by telling me about Grandfather and the interned missionaries. In

1914 when the war began, the German missionaries in the Jaypore region were interned. The young men of military age were sent to a prisoner-of-war camp, and the older missionaries were put under house arrest in a large bungalow. These missionaries appealed to Grandfather's mission to come to their rescue, and after being turned down once, two of Grandfather's colleagues said they thought at least one man should be spared to help. According to Grandfather, they said, "I am willing to go, but do not send me!" This statement became a joke. Grandfather wrote that a voice within urged him to offer himself. "I heeded the voice and did so," he penned. "I said, as did the other brethren, 'I am willing to go.' But I added, 'send me.'"

Though he was a German himself, my grandfather did not hesitate to go. He even took my mother and my aunt along:

I might have hesitated to offer my services to the Jaypore field because only recently I had been left alone with my two young girls, but my faith was in the Lord who I believed had called me to this work. My Canadian citizenship came in handy; no one but a British subject would have been entrusted with the job given to me. I had brought my motorcycle with me. The roads were none too good; there were small streams unbridged and other difficulties. However, we got up the mountain and went from station to station. I was told that there was a man-eating tiger on the lookout for food, but that I need not fear as he would hardly attempt attacking a motorbike. Sometime later this tiger was shot by a Methodist missionary, and when he was cut open his stomach contained all sorts of valuables, such as gold bracelets, which he had collected when devouring his prey.

After the armistice in 1918, he returned to his field and remarried "for the sake of my children who were so much dependent on me, and for my sake, and the sake of the work." He married a missionary nurse saying, "It was the only right thing to do."

He evidently returned to a great deal of tension, as merger with the American Lutherans was being discussed. He had grave doubts about merging. The history of the Lutheran Church in Rajahmundry was rooted in Europe and was wrought out of a different spirit than that in Guntur, which was American, he felt. Not everyone agreed with him and one council member remarked that, "When I get to heaven I am going to drag Neudoerffer to the throne of grace and tell the Lord what he said!" Grandfather replied, "I'll be glad if you tell the Lord, but let us have patience and wait until we get there!" Though church unification was not resolved, it was decided that a new seminary would be located in

Rajahmundry. Grandfather was to go on furlough, "prepare himself in Practical Theology," and return to Luthergiri—Luthertown, as the mission headquarters in Rajahmundry was called.

But Grandfather hardly became settled in the mansion before he made what he considered to be the biggest mistake of his life. In 1925 the Principal of the Waterloo Theological Seminary in Canada asked Grandfather to come and teach there. In spite of his own misgivings and the warnings of fellow missionaries, he went and was desperately unhappy. He stayed for five years even though, not surprisingly, he did not get along with the rest of the seminary faculty. He called it a "very unpleasant relationship," but added that, "there were other elements at work against me which disturbed my peace of mind and added unhappiness." The cruelest blow came in 1930 when his second wife died and their only son, William, who was ten, drowned:

On top of everything else, the Lord in His eternal wisdom decided to take from me my wife and only son. All that was happening to me I looked upon as a chastisement by the Lord for deserting the work to which He had called me. Once this became clear to me I wrote the Mission Board that I was ready to go back to the field to which God had called me.

The mission board accepted his resignation, but before Grandfather returned to India he married for a third time:

To climax my readiness to go forth, I married again, for my own sake, for the sake of the girls, and for the sake of the work. If anywhere I needed a helpmeet it was out in the work at Luthergiri. I was absent from my work in India from 1926 to 1931. So I returned to my God-appointed task which I unwisely left. This sort of backsliding is hurtful to the soul and works havoc with one's whole life. We got back for the opening of the seminary in 1931.

This third wife of Grandfather's was the Grandmother I knew. She was a Dutch nurse, rosy-cheeked, buxom, and extremely kind. My sister and I never called her Grandmother, but Aunt Marie. I remember her always in the background, cheerful but saying little. My grandfather outlived Aunt Marie too by many years, his faith undimmed.

Many years later, Grandfather added a postscript to his journal—a brief fiery protest at being retired by the mission board after fifty years in the "vineyard," as he put it. A rebel to the end, he proclaims the board action a "heresy," defining heresy as "an erroneous belief in regard to some religious doctrine or truth." He concludes, "Retirement rules have only a place in the life of hirelings."

Our little family was subject to his larger-than-life presence while we lived in India. I would always see elements of him in my mother—stoic, tireless, uncomplaining. For a long time, I was embarrassed for Jesse because he took himself so lightly—because he wasn't like my grandfather.

Jesse was the last of Will and Alice's sons. He was born in a tent five miles by oxcart from the nearest village in 1898 and was deposited in a Baptist boarding school on Will and Alice's next furlough. Not much is known about Jesse's early life. Only three of the brothers—Frank, Charley, who returned to India as a medical missionary, and Jesse—ever struggled their way through a college education. Jesse's closest brother, Bill, ran away to Canada and joined the Black Watch when he was seventeen. Bill was wounded in France in World War I and decorated for gallantry in action. Greatly admired by Jesse for his toughness, independence, and charity, Bill was a major influence in Jesse's life. Of all his older brothers, Bill was the one that Jesse turned to most often for advice. In 1917, Bill wrote to Jesse from a hospital in London, where he was recovering from his wounds, and on his recommendation Jesse bummed his way to Oregon to attend college.

Jesse was about 5' 9" tall with broad shoulders and strong legs. His leg strength came, he said, from running to school barefoot in deep snow and from farm work. His fine, sandy hair began receding when he was in his early twenties, and his eyes were a weak, pale blue.

My father said he was an athlete at McMinnville College, that he ran the one-hundred-yard dash in ten seconds flat and broad jumped twenty-two feet. Jesse may have enlarged the truth. An old chum of his who was a high hurdler himself says he vaguely remembers Jesse ran sprints. And it is true that he coached track when we came to America. But no one remembers any record-breaking performances of Jesse's. What is known for sure is that Jesse graduated from McMinnville College in June 1922 with a bachelor's degree in science.

According to the 1922 yearbook, *Oak Leaves*, he was a member of the Dramatic Club as a sophomore, junior, and senior. He was a college orator his junior year. Jesse also served on the staff of the *Review*, the campus newspaper. He was editor his junior year, 1920–1921.

Jesse was called "Jake" all of his life until he met my mother, who disliked nicknames. He taught science and mathematics in America, though Wamps, the college chum who got him his first teaching job in Hood River, Oregon, says science was "foreign" to Jake in college.

There was a lovely girl who hooked up with Jake and his friends. To his surprise, Jesse was the one she fell for. They became engaged when he graduated from McMinnville College. Jesse had carefully saved enough for a year of art school in San Francisco, where he hoped to refine his skills and make professional connections. His mother accompanied him to San Francisco, but before he left he cached little sealed bottles with coded messages in the campus shrubbery for Evelyn, the girl. He gave her the code key before he and Alice left on the train.

When he returned from San Francisco, Evelyn broke off their engagement and returned the small ruby ring Jesse had given her. Most people agree it was because Jesse wanted to be an artist, while Evelyn wanted him to be something more practical. Alice died in 1926, and after Jesse had taught for two years in Hood River, he left for New York.

Jesse loved the East. Though his drawings and paintings were rejected in New York City as being without individual style, he was encouraged to continue developing as an artist. Jesse was a romantic, but I do not think he was actually prepared to live in poverty in a garret. He took a well-paid teaching job in a private boys' school in Woodmere, New York, and in September 1929, he was riding high. He wrote to his brother Bill:

God, but it is hot in this burg (94°) and no relief in sight! I have been in Philadelphia since Sunday and will leave for New York Friday, and then on to Connecticut for a convention. But I will pass by such minor events—the lobster dinner in Newport last Friday night, the day shopping on Fifth Avenue, the night in New York and what we saw and did, the ball game between the N.Y. Yankees and the Athletics of Phillie, and the hot date I've got for tomorrow night—and come down to brass tacks.

The East is really different in many ways from the West. I feel it strongly and at times question myself as to my ability to adapt myself to it. However, I believe I can. Your kid brother, Jake.

But by 1932, Jesse was barely hanging on:

You may know that I wasn't able to land a teaching job this fall, and so the Depression has taken on a more serious aspect to me. Before this fall, the word depression *was more or less a figure of speech, for I hadn't really felt any crimping in expenditures or good times. Now that I have to wiggle along on a small fraction of what I was making last year, well that's a horse of another color. Still, I find that I have been favored by having good friends, and so I don't have to sleep on a park bench. I get my room for being a sort of handyman around the place, and the school bus that I drive keeps me in enough money to supply a meal ticket.*

Jesse went on to say that, though his college board record was good, there were simply no teaching jobs available:

It could be a lot worse. I've got a roof over my head and enough to eat so I'm not complaining. Let's hope that things aren't so bad when school opens in the coming year. I can't say that I like the work that I am doing, for it isn't the most pleasant thing to be driving a bus in a community where you are fairly well known and have been connected with one of the leading schools for two years. People give you that condescending squint, filled with false sympathy, and ask how you are getting along. But, damn their eyes, I'm still making an honest living, even if it isn't at a white-collar job, and they can go jump right in the old Atlantic Ocean, for all of me.

But things got much worse in the next two years. Bill, who was operating a nursery in his backyard, must have tried to boost Jesse's spirits, for Jesse wrote in January 1934:

Don't take too much stock in getting an order of brides or roses from me, for I'm not in the market for roses or brides. It would be nice to have someone to fight with, and to love as well, but times are too hard to give it any serious thought. Getting too set in my ways to dare it now, and more than likely I will go on mending my own socks as long as I live.

Then, out of the blue, three weeks later:

This may come as somewhat of a surprise to you, so I will break it bluntly in order that you can get the shock all of a sudden and have it over with pronto. I am sailing on the Berengaria from New York a week from today for points east! Somewhere east of Suez, as Kipling would say, in fact to India. Now ain't that something: to be going halfway round the world to get a teaching job! But, after thinking it over for hours and hours I came to the conclusion that I might as well grab the chance. Always was a rolling stone and have had a yen to see that part of the world, and this looks like a good chance to fulfill that wish. I get my transportation paid and all I have to do is get seasick, which I don't do very easily as a rule—but you never can tell.

I haven't got time to write much just now for there are so many things that have to be done before I leave this neck of the woods a week from today. I don't even know the address of the school to which I am going, for I haven't received my final instructions from Boston yet. I'll be seein' you some day, but I don't know when.

So Jesse sailed reluctantly to India, and toward my mother, Ernestine.

My mother's young adulthood in the United States and Canada is shrouded in mystery. She left no letters. Unlike Jesse, though, who was left in America when he was only a child, Grandfather Neudoerffer kept both her and my aunt Theodora with him in India until they were ready for secondary education. Then they were sent to a Christian boarding school. While Grandfather was teaching at the theological seminary of Waterloo College, my mother applied for admittance to Wittenberg College in Springfield, Ohio. Her application describes her as being 5' 6" in height and weighing one hundred and twenty-five pounds. Her place of birth is recorded as being south India, and her father's occupation is listed as "professor." Her deceased mother is named as Julia Vander Veer of Denver, Colorado, who was a graduate of Johns Hopkins Medical School.

Under the category "list in order of your preference, the student activities in which you have participated," my mother checked three: "Athletics, Music, and Girl Guiding (Scouts)." Under "scholastic honors you have received," my mother wrote, "prizes in music."

She noted that her favorite courses were English, history, and geography, and that she disliked Latin, chemistry, and physics because "they are practical and require no imagination." She also says that she previously attended one other college, but could afford only the freshman year.

The application asked what the applicant planned to do after graduating from Wittenberg. Mother stated that she planned to get a master's degree after teaching for awhile. Asked the reason for her vocational choice, she replied: "I couldn't bear to be a stenographer."

In the 1930 *Wittenberger*, Mother is pictured front row center in a photo of the Cosmopolitan Club, a club for foreign students, and the affiliations noted under her junior picture list only the Cosmopolitan Club and two years of YWCA.

It occurred to me years later that Mother was a flapper as the dictionary describes the term: "a young woman of World War I and the following decade who showed freedom from conventions." She smoked heavily most of her life, and on at least one occasion my aunt Theodora moved out of the apartment they shared—causing Grandfather much concern.

Grandfather arranged Mother's return to India several years later and her employment at the school in Kodai, but I do not know if the original idea to return was his or hers. I do know that Grandfather's ideas and opinions contributed to his powerful influence in our lives as long as we lived in India. He was a great admirer of the British colonial system, and he justified his belief that India could never be self-governing by his observations of the people. Though he loved them as unruly children, he did not hold their cleanliness or their ambition in high regard:

The masses were illiterate, poor, ignorant, superstitious, apathetic. They did not seem interested in life and cared not whether they lived or died. Pessimism is ingrained in their flesh and blood. Their worship seemed largely mechanical.

Grandfather Neudoerffer was not a feminist, but did deplore the plight of Indian women. In 1924, he commented:

The Indian woman has no voice and no choice; she is downtrodden and looked upon as a useful animal to serve in raising children. Hindu literature makes statements like these: "It is a tragedy to be born a woman. Innumerable sins of the former birth have come home through her." There is no doubt that India had some very noble women who have fought against the degradation heaped upon their sex, but still much has to be done to correct the Indian's idea of marriage. Indian marriages are mostly arranged within their own community or sect. This is true of Christians too. The many marriages I have performed have all, with one exception, been among relatives. There are reasons for that— property and jewelry (of which there is plenty!) should remain within the family. These may not be good motives, but they exist.

Missionaries had most of their successes with Untouchables of the Hindu religion. This was because these outcastes had little or nothing to lose, and everything to gain, socially. Even many Untouchables refused Christianization, however, because in the Hindu faith an Untouchable's lot is only a punishment for misdeeds in a previous life. If an Untouchable lives out his terrible and humiliating present life without complaint, it is believed that he will be amply rewarded in his next incarnation.

Like most young children I told lies to avoid punishment. I do not remember if my grandfather took me to task for these lies, but he felt he could ferret out sincerity and truth in Indians by looking at their faces:

The district workers heard of my appointment to their field and arranged for a welcome meeting. It gave them a chance to look into my face and also gave me a chance to look into their heads and hearts. I have most of my life judged people by their facial expressions. As a college student I was very interested in Lavater's book on the study of faces.

Grandfather loved me and had grand hopes for me, and I thrived on his dotage. Looking back, I try to recall some lightness in him, some airy quality, some wit. He had none that I can remember. Irony, yes, and a robust sense of joy when going about his work and when among his charges. But he was forever formal, German; everything he did had weight. His griefs, of course, must have contributed to that weight. After my grandmother died and Grandfather wrote to friends about her death, he could not bring himself to ever speak of her again.

Two

O N HER RETURN TO INDIA, my mother went first to Rajahmundry and from there to the school at Kodaicanal. It was there that Jesse met her—or she met Jesse—for he arrived first. Jesse had planned to spend some time in Nellore before reporting to work. This was the same Nellore where Grandfather Manley had served, where Jesse had been born, and where his brother Frank was now the missionary. However, Frank's wife was gravely ill when Jesse arrived, and another brother Charley, the medical missionary, had not yet arrived. So Jesse went alone into the hills. More coincidentally, the little Kodaicanal school was the same one that Ernestine and Theodora had attended as girls. In fact, my mother and father were born only forty miles apart from each other—both of missionary families—and yet they never knew of one another until they met in Kodaicanal in 1935. Jesse's first letters to America were homesick ones. On August 5, 1934, he wrote to Bill:

I got the papers that you folks sent me, and it was very thoughtful of you to send them out, for it is certainly good to hear about what is going on at home. I begin to appreciate what that means after being over here for only a few months where I don't see a paper very often, and only once a week do I get to see a paper of the good old U.S.A., and that contains news that is a month old!

It is still too cool for comfort in this part of the world, and I often wish that it would warm up a little so that I wouldn't have to build a fire at night in order to keep warm. I see from the papers that the folks back in New York are having rather a hot time of it, and when I write to tell them that here in India just a few degrees from the equator, I wear wool socks and a heavy lumber jacket all day and build a fire at night— well, they just don't want to believe it. But it is because of the altitude that we are so blessed with a cool climate, for we are a little over 7,000 feet above sea level and that makes a great difference.

Well, folks, drop me a line and let me know how things are getting along in your part of the world. I am in the best of health and enjoying life, although there are times when I do get the blues something terrible. I have received notices of two darn good jobs right near to home since coming out here, and that hasn't added any to my peace of mind. But I try to forget that. I came out here to do the best job I know how and also to see this part of the world again, and so what's the use to pine away for old Broadway and the many pleasures that can be found in little old New York. I can't have them both, and so while I am out here I might as well make the best of it.

Jesse went to the school at Kodaicanal, the small hill town, as a math and science teacher. In those days most Britishers sent their young children home to England, but this boarding school in the healthy mountain air allowed prosperous families to keep their children in India. When Christmas vacation arrived in December 1934, neither Charley nor Frank were in India so Jesse set off alone in a third-class compartment to see northern India and the Vale of Kashmir. Third-class train travel was very cheap. Jesse paid ninety rupees, which came to about forty American dollars, for the four-thousand-mile trip:

Went up to Darjeeling (get out your map) north of Calcutta and took a look at the Himalayas. Didn't get to see Everest, for it kept its head hidden in the clouds. But since Everest is about 150 miles away from Darjeeling, about all that can be seen of it under the best of circumstances is a blob of white that resembles an ice cream cone and leaves you with the satisfaction of being able to say that you have seen the mountain. Kenchinjunga, which is only about thirty miles away and only a little less than a thousand feet lower than Everest, looms up in a way that seems to take the breath away. We were over 8,000 feet in elevation, and it was hard to realize that Kenchinjunga rose over 20,000 feet more into the cold, rarified atmosphere.

Stopped a day in Benares and watched the faithful Hindu bathing in the sacred Ganges. The Ganges is the most filthy river that I have ever seen, bar none, but these poor misguided souls come down there imbued with the idea that if they but wash themselves in this sacred flood and drink some of its purifying water—presto—their sins will all be washed away. The burnings are too barbaric for words. I believe that it is quite fitting to cremate a body, but to do it the way these folks do it is rather revolting to our minds. Of course the fact that the remains of bodies and all sorts of other contaminating things are in the water doesn't in any way deter them from drinking it—it's sacred.

Saw the Taj Mahal by moonlight, because the trip was planned so that we would be in Agra when the moon was full. It is beyond my powers to describe the view of the Taj by moonlight, for it certainly lives up to all that has ever been said about it. I don't wonder that it is considered one of the Seven Wonders of the World. But when one stops to realize that all the many marvels of India were built with slave labor, the sweating toil of thousands of poor devils, and the human lives that have gone into the construction of Rajahs' dreams—well, it seems to rob them of some of the beauty that they might otherwise have. It is said that the designers of the Taj had their eyes put out so that they couldn't duplicate this marvel in marble.

I don't know just how long I will stay out in this country, but I believe that it won't be longer than another year and a half. I don't think much of the sap that they have at the head of the school, nor do any of the rest of the faculty, and I couldn't stick it for five years. I didn't come out here with any idea of making money, but I can't afford to stay here too long. I had a swell offer of a good job in a wonderful school right in the neighborhood where I had been teaching—after I got out to India! The irony of fate. But such is life.

Glad to hear that all your family is doing well, even though the Depression has taken a healthy swat at them. Hope you all enjoyed Christmas and that the New Year will be a lot better than the old one. Love to all, Jake.

And 1935 was a better year for Jesse. Shortly after this letter was written, my mother arrived to supervise one of the school dormitories, and their courtship must have begun soon after. It is said that Jesse's classroom looked out over the area where Mother worked and that he used to kiss pieces of chalk and toss them out the window to her.

My mother and father were an unlikely pair—fair, weak-eyed, balding Jesse, and the tall, dark, stately Ernestine. Mother was often mistaken for an Indian, with her high cheekbones and full, wide lips. Her black hair was as long and as coarse as a Sikh's. I used to watch her, fascinated, as she tied it into a bun. She would tell me of the Sikhs as she wrapped her hair around a comb: they were a tall warrior-caste, she said, very clean, chaste, and they abstained from tobacco and wine. Sikhs were baptized with a two-edged sword and wound their long hair around a short dagger that served as comb, she would explain.

Grandfather Neudoerffer as a young
missionary in the field

Grandfather and Aunt Marie

Ernestine and Theodora

Julia van der Veer's graduation
photo from Johns Hopkins

Grandfather and Grandmother Manley in Madras, ca 1910

Grandmother Manley and Jesse

Will and Alice Manley's wedding photo

Within a year Jesse and my mother were married. The marriage came without warning to members of Jesse's family and must have surprised Bill most of all, for he had always been privy to Jake's innermost thoughts. But it was to Bill that Jesse finally wrote, on Christmas stationery and in his own hand. It took Jesse three paragraphs to get to the point, and even then he didn't say much:

It will soon be Christmas, at least by the time you receive this little note; hence the decorations. Hardly seems like Christmas in this part of the world, for although the cool season is on, it is still quite a little warmer than in your parts.

Very glad to hear of Mary's good work in school, but don't neglect the algebra and arithmetic. I would more than likely find it difficult to recognize my little niece and nephew in Hillsboro.

You may wonder what I am doing in Rajahmundry. Well, I'm visiting with my wife's father and mother! Charley was best man and Frank gave the bride away. So I'm a poor henpecked man now. I've got me a wife, finally. I'll send you some snapshots in the near future, also an official announcement at the same time. Love to all.

They had just returned from their honeymoon to the fabled Vale of Kashmir. It was much the same area that Jesse toured the year before by third-class train and was probably Jesse's idea, but this time they rented a houseboat and saw northern India in more comfortable style.

Mother kept a diary of their honeymoon trip. It is beautifully and carefully written:

Aboard the Silver Jubilee

Jess and I are sitting at the entrance of the little channel leading to the Manasbal lake. A superb view is before us. A narrow valley flanked on either side by barren mountains rising high. The lake itself on this side—and I expect on that—is fringed by dead lotus pads. They must be a beautiful sight in bloom. The other side of the lake is bordered by poplars, chenars, and willows. Colors of yellow, gold, bronze, all shades of green blend as only nature can. In front of this border the limpid, transparent water gives such a clear reflection that one wonders where truth ends and reflection begins.

For remembrance I want to note that the chenar tree was brought over by Nur Jahan when she came from Persia. Can't you imagine a lovely young girl, loved by her family and loving her home and surroundings, having to leave all that to come afar to marry Jahangir and live in an unknown, strange land, wanting to bring some remembrance with her? Here the river is very wide, and our coolies are walking through water above their knees to pull us. I don't see how they can bear to. It is five days since we last saw a newspaper. We are so isolated from civilization that the whole world could have crumbled away and left us and we would know nothing of it. The odd but delightful purple shade in the evening light last evening transformed the ordinary, barren hills into something mysterious, dark, unknown.

Mother made numerous references to the filth of the villages and the rivers, the smell of ganja in the air, and the packs of roaming dogs. However, these never spoiled her fascination for the land. Jesse contributed drawings to Mother's journal:

A perfect line of silver-trunked, lemon-yellow-leaved poplars along the right. Jess thinks they have been planted to hold the bank in time of flood. Here is a break in the line, where women and cattle may come down to the water, and just behind is a lovely tree, a green shade just ready to turn yellow.

We passed a vast edifice. All around were Moslems commencing their prayers. How many are really sincere? I may ask the same of Christians. How futile is the creation of these monuments and tombs to shelter the treasured bones! Rather should we cultivate ourselves in the memory of our friends that they will recall us with kindliness and love.

Armistice Day—at Srinagar! Sitting atop the mountain at Gulmarg. We are very fortunate for we see the famous mountain of Nanga Parbat (26,600 ft.). In half an hour it will probably be concealed behind the clouds and then seen no more. It towers up to its majestic height, glistening white; it looks, indeed, a treacherous mountain and we think of the ill-fated German Nanga Parbat expedition of this last summer. [Nanga Parbat had not been successfully climbed by 1935. Fourteen climbers and seventeen porters had died attempting its ascent.] *Ali says* Nanga *means "bare, with no clothes on." Because the mountain has no trees, I suppose.*

November 11

About 1:30 we set out for Nishat Bagh. Well bundled up in the taxi shikara *(boat).*

Passed through three sections of the Dal Lake, giving us a close-up of the entrance to the Maharajah's palace and his summer bathing section, which is marked off by floating logs, chained to each tree and separated by posts.

Men collecting lotus roots, by use of small, curved knife on the end of a long pole.

Two large stones here, along the bank—Ali says they represent a banker and a matting man who told lies and therefore turned into a block of stone. A similar stone farther along is of a milkman who suffered the same fate.

Kingfishers—iridescent, blue-and-gold-backed ones. Here is one diving in—up he comes with a little four-inch fish, which he devours with a gloating, satisfied gleam in his eye. Here one stops about 6' above the water line, incessantly fluttering his wings until the exact moment, then down like a plummet he goes and emerges victorious.

It is a very misty day, but the reflections are as clear as ever. Mt. Mahadin towers above us, and below us in the water.

November 13

At last we come to the open place where merchants having their wares spread out upon mats mingle with pious Moslems saying their two o'clock prayers facing Mecca. Merchants sell everything conceivable—from rock salt to jewelry to razors and "hair-removing soap." Regardless of all this hubbub, the call to prayer continued at the Nagrat Bal, a mosque of age containing a hair of Mohammed. Such utter indifference to surrounding crowds and noise, and such complete religious absorption of a crowd have I never before witnessed. A Mullah was expounding the Koran (on a soapbox) and the crowd listened, absorbed. Then he would repeat it, so would they, and all would break out into a really beautiful chant of part of the Koran. Some of the men (no women, of course) were so utterly lost in their surroundings that it seemed almost mystical. One man was crying like a child, and all looked rapturously toward the Mullah and Mecca.

Jesse loved strange names. He would collect them and save them to use later on. The names Jesse deemed worthy of saving generally amused Mother too. One of their all-time favorites was "Suffering Moses," a small shop in Srinagar. They used to double up with laughter over that name years later in America. When I would complain or whine, which Jesse called "bellyaching," they would point at me and say in unison, "Suffering Moses," and then laugh so hard they cried. I never knew what they were laughing about. Jesse applied "Suffering Moses" to chronic complainers, though not to their faces.

Sometimes Jesse collected whole lists of names and sometimes he made up names for people or things. Mother noted many of Jesse's curious names, real or created, in her diary:

This is where the boats are repaired. What a collection of house-boats—and names. "Golden Hopes," "The Joyful Jacob," "King's Throne," "Swastika," "Iron Duke," "Black Prince," "King David," "Cherry Pipe." "Paul Reveres" Jess aptly names all the lads and men we see astride hill ponies. They do look rather ridiculous for they tower so far over the pony.

Jess has named two of the crew "Appleseed" and "Nightingale."

November 17

Camels! Disdainful, arrogant camels, thirty-two of them, carrying beds, rugs, tent equipment, children, pots and pans, even chickens—everything for their people. The women all dressed like Bedouins, in draped black. The children and men leading the camels, or watching that the goats, cows, and calves keep to the path, are dressed in beau-tifully-folded, filthy padded coats or quilts. Wooly camels—some very dark—led along in "chains," by ropes tied to their nose pegs.

India will always mean color to me—and color spelled in capital let-ters! Saris, scarfs, turbans of all shapes, sizes, and modes of putting on, trousers, shirts of all colors and all shades of colors. How these folk adore orange, red, scarlet, crimson, reds verging on purple—brilliant blues (never a navy blue—better, black!), greens, and delicate, fairy pastel shades.

Jess and I took a walk through the bazaar. How I was stared at—a brazen white woman walking the streets.

November 18

At last I have seen the Taj Mahal. I cannot rave, for it is no more beautiful than I expected, or no less beautiful. I have seen so many pic-tures of the Taj and read so much of it that I was absolutely prepared for this marble beauty.

The surrounding gardens are a perfect setting for this marble jewel. And here are little wrens and hummingbirds hopping about.

November 20

Bezwada. The last lap has begun. It is good to be in the south again—good to see these modes of dress (and undress), good to see the lush green paddy fields, and the ripening grain, the modes of irrigation and transportation to which we are accustomed, good to hear the soft tones of Telegu, and above all, good to know we will be home soon.

Outside we hear the raucous cries of the vendors—we are almost home. Soon we will cross the Godavari, see my folks, and only the splendor and beauty of Kashmir, as a well-remembered dream, will tell us that we have been so far away.

My parents had wonderful memories of Kodai. Jesse was thirty-six at the time and Mother was twenty-five. Mother worked in the infirmary with the resident students while Jesse taught mathematics, and both of them had plenty of time for the bracing mountain hikes that they loved. Teachers were always accorded the utmost respect in India. Jesse was always deferentially addressed as "Doctor" or "Professor" wherever he went. Jesse always said that he never had students in the United States like those he taught in India, but that was understandable as his English and European students came mostly from well-educated families and had traveled and learned about other cultures.

One of my earliest memories is of being at the hospital with my mother when my sister was born. I was a little over two years old the day that Margaret was born in Guntur, a center of the British government on the plains. The Lutheran Mission headquartered there, and Kugler hospital, where Margaret was born, was at that time the largest mission hospital in southern India. Margaret was a small, golden child, fair and blue-eyed like Jesse.

The difference in my sister's and my sizes and complexions was obvious when my mother gave us both daily baths in a small, zinc tub. Native nurses used to gather round to watch as I stepped naked into the tub. Mother always gave me a coffee can to "pee" in first. This was a great source of amusement to the nurses and a great source of embarrassment to me.

But then children, especially white male children, were always the center of attention in India. Such children were sent home to either England, Europe, or America, and the few that remained were spoiled terribly. In addition there were so many adults who either had no children of their own or whose children were boarded out that they lavished all of their attentions on the few that remained.

There was a large, lovely lake in Kodai that was the town's pride. Punting on this peaceful lake with its shaded inlets was as much a part of weekly recreation as polo was in military communities. The English punt is an unsinkable, shallow-draft boat, propelled by a pole from the stern or rowed. When we went punting on the lake, Jesse steering, he used to rock the boat gently from side to side, which terrified me but only made my sister giggle with delight. Every afternoon Mother and Jesse hiked six miles around the lake. One day the setting sun struck our house in such a way that it appeared to be on fire, and they ran all the way home. This fear of fire was magnified in the hills where there was ample tinder and few resources to fight fires with.

Since both Jesse and Mother were occupied at the school all day, Margaret and I only saw them at tea time when we joined them for tea and crackers with jam. Jesse called these our "crumpets." Throughout the days we were cared for and watched carefully by Mary *Ayah*, our native nurse (*ayah* means nursemaid in Telegu). I can see Mary clearly in her multicolored *sari*, adorned with a nose ring, bangles on her wrists and ankles, her teeth stained red from chewing betel nut. Mary was mission educated, very gentle, and sweet natured. She identified with small children and played games and read nursery rhymes to my sister and me by the hour. When I angered Mary *Ayah*, she went and sat cross-legged in a corner and knit until I apologized to her, and then our games would begin again.

It was Mother who taught Mary *Ayah* to knit, and Mary was proud to have such a skilled instructor. Mother was well known for her speed and dexterity. She was soon hired to teach as well as to function as the school nurse, and she used to knit while students were taking tests. The students knew they could never cheat because even while knitting, she could monitor their every move. Years later my mother was able to knit and watch television at the same time.

Mary *Ayah* took Margaret and me for long walks during the day—pushing Margaret in her pram. We found a shady spot, and Mary and I read through Robert Louis Stevenson's *A Child's Garden of Verses*. However, Mary *Ayah* was not young and often would doze off on a warm afternoon. One day in Kodai, while she dozed, I ran away. Mary *Ayah* awoke in a fright, tearfully informed my parents at the school, and a search was organized. I was finally captured several miles away in the village bazaar—babbling happily away with the vendors and eating forbidden (probably for good cause) delicacies that the villagers had given me.

When my sister grew a little older, our family went on long bicycle rides through the hills. Because I was older and heavier, it always fell to Jesse rather than Mother to carry me on his shoulders or to transport me in the basket fixed to the handlebars of his bike when we went on excursions. At those times, I always thought I detected a subtle disappointment in him.

Life at Rajahmundry on the plains was very different. I knew that I was my grandfather's favorite. We inspected the mission compound together, and the natives argued over who got to hoist the little master on their shoulders. I accepted their obeisance as would a child monarch.

The plains were in every way more exciting to a little boy than were the mountains. Here you could feel the raw energy of India. In this hot and dusty landscape there was something primal and elemental that made you shiver with excitement. Since I had no playmates, I imagined myself a Bengal Lancer or great white hunter on the mission grounds. Over the plain I galloped, whipping my leg as with a crop, or stealthily stalked the low tawny hills that were the color of lions. The air was full of smells: of cooking, of hot dry grass, and always of cow dung. I remember the lines of fire smoke at sunset and the cows being herded home. They kicked up a pale gold dust.

It is said that in India both twilight and death come suddenly. In Rajahmundry, twilight always came very quickly, and then it was suddenly dark, and a hazy mist rose up from the delta. The month of April was followed by six months of heat when everyone who could went to the hills. Then the rains arrived with the return of people from the hills. The only truly comfortable months in southern India were the early months of each year.

Death could come quickly from insects, plagues, or animals. An old saying went that you could eat breakfast with a person in the morning and bury him or her in the afternoon. On the plains they would be buried immediately if they died in hot weather, for there was no electricity or refrigeration.

There were a multitude of insects in India, but on the plains, scorpions and centipedes were the most feared. One day, when I was being put down for a nap, my mother suddenly but calmly ordered me to stand on my bed. There was a large scorpion crawling across the floor that she efficiently dispatched. If for no other reason, my grandfather was a hero to me for the way he shrugged off scorpion stings although they laid him low many times. Mission laundresses, scrubbing clothes in huge washtubs in a large enclosed area at the rear of the bungalow, regularly slopped centipedes out of their tubs and squashed them underfoot.

By the time I was born, tigers no longer roamed out of the jungles onto the plains. They were not even hunted for sport much except on maharajahs' estates. Occasionally, though, a procession bearing a dead tiger hung between two poles passed by the mission. The tiger was a man-eater—usually a crippled animal—who marauded nearby farms for easy prey and was shot by a government hunter. In the hill stations, though, panthers and an occasional tiger still prowled the *sholas* of the hill country.

The animals I feared most—even more than poisonous snakes—were the packs of wild, mad dogs that ran snarling and slavering over the plains. They were mangy, rabid, and ravenous, and we called them "pi" dogs—a shortening of "pariah." Frequently they awakened me in the middle of the night as they ran snapping and howling past my window. Then the servants would begin shouting and raising an alarm, torches were lit, and men gathered in the yard with rifles. I would hear my grandfather's footsteps pounding down the stone staircase, and the men would all run off into the night. For a time all would be quiet, and then from far away I would hear the spattering of distant gunfire. Then all would be quiet again. I would lie in bed, my heart beating with excitement, until I heard the men returning triumphantly, my grandfather's deep, steady voice among them. In the morning, after a pi dog hunt, I always hurried to the rear verandah to look out over the westward plain, and I always saw a flock of vultures—some circling lazily, some feeding furiously on the slaughtered dogs. Everyone was terrified of these mad dogs.

The delta country was a breeding ground for insects of all kinds, and malaria and dengue fever were endemic. My parents took two grains of quinine daily and still had intermittent bouts of malaria. In later years, Mother grew hard of hearing from the long-term effects of quinine. The many types of insects added greatly to one's general discomfort, not only those insects that bit or stung or stank when squashed, but others that destroyed—bored through books and ate through furniture. It was said that if you left your boots on the floor at night, you lost the soles by morning.

The humidity was at its worst in eastern India. Autumn was a time of almost universal sickness. Skin infections—eczema, impetigo, and prickly heat—were commonplace. I remember having prickly heat so badly as a child that I would have scratched my skin off if my parents had not wrapped my hands. In America my case of California poison oak would seem trivial compared to India's prickly heat.

Of course at the mission we were shielded from India's worst horrors—armless and legless beggars, and the lepers of the villages and bazaars. When I came across a sick or crippled person, my servant led me hurriedly away.

A government doctor visited the mission periodically. He would erect a tent on the grounds, and all the native Christians formed a very long line to be examined and treated. Often the doctor gave painful shots for cholera, diphtheria, or smallpox, and I was never exempted. I still have a quarter-sized scar on my left arm from a childhood inoculation. One day the doctor came to Grandfather's mission and the usual long line formed—whole families appeared with babes in arms. The doctor seated himself next to a large jar of disinfectant and placed a pair of long surgical scissors and forceps on the table. I watched in fascination as each man, woman, and child who still had a set of tonsils sat opposite the doctor and opened their mouths. Very quickly he probed into their throats with the scissors, snipped off the tonsils, lifted them out with the forceps and plunked them into the jar. It was all very efficient and businesslike and was accompanied by very little crying.

The heat arrived in mid-April. The wind dropped, the sun got sharper, the shadows turned black, and we knew we were in for five months of discomfort. We never got used to the heat. Every time we walked outdoors on the plains during the middle of the day, the sun slammed down like a hammer. Absolutely no one went outdoors between sunrise and sunset without wearing a topee, which was not to be confused with a pith helmet. Topees were heavy helmets, made of solid cork. Pith helmets were more stylish and worn by the British army when on parade. Even I had a boy's topee and Margaret had one too.

Many nights on the plains the heat was so oppressive that we took our beds and mosquito netting outside, and we slept under the stars—listening to the jackals. We were taught that jackals howled, "I smell the body of a dead Hindu! Where? Where? Here! Here! Here!"

When I think of my grandfather's mansion, it is from the perspective of a very small boy. The rooms were massive, with high ceilings, stone floors, and dark panelled walls. The house was kept very dark, and curtains were always drawn and doors closed. The house seemed cavernous. At night, when the kerosene lamps were lit in the passageways and in the large dining room—casting shadows on the walls and gleaming off the teak dining table—I felt as if I were living in a medieval castle.

The mansion was darkened to keep out the heat. While we were usually in the hills during the hot season, Grandfather seldom left the mission throughout the long summer months. In his office, in the evening, his work would go on. Once when we were in Rajahmundry for some now forgotten reason during the summer, I passed my grandfather's office, which smelled of port and cigars. He was hunched over his desk writing, his sleeves rolled up and held in place with black garters—his arms covered with sweat.

The only apparatus for keeping air moving in homes was the *punkah*, a long pole stretched high across a room with a six-foot-wide matting of bamboo hung from it. A rope attached to the *punkah* ran through a hole in a wall to a servant seated outside who pulled on the rope and made the *punkah* move back and forth. The quicker the *punkah* moved, the more air circulated in the room. This servant, or *punkah-wallah*, would often lie on his back and operate the *punkah* with his big toe, since it was tedious, monotonous work—and often he would go to sleep too. The first Telegu words I learned to speak—or, rather, shout—were "*punkah-wallah!*" I learned them from Grandfather who shouted them often, particularly when our family was at dinner and the *punkah* began moving more and more slowly and erratically.

Grandfather had a great many servants at Rajahmundry. This was partly because servants were very cheap. Depending on their status, servants received from fifteen to twenty-five rupees a month ($5 to $10 in American currency). Mostly, though, the large number of servants was due to the caste system. Though the mission servants had been converted to Christianity, there was still a hierarchy. They simply would not perform a task that was beneath the Hindu station into which they had been born. Grandfather had a personal secretary, a driver, several cooks and serving people, dusters, water-carriers, laundresses, gardeners, and sweepers—the lowest caste of servant, who cleaned the primitive latrines called "thunder-boxes." Grandfather Neudoerffer never minced words whenever he had to use one of the thunderboxes. He always said, "I am going to the pot."

Europeans in India either loved or hated the curried foods that were so common in southern India. My family loved them. Years later, when we had company for a special curried meal, my mother would make an extra hot batch of rice and curry that she called her "blue plate special." Our guests got a milder, fancier version. Rice and curry has never been sufficiently hot for me unless the sauce makes my eyes water and my nose run. However most Europeans ate lots of rice and curry, if for no other reason than to make the meat tastier. Since the slaughter of cows gave great offense to Hindus, beef was hard to come by. In any event, meat had to be eaten on the day the animal was killed, and so all varieties of meat were tough. We ate tough mutton and tough chicken and what little beef we did eat was tough too.

Dinner was prepared by cooks and served by native waiters and was a formal affair, especially at Rajahmundry. Cooks, particularly, took great pride in their station in life, and a good one was in demand in any European community. Dinner usually began with a soup course, followed by either mutton or chicken curry and rice, and ending with a custard dessert. Eggs were about the size of pigeons' eggs and were scarce. Yeast for bread making had to be imported from Bombay. Butter came in tins and was always oily. When butter was unobtainable, water buffalo butter, with coloring added, was substituted. (This made our family's transition to uncolored margarine during World War II fairly easy.)

Not that our meals didn't have some variety. One of my favorite special dinners was Grandfather's homemade German sauerkraut and sausages. He pickled the cabbage himself and churned it in a large barrel. Vegetables, salads, and fruits had to be washed. Drinking water was always boiled. After dinner, Grandfather retired to the library for a glass of port and a good cigar.

But our visits to the mission really revolved around Sunday church services. The church itself was a large stone structure built by hand and was a source of great pride in the local Christian community. On Sundays, I dressed in my best little sailor suit or another hated outfit that resembled nothing more than a knee-length dress over tights. I remember the resounding martial timbre of the congregation singing "God Save the Queen" as the processional. Grandfather wrote seriously and solemnly all week on his sermon. The native Christians dressed in their Sunday finest and joined in the peculiarly militant hymns: "The Son of God goes forth to war/ A kingly crown to gain/ His blood-red banner streams afar/ Who follows in His train?"

Grandfather dominates my remembrances of life on the plains. My mother and father are background figures. But I do remember my longing for companionship other than the servants, since I was not allowed to play with Indian children.

Jesse used to dress me up in silly outfits and costumes. I still have a picture that Jesse took of me after one of his costuming jobs. I am attired in too-large pajamas, with a skullcap (bought on their honeymoon) on my head, large round glasses, and pulling my favorite "dum-dum" toy. The toy itself was nothing more than a miniature covered wagon with a drum head and drum stick inside. When I pulled the wagon and its wheels turned, the stick beat on the little drum and went "dum-dum."

In late September or early October, monsoons arrived on the plains. Hot wind blew day and night from the huge, open plain, and then the clouds began to bank up and up and there was a great feeling of pressure in the air. Then the rain came down with terrific force, and this went on for two or three days at a time. The hot, dry climate was replaced by a humid one. The air got very sticky, with a more-or-less constant rain for a few months. Soon the Godavari ran two miles wide.

Our family was seldom on the plains during monsoon season; it was far too unhealthy. Most people who could do so left the plains in March and only came back when the monsoon had broken, so they were away for the very hot and the humid months.

We did spend Christmas at the Rajahmundry mission, and it was always a production over which my grandfather presided. Visiting mission officials, dignitaries, guests, and our family sat on the spacious front verandah before twilight. We were served a sumptuous Christmas dinner with much toasting of punch. The large crowd of Indian Christians who gathered for this annual celebration sat packed together on the ground, eating their meal off large plantain leaves and without benefit of silverware, as was their custom. There were many speeches during and after dinner and much applause. After these, the Indian families were invited to form a line—a very long one—and were greeted one at a time by my grandfather at the top of the bungalow steps. One by one they filed past the verandah, and my grandfather presented each man, woman, and child with a small gift. Christmas culminated with a round of carols.

When we left Rajahmundry for the hills, it meant a journey of several days and nights on a train. Train travel was terribly uncomfortable and overcrowded. Hordes of poor Indians with their possessions squatted on the tops of cars, and the stations served as shelter for homeless and sick masses. But railways were the only efficient mode of travel over long distances and rugged terrain.

The railway compartments were hierarchical, reflecting the social structure of British India. They were luxurious in first class, but the summer heat could not be overcome by comfortable accommodations. A train journey always reminded a person of India's size, and discomfort increased with the distances. Our train trips were long and hot and dusty. I recollect masses of Indians and vendors, but I remember the children of my own age most clearly—they cried plaintively, "No Momma, no Daddy, no whiskey soda."

As a child, I was drawn to the dramatic aspects of life. I do not remember leaving the plains in advance of the hot season, but I do remember vividly the descent from the hills after the monsoons. Crossing over the long, narrow Godavari River bridge was terrifying—the muddy river ran dark and full and strong only feet below the train wheels.

I was petrified by large bodies of water when I was a boy. Once, when we were in Rajahmundry, we went for a day at the sea to the "Dolphin's Nose," a jutting coastal headland near Bhimavaram. When we arrived at the beach, I was awestruck at my first sight of the sea and of the Dolphin's Nose where men dove off the high cliffs. I ventured a little way into the surf, but the undertow knocked me off my feet and began to drag me out into the Bay of Bengal—or so I imagined. Jesse and Mother pulled me crying out of the water.

At some point, the "sap" who administered the school at Kodai must have become too overbearing for Jesse. In May 1936, our family made a trip to my grandfather's summer cottage in the Nilgiri hills, and Jesse fell in love with the "blue mountains:"

Here we are in the Nilgiri hills visiting with Ernestine's parents and having a wonderful time just loafing and enjoying the scenery. Kotagiri isn't far from Kodaicanal but it is in a different range of hills and is one of the several hill stations to which Europeans retreat at this season. Believe me, it is a blessing to have these cool hills because the heat on the plains in May is terrific.

We went for a walk through the woods a few days ago and saw some Malabar squirrels, which are the world's biggest. They are certainly beauties too. This brings up the question which you raised: why don't I do some hunting? For several reasons, I suppose. A hunting license is rather expensive, and ammunition and guns are out of my reach. Going on a two- or three-day hunting trip is different in India than at home and takes on the aspect of an expedition. But, all these difficulties could be overcome if a person was keen enough on hunting, which, I guess I ain't! Charley does some shooting and lives in a district where there is considerable game. In fact when I went to visit them for a week last November I slept in a tent with a .32 automatic under my pillow! You can imagine my slumbers, when every night sound set me tingling with visions of a panther stalking up to my bed. Under the conditions, I would have been better off with a squirt gun that couldn't cripple anything, because I'm sure I couldn't hope for a death-dealing shot from my shaking hand. Still I hope to get a chance to go with Charley some time when he goes out for a tiger. I know I'd shake my boots off, but it would be a thrill of a lifetime.

This letter was written one month before Margaret was born, yet Jesse said nothing about her impending birth to Bill and Idylla. His thoughts about hunting are surprising because he continually procrastinated when, as a teenager, I asked him to let me buy a rifle.

Jesse soon obtained a teaching job at one of the English schools near Kotagiri. These schools were all very strict because they were preparatory schools for Cambridge University. Besides, Mother decided it was time for her to stop working and to attend to my education, though I was only three years old.

Kotagiri is a tiny jewel of a village set high in the Nilgiris. The largest village nearby was Ootacamund, or "Ooty," the "Queen of the Hill Stations," as it was fondly called by Englishmen. The governor and his entourage retreated to Ooty during the summer. More British came to the Nilgiris during the summer than did any other nationality, and the cultural and social life of the villages had a slow, sedate, and orderly pace. I especially remember men in white ducks and women in pleated, white dresses playing tennis on bright green grass courts, and the strains of classical music wafting from homes. The view westward from Kotagiri to the plains far below was magnificent, and to the east, mountains, valleys, meadows, and *sholas* were bathed in a blue haze. It was an incredibly pristine landscape—no fences, paved roads, power lines, or dammed streams. On some days the Nilgiris were collared by fog, and we were isolated from the worlds below and beyond. It seemed enchanted.

The village itself was centered around a small park, surrounded by shops and modest villas. No auto traffic was allowed in Kotagiri so people went by foot or bicycle, and the only vehicles were bullock carts loaded with produce for market. The park itself was spacious, with shade trees and a white bandstand with a scalloped facade. There were even two thatched-roof structures supported by poles, under which picnickers could escape sudden downpours. These were usually occupied, however, by sacred cows seeking shade.

Grandfather built his cottage, The Roses, a mile or so outside of the village on the side of a mountain. The garden at The Roses was luxurious, full of exotic plants and flowers. Orchids grew wild, and roses of every variety and description climbed house and garden walls. Terraced and separated into areas with low stone walls, the gardens were Aunt Marie's pride and joy. On the hill behind the house grew custard apples, a large sweet tropical fruit the size and shape of a pineapple, and we ate them every morning for breakfast along with papayas and mangoes.

Although my sister and I had no *ayah* to tend us any more since Mother had taken over our upbringing, our family was attended by two servants.

Ferdinand, the only Christian Indian I can recall who did not have a biblical name, was our cook, and John was our gardener. My memories of being waited upon are not intellectual but physical—of being safe and shielded and not a little superior.

I was rarely left alone, but when it was unavoidable John, a personal convert of my grandfather's, was put in charge of me (though he acted as if I were in charge of him). He died before my eyes one morning when we were alone at the cottage. John was an epileptic, and on that morning he flung aside his gardening tool, his eyes rolled back in his head, he appeared to be lifted up and then flung to the ground by some unseen force, and his body heaved and convulsed with spasms among the flowers. I am told that I ran to the village for help, but I don't remember that. I only remember John, suddenly stilled, sprawled among the roses.

Simon, a mischievous young man who was good at avoiding work, replaced John. Whenever he could manage it, he joined me enthusiastically in my children's games, and Jesse quickly named him "Simple Simon." Simon even made me my first slingshot, which my mother tried to take away. I argued that, as a youth, King David had slain Goliath with a slingshot. Mother insisted that David wielded a sling, not a slingshot. It was only through Jesse's intervention that I was able to keep my weapon. Jesse treated Simon with bemused tolerance. Being a very good woodcarver himself, Jesse admired Simon's craftsmanship and ingenuity in managing to whittle the slingshot frame while he should have been gardening. Eventually my mother prevailed, however, and I never learned to use my slingshot well. One day my friend Simon was several hours late returning from drawing water at our well. Mother found him sleeping down the hillside under a tree and sacked him on the spot.

Wood of all kinds was plentiful in the area, and Jesse did a fair amount of carving. He esteemed Indian woodwork—especially their attention to delicate detail—and he often spent time studying wooden pieces to see how they were fashioned. As for me, I never could find wood, especially sticks, no matter where I searched. It is an old joke in our family that when I misbehaved and was in for a spanking, Mother would send me out to find a suitable stick for the job. I would wander, sobbing loudly, and return in an hour or so with the startling news that in all of the vicinity there was not one stick anywhere. Of course my mother would quickly prove my eyesight faulty and my punishment would be accomplished. As far as I was concerned, this whole procedure was conducted with great solemnity. I only learned a long time later that my parents sent me out on purpose, regularly knowing that I would return with the same lament each time, and that while I pretended to hunt a spanking stick, they watched me with great merriment from inside the cottage.

As on the plains, I had few friends of my own age in Kotagiri. In fact, I remember only two, Jan and Pip. Jan and Pip were Danish, their family having fled Denmark when it was being threatened with invasion by Nazi Germany.

My only other friends were "uncles," two of whom were young American teaching missionaries. Summer and Bill became my friends more for what I perceived to be acts of valor than for their spirituality.

My uncle Summer repeatedly dove off the high cliffs on our excursion to the sea—he seemed to float like a gull in the air, before plunging into the ocean. My uncle Bill actually stared down a panther in the *shola* where we took daily walks. That small jungle was inhabited by wild animals, and people took minimal precautions. Half the pleasure of the daily walk was in listening to the shrieking and shrilling of birds and the growls and howls of predators, but no predators had ever appeared near the trail before. When our family walked, our dog Jinx was always fitted with a spiked collar for protection, and my parents always carried walking sticks. One day, however, Uncle Bill was strolling through the *shola* alone when he came face-to-face with a panther. As he later told it, he stared in shock at the panther for some moments, then backed away slowly around a turn in the trail, and then ran like hell. Two days later, he and Uncle Summer went back with guns and killed the panther. This sort of action was guaranteed to gain my admiration.

The closest call my immediate family had in Kotagiri was the one time Jesse discovered a cobra in our bathroom. Jesse wisely shut and barred the door and declared the bathroom off limits until the cobra departed of its own free will, which it did soon enough. This common-sense approach was one not guaranteed to win my admiration.

Most daylight hours were reserved for my schooling, over which Mother presided. I began to read voraciously and am told that I was a wizard at mathematics by the time I was four years old. I cannot make simple calculations now, but such is family legend. On Jesse's urging, I was sent briefly to a local school to mingle with children of my own age, but that experiment did not work out. Shortly after I enrolled, I was cracked in the head by a runaway swing, ran howling home to Mother with my teacher in hot pursuit, and that was the end of that.

The books on which my mother based my education invited me to aspire to courage and honor. Because Jesse confided the Manley family origins to

Little Master with dum-dum toy

Our family on the veranda
in Rajahmundry

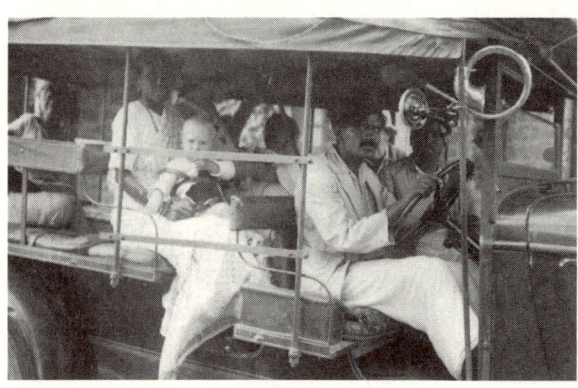

Mary *Ayah* and my sister
Margaret on a bus

Punting on the lake
in Kodai

Jake and Ev

Uncle Bill in the Black Watch

Mother, bottom right, in the *Wittenberger*

me, my tastes ran to medieval stories. He related that the Manley family was one of the most ancient of the landed gentry of England. The first Manley was a companion-in-arms to William the Conqueror and accompanied William from Normandy to the conquest of England in 1066. His name, Jon de Mandelie, appears on the "Battell Abbey Roll," the official list of the knights that attended William. According to Jesse he was a knight in the first Crusade, and so the family crest is a Saracen's head. Mother agreed that knights errant were especially brave because they traveled alone and were not owned by any king or baron. She also taught me about the heroes of the Old Testament, most of whom had human frailties, she said. I did not admire Sampson, who let a woman fool him, nor even King David particularly. My favorite character was Absalom because he was dashing and led a rebellion.

When I was very young I assumed I had been named after King David because we were a religious family and because my father's name was Jesse. Mother explained to me, however, that I was named for King Edward of England who had abdicated his throne for love and whose nickname was David. My sister Margaret was named after Princess Margaret Rose. In those days, Mother followed the members of the royal family as if she were related to them. She introduced me to other sorts of books too. I had my fill of Dickens, whom I disliked because his stories were so depressing and full of squalor. We read *Black Beauty*, all the Pooh stories, Kipling, and Robert Louis Stevenson. Perhaps the most important thing that Mother taught me was to use my imagination. She also taught me that in imagining, there is a difference between reverie and invention. Jesse did not have any patience with unimaginative or stupid people either. If he did not call them "saps," like his ex-principal, he called them "jackasses." More than anything, he hated hypocrites.

On any given weekend, Jesse and Mother and several other families would set off on a camping trip in the Nilgiris. Our hikes were always into wilderness unmarked by trails. When we found a likely spot—usually on some forested bluff—tents were set up, ditches were dug for latrines, and clotheslines were strung for laundry. Unlike the gentry in Isac Dineson's *Out of Africa*, who dined at tables covered with white linen and drank out of crystal glasses when "in the bush," we spread blankets on the ground. Jesse provided the special wonder of those trips for me. After the adults' tents were set up, Jesse would build a small hut of leafy boughs for my sister and me to sleep snugly in. My uncle Summer was a violinist, never quite good enough for the concert career he envisioned, but who played wonderfully nevertheless. After the singing and the storytelling were over and everyone went to bed, Summer sat by himself and played his violin long into the night. I lay awake in Jesse's hut and marveled at the beauty of his music. Then, when Summer had played himself out, a nightjar's song would replace the violin, and I fell asleep to different, but no less lovely, music.

Long, languid tennis afternoons were also a staple of life in the Nilgiris. The lawns of the courts were as green as emeralds and were immaculately manicured. There was always punch and sweets and beer, and no one took the competition very seriously except Mother. She possessed a wicked underhand serve and used it to good effect.

One day in 1939 Mother and I were sitting on a blanket and reading in the Kotagiri park. I had graduated from sailor suits to khaki shorts, shirts, hiking shoes, and long wool socks. Jesse cut my hair in the British style, and with my topee on I must have looked like a proper little English gentleman. On this particular day, Mother and I were deep in some book when Jesse arrived hurriedly on the scene. There was talk between them of Germany and England, and I was hustled home where my parents secluded themselves in discussion. For several days afterward friends came and went, and my parents seemed tense—especially Jesse who normally could find time to lighten up any problem. As it turned out, the day that Jesse hurried to the park was the day that Germany invaded Poland. On September 4, 1939, Britain and France announced a state of war with Germany.

Not long after the announcement we had a family meeting and I was told that our family was going to leave India. Since war had been declared between England and Germany, my parents felt we would no longer be safe there. In retrospect the prospect of the Wermacht storming through the Khyber Pass seems ludicrous, but it was a very real concern then. Britain's finest, most seasoned officers and troops were stationed in India, and everyone knew that they would be the first troops reassigned to a European war. This would effectively strip India of the British military presence and leave her civil employees, teachers, and to a lesser extent missionaries, open to threats of German invasion and to internal warfare. Ghandi's influence had rallied the Congress Party to England's cause in World War I, but after being imprisoned and scorned by the British for his pains, he would not lend his support to their cause again. So, at least partly, we left because India's course was set toward independence even then.

I had mixed emotions about my parents' decision to flee India for America. On the one hand I considered it cowardly because America hadn't entered the war yet. On the other hand, I knew that America would offer me some playmates my own age.

My father would leave as soon as possible for America. He would spend a year there studying so that he could teach in the United States again. In the meantime, Mother, my sister, and I would wait in Kotagiri until we could join him. It puzzled me that we did not even travel to see Jesse off from Calcutta, where he sailed on a Japanese ship for America. The ironies of fate decreed that within three years Japan posed a greater threat to India than Germany ever did, and within four years the same Japanese vessel that carried my father to America was sunk by an American submarine while transporting troops in the Pacific Ocean.

Three

IN THE YEAR THAT FOLLOWED, my mother's tutoring intensified, and I spent long hours studying at my small desk. It seems strange to me now that I did not study any books about America. My reading, almost without exception, still consisted of European adventure stories—Kipling, Dickens, Sir Walter Scott, Dumas. Poetry was now required reading, and Tennyson's "Idylls of the King" and Alfred Noyes' "The Highwayman" were favorites of mine. I acted out some of these stories. My still-scarred knees were wounded besieging high garden walls.

Mother told me I must be brave and that I was the protector of our family while my father was away. When Mother was not teaching me, I spent many hours with my uncles, who seemed more serious and preoccupied than before. One uncle, an American citizen, was leaving soon, and in the not-too-distant future I wrote to him in England where he was stationed as a gunner on a B-25 crew. Though he was a missionary, this uncle went to war rather than become a chaplain.

The ranks of Europeans (for all white foreigners were considered "Europeans" to native Indians) had thinned by the time Jesse sent word for us to set sail for America. We were given a small going-away party at The Roses that seemed more like a wake than a festive occasion. I sat among packing crates and luggage and ate cake and shook hands. Someone gave me a flashlight as a good-bye present. It was a thoughtful gift because there was no electricity in India, and the gift giver no doubt thought there was no light in America either. My sister's going-away gift was a miniature tea set.

We left the next morning by bullock cart for Ootacamund and from there by train to Rajahmundry. There were more good-byes at Grandfather's mission; his servants shook my hand gravely. I was hugged by my grandparents but received no advice from Grandfather. Grandfather did not commiserate with us, nor did we expect him to because we knew that he and my aunt Theodora, who was now the director of nurses at Kugler Hospital, would be having the worst of it by remaining in India.

I have always singled out my grandfather and my mother as being stoic, but perhaps that is an illusion of remembrance. Perhaps everyone was more stoic and less complaining then, less apt to bemoan their fate and "belly-ache." It is said that life is more complicated now, but I question whether that is true. I do know that our family was leaving everything familiar behind and crossing the ocean to an uncertain future, yet no one cried. Jesse used to say, "Complaining never did anyone a damn bit of good."

We did not know it, but during the year that Mother, Margaret, and I waited in Kotagiri, Jesse had a rough time of it in the United States. He was given bad advice regarding the classes he needed to renew his credential, his cash was running low, and he feared he would be jobless when we arrived:

Thanks for the birthday card, Hillsborians; it was nice to be remembered.

I have transferred my allegiance to San Jose State College as Stanford is too expensive for my income, or lack of it. I was under the impression that I could complete my work in three quarters but found out it will take five instead. I had very poor advice or guidance when I enrolled in Stanford, and therefore I wasted $120 and a lot of time. They were quite verbose in expressing regrets, but I was the loser and decided not to hand any more checks for tuition in Stanford. So I am going to enroll in San Jose State in the fall and have my credentials in two terms at a cost of about $25 a term.

This change in plans won't set me back very much and will save me a lot of money. Stanford's tuition fees are $115 a term, plus other fees that run anywhere from $2 to $10. Five terms of such extravagance would set me back so far I'd have to reach up to touch bottom. San Jose State is about one fifth as costly, so it's an easy choice. How's the shooting eye these days, Bill? Knockin' 'em cold, I hope.

And, almost one year later:

Was very glad to get your kind birthday remembrance. Wish I could get up to see you some time this summer, but I really don't see how I can do it. It's the old question of money. That particular commodity has been going out all this time with me and none coming in, and believe me I have had to hang on to it until the old eagle has almost been strangled several times. The powers that be at San Jose State are all optimistic about my finding work for this coming fall, and I wish that I could share their optimism. As yet, nothing has developed except writer's cramp and hopes deferred, neither one of which makes for peace of mind.

To top it all off, I have just received word from Ernestine that she is sailing on the twenty-third of this month! Now, I should be walking on air and performing all sorts of gymnastics upon the receipt of such news. But it has filled me with conflicting emotions that take me up into the blue-tinted skies and then plunge me into the depths. I haven't a job, and if they should arrive in August and I was still on the hunt for work—well, draw your own conclusions as to how you might feel.

Will keep you informed of developments, and hope that I can soon report that all is well and the future rosy.

Mother, like Jesse, loved to be at sea. The ticket she bought for the three of us on a Dutch freighter cost $300. Jesse spent the summer in Palo Alto working as a gardener for his sister Eva and her husband. He got his room and board in return "for keeping things in order," as he said. So his Kansas upbringing saw him through the Depression as a handyman and now as a gardener.

The ship we boarded for our voyage was the *Bloemfontein*. I did not know that it was a cheap passage, but assumed that this particular ship had been chosen especially for my entertainment since the freighter was also transporting a cargo of wild animals bound for the San Diego Zoo. There were very few passengers besides Frank Buck (as we called the hunter who had captured the animals), his young daughter, Mother, my sister, and me. The *Bloemfontein* might have been a luxury liner for all I knew—there was so much to explore aboard her, and there were no servants to watch over me. I inspected the toilets closely, for they were marvels to me, and the showers also. I stood on deck and craned my neck to see the solitary sailor perched high in the crow's nest, and inhaled the smell of diesel fuel that ever since has reminded me of the sea. Even the maze of below-decks passageways were wonderful to explore, accompanied by the thrum of the engines that vibrated the steel bulkheads of the ship.

In reality, the *Bloemfontein* was a drab and dismal little ship, painted grey and sailing under a full blackout. Holland was by now at war with Germany, and there was widespread fear of far-ranging U-boats. Although the animal cages were lashed down on deck in full view, we were not allowed to inspect them: several cages imprisoned bewildered, angry tigers and leopards.

On the second or third day at sea, we were summoned on deck for lifeboat drill. I was so seasick that I could hardly stand, but I was ordered to attend the drill nevertheless. The ship's officers took the U-boat threat very seriously, and we were all strapped into life jackets and loaded into the lifeboats before the drill ended. Once I was over my seasickness I loved the sea and that ship. I spent hours walking her decks from bow to stern watching the changing colors and moods of the sea and the seabirds and fish that accompanied our passage.

The great white hunter's daughter immediately fixed her attentions on me—this was no great compliment as I was the only boy on board—and she attempted to order me about as if I were courting her. She followed me everywhere and when I stubbornly (or in a panic) resisted her advances, she threw my flashlight overboard. This was my first encounter with a woman scorned.

The drowning of my flashlight did not displease my mother. Since there were very few passengers on the *Bloemfontein*, my mother, Frank Buck, and other selected adults were usually the captain's guests for dinner. She would leave for the captain's table after giving my sister and me a bath and putting us to bed. As soon as she left, I would get out my flashlight and read with the covers pulled up over my head. Once or twice the book I was reading transported me so far away that I did not hear my mother reenter our cabin. On these occasions she spanked me soundly. I used to wonder why she punished me for pursuing the knowledge she so encouraged. But maybe Mother feared that my flashlight's beam might attract prowling submarines.

We disembarked at Rangoon long enough to visit a Buddhist temple. We removed our shoes to enter the temple, and I was disgusted by having to squish barefoot over its muddy floors. I am sure that I told everyone who would listen what I thought of a religion that would countenance such unhygienic practices.

We did not go ashore in Borneo because, as Mother said, "The place is still full of headhunters and cannibals who would love to shrink our skulls and boil us for breakfast." I protested that I could lick my weight in headhunters given the chance, but we remained on the boat.

Meanwhile, in the United States, Jesse completed his undergraduate studies. He even found a job. The only problem was that he lost us. He explained to Bill:

I have finally located a job for the coming winter, and it is at a small school only four miles from Grass Valley, which is a very nice little town. My burg is called Nevada City, and it is right in the center of the old gold rush days of '49. It is beautiful country and is simply redolent with "tall stories" about the old times when bewhiskered prospectors roamed the hills with their trusty six-shooters, a pack horse, and shovel and pick. There is a gulch that leads away through a pleasant meadow from the school that produced over a million dollars worth of gold in those stirring days. The hills are heavily wooded, and I believe that we will enjoy the many trails that lead over romantic paths through the tall timber. It won't pay a great deal of money, but it will be a beginning and that is a difficult thing for an outsider to do in California. But once I have got on the inside and have had some experience in the California system, I will be in line for something better. This coming winter, though, I will have to sail pretty close to the wind. However we will be able to make it since Ernestine is a good planner and knows how to cut corners. Anyway, we are going to enjoy ourselves in the process.

At present the family is out on the Pacific somewhere between here and Manila—I believe. Several months ago I got a letter from Ernestine saying that she was coming on a cargo boat of the Java Pacific Line. At the time she didn't know the name of the boat or its exact date of sailing. An airmail letter from Calcutta told the name of the boat, its date of sailing, and date of arrival in San Francisco—but the.......censors had blacked that information out! So I still don't know just when to expect her or just what boat she is coming on. However, the Java Line has a boat due here about the twenty-fifth of next month, and so I am going on the supposition that is the one that she is on. I hope to get some word from her after she has been in Manila or Honolulu, because it won't have to go through the censors' prying ways from such ports. But since she feels that she has told me all about the boat, she may not say anything more about it! Oh me.

At any rate I won't have to meet the boat empty handed and be forced to take them over to the local soup line for their first meal ashore. That may sound funny, I know, but when the days and weeks slipped by and no job turned up, it began to look rather dark. You see I have reached the age of forty-two, when men are considered old and decrepit and of little use. Well, it was a long gamble I took when I left the rest of the family out in India and came here looking for work, for I knew that I was soon to join the ranks of the has beens, and if I didn't get over here pronto it would be just too late. So here I be and now that I have got in and the family is on the way, I am just about the happiest man in the whole United States. I will keep you informed about the expected

*arrival of the family, and some day we will get up your way and have
an old time gabfest. Love, Jake*

The *Bloemfontein* steamed from New Guinea toward Hawaii, where a
new culture shock awaited me. Some passengers whose destination was
Honolulu were replaced by a family of Americans for the final leg of our
trip. (The *Bloemfontein* also disembarked one animal trainer who had been
mauled badly while feeding a tiger.) The American family included two
boys about my age, and for the first time in my young life I realized that
everyone in the world did not dress like a proper *pukka sahib*. They were as
amazed by my khaki uniform, bobbed hair, and serious demeanor as I was
by their gaudy Hawaiian shirts, long trousers, and exuberance. On our first
day out from port, these boys produced a couple of cap guns—weapons I
had never seen and that looked and sounded lethal to me—and pursued me
all over the ship whooping and firing at me. I ran terrified over the decks
and through the passageways, while the passengers and crew laughed in
delight. My mother finally arrived on the scene and broke up this "game,"
but I remained an object of ridicule and scorn to the Americans. As for me,
I wished that I could set a tiger or two loose after them or, better yet, return
to Borneo and feed them to the cannibals.

Our voyage from India took about six weeks, and in its last stages
Mother, Margaret, and I stood in the ship's bow waiting for our first
glimpse of America.

Mother somehow got word to Jesse that our ship would dock in Los
Angeles rather than in San Francisco, but our reunion was complicated. The
ship sailed around a concrete breakwater into drab San Pedro Bay. I don't
know what I expected, but there was no Statue of Liberty, no Colossus of
Los Angeles, not even a big sign saying "Welcome to America." In fact, the
shoreline was not even as dramatic as Calcutta's but was dominated by
squat, grey government buildings and the cranes and dry docks of a huge
shipyard. When the *Bloemfontein* at last docked at a pier and all of the other
passengers had exited by the gangplank, Mother, Margaret and I were
detained on deck by an American immigration officer.

While awaiting our arrival, Jesse lived with my young cousin Gertrude
and her husband in Los Angeles, daily checking shipping schedules for
news of our ship. Gertrude remembers the *Bloemfontein's* docking. "When
it was the time you were to come back, John [her husband] and I drove your
father to San Pedro to meet the boat. We watched through awful steel fences
across the water expanse to see Ernestine and you kids on deck. We all
paced, as she was not allowed out on shore for a long time. Poor tortured

Uncle Jake. Finally, Margaret was released, and after Uncle Jake talked to an official, we drove back to our house in Los Angeles with your father and sister but without you and your mother."

Of course I did not know—and neither did my mother—that Terminal Island in San Pedro Bay was, along with San Francisco's Angel Island, California's cousin to Ellis Island in New York. The fact of the matter was that we were being held in a federal prison as illegal aliens. Mother and I were escorted to a spartan room on an upper floor of what appeared to be a gloomy stone fortress. A Mexican woman who I remember as being large and friendly shared our chamber. She was about Mother's age, and they spent the long hours talking together—the woman in broken English—of India and Mexico. I spent most of my waking hours looking out the single window at the ocean we had just crossed and at the ships entering and leaving the harbor. Mother tried to buoy my spirits by making an adventure out of our circumstances, and I pretended that I was the prisoner of Zenda plotting a daring escape.

The door to our small room was not locked, and we were allowed to walk twenty yards or so down the hallway before our escape was blocked by a barred steel door. Here, at the barrier, and with a guard standing watch, Jesse and Mother met every day to discuss our release. After several days, Jesse appeared with Frank Buck from the *Bloemfontein*. He must have had influence with the immigration authorities because the next day we were freed.

Mother was outwardly calm throughout our internment, although it must have been degrading to her. For my part, I was not bewildered by our circumstances. I just assumed internment was a normal part of moving to America—except for little girls who were always given preferential treatment anyway.

Four

A MILLION YEARS AGO the Sierra Nevada range of mountains, then one huge block of granite, was lifted up, tilted, and gradually eroded over the centuries. This gradual wearing away gouged mountain valleys, and snowmelts from the range's peaks carved many streams on the western slopes. Nevada City lay in one of these high valleys at the confluence of several mountain streams.

Perhaps Jesse thought that Nevada City's climate would approximate that of the Indian hill stations of Kodaicanal and Kotagiri. The city nestled at an altitude of 2,600 feet, and the mountains and valleys were forested. But winters in the northern Sierra were more like winters in Oregon: rainfall averaged fifty-three inches annually, and my sister and I were often sick.

Our first home in America was a small furnished cabin north of town. Scattered among other cabins in a grove of conifers, it had a feeling of the north woods about it. For the first time I lived in a wooden house, and I loved the smell of the knotty pine and the give of floors that creaked underfoot. It also had an icebox, electric light, and indoor plumbing.

When I scouted out back beyond the grove, I discovered an old abandoned gold field. Its pockmarked soil had a whitish cast, and its surface blew off a fine dust in the slightest wind. The soil near our cabin must have been more promising, for Mother promptly marked off two garden plots. One plot surrounding the cabin she planted with flowers, and she seeded a large vegetable garden a little further away. She spent long hours in her gardens. This was the first time I saw Mother stoop to manual labor. She cut an unusual figure. While gardening she wore a modest, long dress and a large straw "coolie hat" tied firmly on her head. Though her long dresses would give way to slacks and then to shorts, Mother wore her coolie hat until it completely unraveled.

Gold Flat School, where Jesse was to teach and I was to study, perched on a wooded ridge about four miles from our cabin. In the fall, Jesse and I walked together to the two-story schoolhouse each morning, then he climbed the outside stairway to the second floor where he taught grades five through eight. The ground floor held grades one through four and, at first, no one knew quite what to do with me.

Since I had no formal education—only Mother's tutoring in India—I was finally given aptitude and I.Q. tests, and to Mother's delight scored very high in them. So in the fall of 1940, over Jesse's mild objections, I was placed in the third grade when I was six-and-a-half years old.

My first day at school was a disaster. I arrived in my best "little master" outfit—khaki shorts and shirt, long socks, and high-topped shoes—and sporting my "bonnie Prince Charlie" haircut. My classmates howled and guffawed at my European pronunciation of words like "tom-ah-toes," and my teacher despaired of my English spelling and my penmanship. (Rightly so in the case of my writing, for I had been taught by Mother, and no one could ever decipher her writing effortlessly; it was as if her mind raced ahead of her pencil, so that her written characters all seemed to be blown flat by a strong tail wind.)

No one explained to me the custom of raising one's hand for permission to use the bathroom (actually an outhouse with a thunderbox at Gold Flat School), and so, partly because of ignorance and partly because I did not want to call any more attention to myself, I quietly "pooped" my khaki shorts in class. I couldn't completely wash myself off at recess, and by the time we gathered for a baseball game during P.E. in the afternoon, my classmates were giving me a wide berth. The baseball game itself was a fitting climax to a day of ignominy, as the mechanics of the game so puzzled me that I was once again the butt of jokes and uncontrollable laughter.

In the two years that we lived in Nevada City I never made a close friend at school. My only playmate was another immigrant boy whose family moved into one of the other cabins. His father had been a civil servant in the Philippines, and like us, they left due to rumors of war. My friend and I swapped lies about our heroism, and he told me that he once hunted caribou in the Philippines. Since caribou could not compare with the panthers and tigers I hunted in India, I assumed lordship over him and ordered him about whenever the opportunity arose.

The gold field out back of our cluster of cabins became my constant playground. When Nevada City was a boomtown, miners sunk shafts from several feet to a depth of about twenty feet trying to uncover gold deposits near the bedrock. Then, from the holes, they radiated horizontal tunnels, like spokes—a process called "coyoting." The dirt from the holes and tunnels was still piled about in mounds. Although most of the tunnels were caved in and the deeper holes were filled up, there were still enough of the old mines left for a youth to go exploring. The pockmarked old gold field looked like battlefield to a small, imaginative boy. The holes were bomb craters to me, and the hulks of old gold-mining machinery were charred and rusted tanks and airplanes. From my command post in one of the deeper holes, I would plan my army's strategy, and then with a blood-chilling war cry, I would lead my troops out of the crater in a charge against the enemy.

One day I was busy shoring up my army's defenses by digging into one of the old tunnels. Mother caught me at it, and fearing a cave-in, she marched me straight back to the rear.

Eventually I decided to run away. I don't remember why. It might have been the treatment I received at school, anger at my parents over some trifle, or simply boredom. But I remember announcing one afternoon that I was going to get a job on a tramp steamer and sail back to India. "I promise I'll write to you, and maybe someday we'll meet again," I said.

Actually, I hoped they might suggest I wait until after dinner or even sleep on my decision. But Jesse said, no, no, a bold plan like mine should be implemented while the fires of independence burned brightly. "The main thing you will need on your journey," Jesse said, "is a good stout pole to carry your provisions and for defense in case you meet any robbers."

He promptly went outside to whittle a stick while my mother, apprehensively I thought, prepared some sandwiches and fruit. Margaret went into our bedroom and peeped around the door frame.

"Here we are," Jesse said, reentering with a long stick. "Now we'll just wrap your provisions in this kerchief and tie the bundle onto the end of your pole so that the load is distributed evenly."

He showed me how to sling the apparatus over my shoulder and to balance it.

"It seems awfully light for a long trip," I remarked.

"You mustn't take extra supplies or clothes, not even a spare jacket, and only a minimum of food when destiny calls so abruptly," said Jesse. "Strike out boldly, and you will be rewarded for the fine and heroic deeds you are sure to accomplish."

With this, he ushered me out to the sidewalk. I barely had time to say goodbye to my mother and sister—and certainly no time at all for the tearful farewell I had envisioned—and Jesse told me how much he admired me.

Then with a pat on my back and a solemn shake of my hand, he bid me farewell and Godspeed. With this he disappeared back inside our cabin.

I walked a couple of miles before I ate all my provisions. Then I began to feel very lonely and afraid. In my own defense, I waited until evening to return home. It wasn't easy. I thought of the warm wood stove and the fine dinner my mother must have been preparing, and our little cabin seemed cozier than ever before.

As I reached our front gate, Mother and Margaret rushed out to greet me as if I had just returned from a far land. Jesse, too, seemed satisfied that I had accomplished something. Miracle of miracles: there was just enough dinner left over to feed me, and a slice of pie to boot. I had a hot bath and went to bed, promising to tell Margaret about my adventures in the morning.

After I was banished from my gold field battleground and following my aborted journey, Jesse decided to build me a box kite to keep me occupied. He fashioned it carefully, and when it was completed it was a beautiful creation. Like all of the objects Jesse ever made with his hands, it was far too fine a piece of craftsmanship to be put to practical use. Everything he made had to be seen to be believed, especially since he always used the most primitive tools. And since these works of art were made so finely, they battered and broke easily in the hands of a boy.

In Jesse's hands, the kite soared and sparkled in the sky; in mine it swooped and darted dangerously until one day it crashed beyond repair into a tree. I remember looking at the wrecked kite, its colorful fabric shredded and its struts splintered. Jesse comforted and reassured me—it was only a kite, he said—but he never built another.

My school year was interrupted that spring. Mother and I traveled to Vancouver to unravel our immigration problems. Mother and I were granted some sort of temporary visas in San Pedro, but the authorities were not finished with us. So we dutifully boarded a train bound north. Contrasted to the dramatic landscapes of India—vast unbroken plains, abrupt mountains, dense jungles, brilliant dome-like skies, and vivid colors—the trip through Oregon and Washington was like a journey through a forested kingdom. The stately snow-capped peaks of the northwest territory filled the train windows one by one—Shasta, Hood, Ranier. We traveled through the beautiful Willamette Valley that my father loved, and crossed the wide Columbia River. Even our train was sleek and luxurious compared to Indian trains, although we traveled in the cheapest possible class.

As I dig up old thoughts and emotions—how I felt on the trip north and the general feelings I had even amidst all that splendid scenery—I find that they were mostly unspoken feelings of unease and the beginnings of a sense that the dragonslayer was, after all, a child. Alone for the first time with my mother in strange territory, her "little protector" felt that he would be inadequate in an emergency. Yet these Americans were friendly—far more easy-going than most of the English civil servants and missionaries I had met. I know now that my feelings were brought on by my mother's apprehension. For the first time, Mother showed vulnerability, her eyes would mist over and she would look away from me and out the train window. Of course, this only strengthened my youthful resolve to protect her at all costs, though in my heart I quailed.

I remember Vancouver as a gray and rainy city. Our hotel was in the poorer part of town where the government buildings were located. I don't remember how many days we spent there, but they seemed endless. Mother was away "taking care of things" all day, and I was left alone in our room to fight the Battle of Britain with a small silver airplane that Mother bought for me in a five-and-dime store. At lunch time, when she returned to the room, and in the evenings, we dined on white bread sandwiches filled with Kraft sandwich spread. I loved the sandwich spread and the novel soft white bread. Far from my understanding that it was a necessity, I thought it was a rare treat, and Mother nourished that illusion by pretending that we were on a sort of holiday and we could "picnic."

At last our business in Vancouver was concluded, successfully, I thought. Mother was in a much better frame of mind on our trip home, and her old confidence seemed to have returned. When we returned safely and school had closed for summer vacation, Jesse wrote to Bill:

It is a cold, clammy, damp morning, and even though it is no doubt unusual for California, there is little consolation in the fact. Seems to me that we have had a lot of "unusual" weather this past year. But what to do?

Ernestine's sister has been with us for the past two weeks and leaves us this noon for points east. She has brought along a lot of things, but the thing that interested me most was the jar of curry powder. Oh boy! Good Indian curry can't be bought for any price in this country, although they make extravagant claims for it when they sell it to you. But even at its best, the real Indian atmosphere is lost without the plantain leaves for plates and fingers for eating. One of the things that I miss most about India is the hot Indian foods—how I like 'em. But you should see Ernestine go for mango chutney—she eats it like it was apple butter. That stuff is so hot that it will melt the fillings out of your teeth if it isn't taken with caution. India gets into one's blood, and after a few years out there it is hard to reconcile oneself to life in the states. Personally, I would have been very glad to stay right on indefinitely and so would have Ernestine, but the kids had to be considered above our own desires.

I have had three day's work since school closed, and it looks as though the opportunities for earning an honest dollar are rather few and far between. I have put an ad in the local paper, but the results haven't been very gratifying. The chief occupation of the people in these hills is mining, and a school teacher has about as much chance of getting a job with them as a snowball has of surviving in purgatory. I have tried to sell some drawings to the Saturday Evening Post, *but received a rejection slip! My drawings are just as good as any of the other cartoons, but the ideas weren't quite up-to-date. Most of the cartoons in the magazines have to do with life in the army or navy, and so I am trying to think up some clever ideas on that phase of life. If you have any bright strokes that you wish to pass on, I'll give you a cut on the check! The* Post *pays $30 a drawing for beginners, and gosh knows how much more for those who have worked up a reputation. I have been told that it is one of the hardest magazines to crash into, so I don't feel too discouraged by a rejection the first time.*

Have you been to the movies lately? David and Margaret went on Saturday to see Gene Autry in Sunset in Wyoming. *We hope to see* The Reluctant Dragon *next week.*

Between Gene Autry in the Saturday matinees and Red Ryder in the Sunday comics, I became Americanized enough to include the cowboy in my list of heroes along with knights, bengal lancers, and great white hunters. To see valiant heroes I had only previously read about in books come alive on a movie screen was astonishing. Up to this point in my life I had only seen two movies. They were both Charlie Chaplin films, and he scarcely fit my idea of a hero.

Since we were surrounded by piney woods, Jesse unpacked his *kukri* knife in order to cut us a Christmas tree. He sharpened the knife on a stone, spitting on the stone to whet it and repeating the story of the *kukri* knife to me. Jesse said a Ghurka gave him the knife, and among the Ghurkas the *kukri* knife was a sacred weapon. It was never to be unsheathed without drawing blood; so when it was sharpened, you pricked your finger slightly just to preserve the sacredness of the knife. He asked me if I would like to pretend I was a Ghurka soldier and have my finger pricked with the knife when he finished sharpening it. I declined, so Jesse pricked his own finger, which I thought was brave of him. Actually, I don't think Jesse ever really pricked his finger, because I never saw any blood. We walked into the hills, and Jesse showed me how to select a perfect Christmas tree. He cut it down with one stroke of the *kukri*, and we slogged home carrying the tree and smelling the green pine needles.

When Christmas day arrived, I was both delighted and disappointed. I received only two gifts, but they cost my parents dearly. I had asked them to outfit me like a genuine cowboy, and the first present I opened contained a cowboy outfit. My parents were used to ordering via mail order catalogues in India, and when they came to America they just naturally transferred their allegiance to Montgomery Ward. My outfit may have looked swell in the catalogue, but on inspection it was unbelievably garish. The chaps were all white and fleecy, like imitation lamb's wool. They itched like crazy besides being silly-looking. The Stetson was red, high-crowned, and made of some sort of pressed cardboard. A vest to match the chaps was included. It was black with tufts of fleece and red stars all over it. Wards threw in a couple of red "leather" wristbands to complete the ensemble. They were made of a cardboard-like substance and had glass studs all over them. The costume didn't look like any of the cowboy outfits other children owned and of which I was envious; in fact, mine made me a further object of ridicule. In Mother's defense, she would not have known what genuine cowboy duds looked like in the first place. Years later, when I was acting in Hollywood and being costumed to play gunfighters on television Westerns like "Gunsmoke" and "Bonanza," I remembered my first cowboy outfit with nostalgia and wished that I had saved it.

My second present was a real beauty. When I opened the package I found a genuine Red Ryder lever-action BB gun. Before I was allowed to fire my new rifle, Jesse instructed me on its safe use and promised to impound it if he ever caught me shooting at birds or cats. I treasured that rifle and never had it taken away from me.

It took Mother years to become fully trusting of American products and even more years to become fashion conscious. If a thing wasn't sensible or practical, to her it had no value or appeal at all. We were poor, but even given our circumstances, Mother seemed to make the drabbest choices possible for a long time. By now she had acquiesced and purchased a pair of long trousers for me via "Monkey Ward." They were made of a heavy, stiff, uncomfortable corduroy, and bore no resemblance to what the other children were wearing. And though they withstood all of my youthful battering, I never could batter much of the stiff uncomfortableness out of them.

Mother believed in practical and inexpensive remedies for childhood ailments too. A doctor was summoned when I developed pleurisy, but not until it had become very serious. When I came down with whooping cough, Mother first treated me with Smith Brothers cough drops (the foulest tasting stuff I can remember, even worse than cod liver oil or castor oil) and punished me when I had coughing fits at night. Finally, in exasperation more than anything else, a doctor was called to treat me.

Some of my ailments were psychological, but I was never happy in Nevada City because I was never really well there. I was a small, rather frail child and seemed destined to grow into medium height like my grandfather, but without his hardy constitution. My schoolmates never did take to me, and I began to blink and stammer badly. Because I was nervous, my scalp started flaking, and my mother treated that condition with bottled mange cure, which caused me to stink. I began to believe that Mother thought if anything smelled or tasted particularly badly, it must be very good for you. She was always suspicious of what she called "doctored-up" (flavored) medicines. When I was afflicted with colds, which was often in that unfamiliar climate, I was given a teaspoonful of cod liver oil morning and night and made to chew on Smith Brothers cough drops.

Jesse tried to cheer me up by building me a wooden wagon. It was a lovingly crafted piece. The wagon bed was hand carved, sanded, planed, and finished. Jesse scrounged up an old frame somewhere, repaired it, and greased the bearings and axles, making it better than new. Although it was lightweight and I easily outraced other children over Nevada City's hills, I never ceased to envy them their brightly colored, heavy, metal wagons.

Then, what seemed like a golden opportunity presented itself to Jesse. His roommate from Stanford, now a teacher in Salinas, wrote of an impending opening at a Salinas school and promised to throw his weight behind any application Jesse might want to make. Whether his friend's promise seemed airtight or whether Jesse and Mother were so disappointed with Nevada City that they were grasping at straws, I don't know. But without any hesitation and without a contract in hand, Jesse quit Gold Flat School, and we moved precipitously to Salinas in June of 1942.

The clearest and happiest memories I retain of Nevada City are of Jesse's and my walks together to and from school. By the heat of the wood stove, I would shrug into my woolen mackinaw and wrap a muffler around my throat. Then, in the cold early morning, with books under our arms and lunch buckets in hand, Jesse and I would set off across the highway and through the woods. Sometimes I got a science lecture. Jesse pointed out poisonous mushrooms and edible plants to me, named species of birds and imitated their songs or described the ecological function of trees. Though he explained the trick of blazing a trail in the forest so that one wouldn't become lost, he never cut into a tree with his pocket knife to demonstrate. I came to understand that to Jesse the forest was as sacred as a church.

Once through the woods, we crossed a mined-out creek on narrow planks. The water in the creek was so clear that you could see the gravel bottom, but its edges were covered with a golden, frothy scum. Jesse crossed first, daily testing the planks, and then waited for me to follow—balancing my books and lunch and tiptoeing precariously. Then it was up the hill to school.

On our way home, I was usually depressed from another dismal day of my classmates' hazing. On these days, Jesse made up stories for me about the forty-niners who used to pan the streams or about Indians who once stalked the forests. The Indian stories were particularly fine because many of them had been taken from James Fenimore Cooper books, though I did not know that then.

I don't remember that my bad days were ever mentioned. But often my father told me of his own boyhood in Kansas when he walked miles barefoot across the prairie in winter to attend school. My favorite character in Jesse's Kansas stories was his black friend, Pompeii Williams. As Jesse described him, Pompeii was huge and incredibly strong for his age, but was gentle-natured. When he and Jesse were schoolmates, they would go off together and share Jesse's meager lunch in a remote corner of the schoolyard, for respectable white boys did not associate with blacks. The other boys would crowd around chanting, "Nigger and a white, nigger and a white," but they would never approach too closely for fear of raising Pompeii's wrath. Jesse said that would have been impossible, for Pompeii did not understand the cruelty behind the words. Pompeii would just grin broadly, which made him look more ferocious than ever, and the other children would run away afraid.

In another story Jesse told me as we crossed the creek one day, he and Pompeii showed up together at the local swimming hole. A gang of youths, who knew that Pompeii could not swim, threatened to swarm over him and forcibly throw him in the deep hole. Genuinely frightened, Pompeii seized two of the ringleaders by the scruff of their necks. He held them out at arm's length over the pond, and with tears streaming down his face, pleaded, "Don't throw Pompeii in! Oh please, don't throw Pompeii in!" The terrified boys promptly agreed not to dunk Pompeii, and he set them down gently, all the while thanking them for not drowning him. "Don't throw Pompeii in" became a code understood only by Jesse and me meaning "Don't provoke me." Later, Jesse showed me an old snapshot of Pompeii. He had on a shrunken suit of Sunday-go-to-meeting clothes and really was gigantic. But what a wonderful smile he had.

At any rate, I always arrived at home somewhat soothed after walking with Jesse. The combined effect of the quiet woods and Jesse's stories about inner strength and human kindness always calmed me and helped me to forget another awful day at Gold Flat School.

******

If fortune did not smile on us in Nevada City, she abandoned us in Salinas. Jesse's job did not materialize because the position had already been promised to a local applicant, and for the first time since their marriage, Mother returned to work. Salinas was the county seat of Monterey County; it was a large sprawling city with no public transportation. Not only did the city's size seem overwhelming, but the climate, too, was worse than Nevada City's—chilly night and morning fog and hot overcast days in summer. This unpleasant weather was fine for raising the crops or cattle on which the large ranches of the area depended, but otherwise it was oppressive. I should have been delighted to live in a "cow town," but these cowboys bore no resemblance to fictional Western heroes. Mostly overweight, with their flashy belt buckles hidden by their sagging bellies, they waddled rather than sauntered down the city's streets. Too, it was our family's first encounter with neighborhoods, those class or ethnic islands that make up a real city. We moved to "Rose Court" in a working class neighborhood. The court consisted of a horseshoe-shaped cluster of squat, stucco, imitation-Spanish-style cottages all joined together by common walls. This neighborhood was chosen, aside from the fact that it was cheap, because it was within walking distance of downtown. We had come a far piece from The Roses to Rose Court.

Jesse went to work as a civilian fireman at Fort Ord near Monterey. World War II was gathering momentum, and the fort was becoming a major launching point for troops being shipped to the Pacific theater. (I was learning that in America war was theater and sports was war.) Since

68

most able-bodied young men were being drafted, the fort was hiring civilians to oversee its day-to-day operation, and Jesse was able to hitch a ride daily fifteen miles away to the coast. He was also issued an olive drab uniform, which I thought was terrific.

Rose Court was part of a good-natured, rowdy neighborhood, full of rough, working-class kids. At first I was overawed by their enthusiasm and stood watching them out of our large front window that faced the street. It was the greatest thrill of my life the day I was accepted into their "gang." After several days of watching them through the window (I had been instructed to stay inside and "guard the house" while my parents worked), I ventured outside to watch.

The Hartnell Street gang was choosing up sides for a baseball game in the street, and one side had come up a player short. Rusty, the captain of the playerless team, called casually over at me, "Hey, kid, you wanna play on our side?" He made no comment about my silly haircut or funny clothes.

"Sure. Where do you want me to play?" I asked this in spite of the fact that baseball's intricacies still eluded me. I stopped playing at Gold Flat School rather than continue exposing my ineptness.

"Listen, kid," Rusty said, in what I was to learn was his most charming manner. "Since you're new on the block, we're gonna let you play right field." Right Field! My heart leaped. The way Rusty said it, it sounded as if right field was the ultimate position an athlete could ever aspire to play.

Right field, as I was instructed to play it, turned out to be on a lawn directly under a neighbor's large picture window. Very few of the gang had baseball gloves, but I stood on our neighbor's lawn rubbing my bare hands together and praying that a ball would be hit my way so that I could justify Rusty's great faith in me. Finally, a well-hit ball sailed in my direction. I retreated back, back, back as far as I could and leaped, but the ball went over my outstretched hands and crashed through the neighbor's picture window.

Usually the streets were deserted during the day as most of the families worked somewhere, and the gang pretty much did as they pleased. However, after the window shattered, the gang scattered. That is, everyone scattered but me. I was too shocked by the crashing glass to gather my wits about me. To compound my difficulties, the neighbor's wife was at home and came rushing out to collar me. She threatened and demanded the names of the other children who were involved. I kept mum, not out of honor, but because I truly didn't know their names, not even Rusty's yet. So she took my name as I sadly pointed out our cottage in Rose Court, and said she would hold me personally responsible for her broken window. I slouched home crying. When I explained the situation to Mother and Jesse that evening I could not even give them the names of my companions, so my folks made an arrangement to pay for the neighbor's window, adding to their financial woes.

The smashed window turned out to be a blessing in disguise for me. The very next morning, after my parents left for work, the whole Hartnell Street gang came knocking on our door. When I opened it, there was much backslapping and talk of what a fine fellow I was for keeping my mouth shut, and I was officially invited to join the gang. The neighbor whose window had been shattered turned out to be heartily disliked by the community, and on that Saturday while my mother was on her hands and knees picking clover out of our pitifully small front lawn, a parade of neighbors who had looked on us as peculiar stopped to welcome us to the neighborhood and to pass the time of day.

Though I hated Salinas, I loved my neighborhood gang. I had found kindred adventurous spirits. One day I invited my friends to our house to show them our Indian mementos, and they ate everything in the refrigerator. After that episode I was locked out of our cottage during the day, so I went up the street to Rusty's garage, which his parents had converted into a clubhouse for the gang. There we all drank Kool-Aid and read comic books like "The Blackhawks," "Defenders of Justice," "Batman and Robin," "Captain Marvel," and "The Blue Beetle" (my favorite because he looked like a knight in scaly blue chain mail). Eventually I was discovered there by my mother when she returned early from work, and was forbidden to hang out at the clubhouse any more. Jesse and Mother did agree that I could subscribe to a couple of "acceptable" comic books—"True Comics" (a sort of *Reader's Digest* for children) and "Classic Comics," which adapted literature to comic-book format. But most days, I simply ignored my mother's admonitions to stay away from Rusty and the gang, and spent my days hanging out at his garage. I was beginning to be more circumspect and devious, though.

One evening when I was playing Blue Beetle and looking for crime to fight, I found myself alone in the junior college football stadium, several blocks from our house. Suddenly I was jumped by four or five Mexican boys who wrestled me to the ground and tried to pants me. This wasn't a uniquely Mexican trick. If anthropologists examined the origins of "pantsing," they would probably find it was once called "loin-clothing" and is as fundamentally cross-cultural as hunting or food-gathering. Luckily, in the nick of time, my gang came shrieking

70

out of the twilight to drive my tormentors off and save me from the ignominy of being pantsed.

Soon after I was approached furtively by another group of Mexican boys. They came from their own neighborhood several blocks away to apologize for their renegade friends' behavior. These boys invited me to visit their clubhouse, which was accomplished by scaling back fences and negotiating a maze of alleys. I liked the Mexican gang's headquarters better than my own companions', because it was more military and organized. They had collected lots of corrugated tin and boards with which to build fortifications, and their clubhouse was a big hole dug in the ground of the leader's dirt backyard. The hole was covered up with boards and cardboard to camouflage it. The result was like a bomb shelter. Candles illuminated this command post, and there were crates on which to sit and plan strategy.

War had been declared in December of 1941, and like every other child of the forties we involved ourselves in war games that we took more seriously than we did any other games. I began a precarious life as a double agent, moving cautiously back and forth between the lines on spying missions. I cannot say why I was disloyal to my own neighborhood gang except that I truly liked the Mexicans and they seemed to accept me without question. In truth, there was nothing to spy on and no important information to exchange except about comic books and baseball. It was all talk and bluff, and the Anglos and Mexicans were more curious about each other than anything else. The Mexicans, whose games seemed spontaneous and animated reminded me of the poverty-stricken Indian children with whom I was never allowed to play, but who seemed so happily optimistic.

I spent a lot of time—disguised—sitting high in the crotch of a tree looking out over the houses and lots that separated the neighborhoods. It was very peaceful in that tree. My perch was much like a crow's nest on a sailing ship, and I often daydreamed that the cream-colored homes were ocean breakers and that I was Amyas in *Westward Ho*, my favorite "Classics Comics" hero. I did not separate people from causes yet—my allegiances were personal rather than political—nor did I play these games with abandon. I was still a fairly serious, withdrawn dreamer.

If I got home late, Jesse was too tired to discipline me. He was working long hours and was not used to hard labor anymore. His days in the rock quarry and lumber mills of Oregon were long gone, and he was the oldest and probably the smallest fireman at the army base. In my case, I always felt a reluctance on Jesse's part to punish me. That was Mother's domain, and Mother was beginning to worry about me.

We attended Jesse's friend's church on Sundays. The friend was a Methodist and the services were a disappointment after the pomp and pageantry of the Lutheran church. One Sunday I put a dime in the offering basket and took out a quarter's worth of change. I used this stolen wealth to buy two miniature metal officers to command my army of rubber soldiers. I coveted my friends' collections of all-metal troops, brigades, tanks, and warplanes; now at last I had proper officers. Since I got away with it once, I repeated my plate picking the next Sunday and was caught. My mother wept at the disgrace I brought on our family, and my father was not too tired to strap me.

It was an especially hot, overcast summer in the Salinas Valley in 1942. The air was oppressive compared to that in the high altitudes of the Sierra or the hills of India. One Saturday, when Jesse had an unexpected day off, my parents took my sister and me to the small, tree-shaded park in the center of town. We spread out a blanket and picnicked under a tree. Perhaps I had asked to come to the park to launch my new submarine. On our journey south from the Sierra we stopped to see Aunt Daisy and Uncle Ed, Jesse's older sister and brother-in-law. Ed was the new manager of a department at the local Monkey Wards and, as in-laws are apt to do with their wife's relatives, he was anxious to show off his position and to share his good fortune.

We were taken on a grand tour of the store, and Ed invited Margaret and me to choose a toy as a personal gift from him. Ed made a large sweeping gesture when he said, "pick anything." Margaret, with Mother's help, chose some modest trifle, but I selected an expensive metal submarine. Mother protested my extravagance, but Ed, who could not very well withdraw his offer without looking miserly, was stuck. He waved Mother off with a generous gesture, and the expensive sub was mine.

On this Saturday in Salinas Central Park I had been promised that I could finally launch my new sub, for the park enclosed a large, circular wading pool. It was a very shallow pool—no more than a foot or so deep. So even infants could splash about in it without fear of drowning, and on this hot day it was crowded. Into this welter of happy children, I launched my brand new submarine, while in a far corner of the park Jesse napped and Mother read to Margaret. My blue steel submarine was about ten inches long with a sharp, pointed bow for steep diving. The sub's engine was wound up with a key, and it was driven by a shiny, sharp metal screw that buzzed beneath the stern. If the diving fins were set just right before launching, this wondrous submarine would slip beneath the water's surface

72

and then speed along with only its periscope showing until its powerful spring wound down.

I cannot adequately describe the havoc my submarine caused that day. It sped forth out of my hands, dove, and sped on—cracking the first child it met on the shins and kept on round and round the pool, careening from child to child. It banged into some with its bow and nicked others with its propeller. Children tumbled over each other like tenpins and wailed and screamed for their mothers and fathers who came running to their rescue.

I stood in shock again as I had in the baseball game. I had only meant to try out my sub and perhaps to impress park-goers with its intricate maneuvers. I hadn't known that it would run completely amok. My parents, too, came running and we all made profuse apologies. The submarine itself was stomped to death on the cement floor of the wading pool by an irate parent—its fins broken and its hull bent beyond repair.

Our whole Salinas summer was not a happy one. My parents always spoke of it as the worst time in their lives together. Jesse especially despaired, for he must have regretted leaving Nevada City so impulsively. He was wearing down from the hard work, and his old doubts about his ability to support his family must have returned. Finally, just before he resigned himself to an indefinite stretch at Fort Ord, an offer of an elementary school teaching job in Healdsburg, California, arrived. Though it didn't pay much, Jesse accepted it. And my family would never again be budged. Jesse remained loyal for the rest of his life to the man who proffered the job, and he refused much better offers from other schools. We at last found a home in America—although Mother always insisted that the main reason we moved away from Salinas was because I was becoming a "juvenile delinquent."

Five

IN 1942 THE OLD EL CAMINO REAL, the Royal Road of the Spaniards, wound north from San Francisco Bay following the coastal range of mountains. As the narrow two-lane highway ran up through the Petaluma plain, fishing villages on Richardson's Bay gave way to cattle, sheep, and chicken ranches. Then, as the Sonoma mountains angled in from the east to constrict the plain, open grazing lands with clustered California oaks were transformed into lush orchards and vineyards. At its northernmost end, the plain met the Russian River, so called for the early Russian settlers at Fort Ross who had plied the river. There were no dams on the river then, and it rushed straight south after parting from the Eel until it twisted through Alexander Valley six miles north of Healdsburg. Then the river met Fitch Mountain at Healdsburg, veered abruptly, circled the mountain in a wide sweep, and altered its course westward toward the sea some fifteen miles away. After altering its course, the river formed a rich bottomland that held as far as the timbered coastal mountains. Before the Russians came, Pomo Indians called the river the Snake.

Healdsburg lay in the crook made by the river's curve, in the shadow of Fitch Mountain. To the north, after several climbing miles, was the deep, wooded Russian River gorge and beyond that the high Mendocino plateau. San Francisco was sixty-five miles to the south, twelve hours away by Greyhound bus in 1942. After 1942, bus service was discontinued until the war's end.

The town of Healdsburg was named after Harmon Heald, who built a trading post at the confluence of Dry Creek and the Russian River to trade with the Russians and Indians in 1852. As the trading post grew into a settlement it was renamed Russian River. As it grew into a town, it was renamed Healdsburgh. Over time the final "h" was dropped.

Healdsburg itself was not built on the banks of the river because the river's plain was far too valuable for homesites. Instead, the town's main street was developed along a tributary of Dry Creek that flowed into the river at the south end of town. A long block of brick commercial buildings were constructed with their loading docks toward the creek and the railroad track that followed its course. The storefronts, bars, hotel, and movie theater in this block all faced West Street and, across the street, a large plaza. In my youth, the plaza was covered with Kentucky blue grass. It was planted with rose bushes, citrus trees, and palms, and boasted an ornate granite bandstand—a lot like the one in Kotagiri, only bigger. Until 1870, the plaza served as a central parking lot for horses and wagons, and the commercial core of Healdsburg just grew up around it.

Except for the bars, which had names like the 339 Club, Buck & Ernie's, Vic n Sis' Nuf Sed, and The Sportsmen's Club, the businesses were all named Plaza something-or-other: the Plaza Hotel, the Plaza Theatre, the Plaza Drugstore, and the Plaza Market. Exceptions were the Bank of America building or the two-and-a-half-story brick City Hall with its bell towers, court, police department, and one-cell jail. Harmon Heald, whose trading post became Healdsburg, sold plots of land to the east of the plaza, and these in turn gave way to regular blocks that grew slowly eastward toward Fitch Mountain. The Northwest Pacific Railroad tracks, laid in 1871, created a man-made boundary to the west and south of Healdsburg, and those boundaries still held in 1942. There was no development on "the other side of the tracks" except for farms. Past the farms to the immediate north was an area that had been called "The Plains" in the old days and that was now the small town of Geyserville. Some seven miles to the immediate south lay the fragmented communities of Windsor and Fulton. They had been collectively called "Poor Man's Flat" once, because so many poor laborers and farmers lived and worked there.

Fitch Mountain, which bordered Healdsburg on the east, had always carried the city's hopes for prosperity, if not for fame. Even though Fitch Mountain was actually two feet short of being a real mountain, it was impressive. Its slopes were heavily wooded, unlike the other surrounding mountains that had been mined for rhyolite and stripped of their timber many years earlier. From the top of Fitch Mountain, Captain Henry Fitch first surveyed his domains. When Captain Fitch married the sister-in-law of General Mariano Vallejo, all the land that could be seen from the top of the mountain became his Sotoyome rancho. As early as the turn of the century, when Grandfather Neudoerffer was arriving in India, the merchants of

Healdsburg were discussing the feasibility of mounting a lighted beacon on the summit of Fitch Mountain to attract tourists. The beacon was never erected, but the tourists came to the mountain anyway. Their summer homes ringed the mountain, following the loop of the Russian River.

Sonoma, site of the Bear Flag Revolt, lay some thirty miles to the south and east of Healdsburg, and Sacramento—the state capital—was twice as far away as San Francisco. In those days, Los Angeles seemed as distant as New York City.

There had been little change in the population of Healdsburg since the turn of the century. When our family arrived in 1942, it was the same as it had been in 1880: 2,000 people. The actual town seemed much smaller than this though, as many residents lived on farms reached by the country roads that twisted out of Healdsburg along the waterways—Russian River, Mill Creek, Felton Creek, Dry Creek, Sausal Creek.

By the time we arrived in Healdsburg, the town had grown east to the base of Fitch Mountain—about eight long blocks. Matheson Street, which intersected West Street at the plaza to form a "T" in the center of Healdsburg, became Fitch Mountain Road at Second Street, the eastern city limits, and continued around Fitch Mountain's ten-mile girth. Here Bay Area aristocrats owned summer cottages overlooking the river.

We first lived in a part of town that dated back to the 1880s. After the 1906 earthquake, most of the homes around our University Street house were rebuilt in the two-story California bungalow style. They were made of native wood with exposed beams and overhanging eaves. Most of them had sleeping porches. As Healdsburg, faced on the east by Fitch Mountain, was squeezed into north-south growth, these old homes were either maintained scrupulously or fell into disrepair.

Byron Gibbs, the new principal of the elementary school that hired Jesse, located the house for us. His own home stood just across a vacant, grassy lot. We rented the house cheaply because it was very old. Mother despaired of it. It was too large to clean easily, our meager household goods (which were mostly Aunt Eva's castoffs) were dwarfed in its big rooms, and there was no space for a garden. But I loved it. I explored everywhere, discovering that the large closet in my upstairs bedroom extended through to my sister's closet in her room next door. I could, cleverly disguised, pop out to surprise her whenever I wanted. The large screened porch that abutted our bedrooms had ample room to race and tumble around in or even, when I obtained my first pair of roller skates, to skate in. Our tiny dirt backyard was dominated by a large scarred oak tree where Jesse hung a swing for my sister and me. When I got to arcing up high, I could kick the house's eaves on my forward peak and touch the garage roof with my toes on my backward swing.

These antics contributed to my mother's discomfort, but she endured them because they at least did not smack of gangs and delinquency. My father, on the other hand, was reasonably content. He set up a woodshop in the garage—we weren't to have a car for years—and it was out of this shop that our furniture began to be produced.

The best part of our new location was the enormous vacant lot next to our house. In summer it was overgrown with grass up to a child's armpits. By lying on one's belly, a boy could snake his way through the high, dry grass, and flatten down narrow, hidden trails. Mr. Gibbs had a son about my age named Teddy, and he became my first friend in Healdsburg. Teddy would belly into his side of the lot at the same time I began crawling from my side. We crept along our trails and created new ones, trying to avoid each other while swatting bugs from our eyes and wiping off sweat, until one of us surprised the other and won the game. By the end of summer the grass in the lot was smashed flat.

This was nothing like the "gang wars" of Salinas, but Teddy would not have stooped to such elemental aspects of warfare. His biological father had been a cavalry officer who was killed in a fall from his horse. Teddy had artifacts to prove it. His mother's descendants were landed gentry and Mr. Gibbs, after he married Teddy's mother, pretended to the aristocracy too. His den was full of leather-bound books, glass-encased rifles and shotguns, paintings, and expensive pipes. More than anything, Mr. Gibbs was squire-like: tall, with a clipped mustache. Graying at the temples, he smelled of pipe tobacco and cologne.

It was an unusually long summer. Because of the war, farmers had trouble harvesting their crops, and the opening of school was delayed until early October. One reason for the labor shortage was that all the Japanese who worked on local farms were ordered to relocation camps by newly elected Attorney General Earl Warren. The Japanese in Sonoma County were well liked because they were content to work for others, whereas in many California counties the Japanese were buying their own farmland. They were not so well liked in those counties.

In early October, Healdsburg's weekly paper, the *Healdsburg Tribune and Sotoyome Scimitar*—commonly called the *Tribune* or just the *Trib*—carried the headline, "Elementary School Hires Two New Instructors." The story read: "…Jesse E. Manley of Salinas will take the duties of seventh and eighth grades from Byron Gibbs, who is the new principal. Mrs. Laura Jo Nichols of Kern County is the new school nurse." Included in the paper was news that a P-38 fighter plane from the Fulton Army Air Base had crashed in a local prune orchard, that old keys were needed for scrap metal, that old nylon and silk hose were in demand to make powder bags for the artillery, and that induction of married men without children would begin in November.

Two men, one German and one Italian, were arrested in the same week for violation of alien curfew laws and transported to the county jail. Fourteen acres of good bottomland planted to prunes, pears, and apples was priced to sell at $215 an acre, and Ben Franklin and Federated Stores were selling chambray work shirts for $.98, men's cords for $3.85, denim jackets for $1.95, and bib overalls for $1.49.

The advertisement for the Plaza Theatre read: "Thursday it's Jungle Love in Gorgeous Technicolor. See Dorothy Lamour in *Beyond the Horizon* with Richard Denny. Also *March of Time* features "Men of the Fleet." Cartoon-Novelty-News. Friday, Saturday, Wallace Beery in *Thunder Afloat.*"

Readers were told that the *Tribune* had been sold, the former owner having left for Hawaii and defense work. The new owner editorialized that Russia alone was standing off Hitler and that "Stalin will go down in history as the savior of the free world." He warned that Japan was winning the war and that "a series of disasters" was befalling U.S. forces.

The farthest corners of Healdsburg were within easy walking distance. Even Fitch Mountain Road could be circled at a leisurely pace in a couple of hours. So our family walked everywhere. Jesse, Margaret, and I never rode to school in a car, even in the rain, in all of our years there.

Healdsburg Elementary School was only four blocks away from our University Street home. The school was a single-story mission-style building painted a pinkish color that resembled the clay of the river's banks. The school's cobbled entrance faced a corner, and the classroom wings angled off down two converging streets to form a wide "V." The school playground between the V's wings was nothing but dirt and gravel. Two tiny baseball diamonds, one at each far corner of the yard, marked the perimeter of the school.

Children were not deterred from playing on the schoolyard's abrasive surface. Before long I had shredded several sets of school outfits, and Mother began sending me to school in old clothes like the rest of the boys. But that came later.

That first October morning, I was led to Miss Mayes's fifth grade class and my American education really began. Miss Mayes had a clubfoot, which she compensated for by use of one special shoe, the sole of which must have been four inches thick. Though she was not young, Miss Mayes rouged and powdered her face heavily and her lipstick was a bright red. She was also partial to dangling metal earrings like Indian women wore—so that she thumped and jangled when she walked. She was a marvelous teacher—an actress, really—and her lessons were delivered with a fine imagery. My integration into the class was easier than it had been in Nevada City. I was still considered somewhat of an oddball and an easy mark, but I had Teddy to introduce me and before long I ceased to be such a curiosity.

I met Jere and Bruce Holbrook, the dentist's sons. They lived in a big house a block from the school. Jere was the "general" of his own army, a group of neighborhood boys that marched regularly in formations and whose headquarters was a wooden backyard fort built by Jere. His best recruiter was his sister, Lorelei, who was his army's nurse. Although Jere was my classmate, I first became friendly with Bruce at a marbles game. Most all young boys played marbles at recess, and marbles were Bruce's forte. I initially traded Bruce a pair of teak elephant bookends for a starter's sack of marbles, including a couple of steelies and several stickers which Bruce guaranteed would make me unbeatable. He threw in a couple of lessons before he proceeded to win all my marbles from me. I bought more marbles from him with more Indian mementos, and my marble-playing career lasted only as long as my collection of Indian trinkets did. I could never get my knuckle up high enough off the ground to snap off straight, crisp shots, and I was beaten regularly.

I was better at keep-away. We chose sides at recess and tried to keep a ball away from the other side by running with it, throwing it, or kicking it. The other side was allowed to do anything short of deliberately breaking bones to obtain the ball. I developed a reckless, physical style of play that won the admiration of my teammates, but the anger and despair of my mother. When she began dressing me in old clothes to go to school, I was happy because I fit in better with the rest of the boys.

Before long, I was invited to join Jere's army, and not long after that I was awarded my first medal. While marching with the army on maneuvers in a vacant lot, I punctured my foot on a nail. Lorelei appeared with a wagon with a red cross on it and took me to the fort to bandage it. Doc Holbrook, or "Holly" as he was called, became our dentist, and soon it seemed as if I was in his chair every week. Jesse, Mother, Margaret, and I all had cavities from the bad water in India.

Practically the first thing Mother did after we settled in Healdsburg was to choose a family church. Jesse seemed as comfortable in one church as another. He attended, but never really got fired up about religion. Mother's choice was the Federated Church—a sort of Methodist-Presbyterian mixture—because the Gibbs and the Holbrooks went there. That was fine with me because most grammar school children were members of the Federated congregation, except for Italian boys and girls who attended huge, old St. John's Catholic Church. Only a few children, mostly from poor families, attended the ramshackle evangelical churches in town.

We all settled into a routine. Mother stayed home and worked around the house, pausing to cook lunch when we all walked home at noon. In the afternoons she hoed and weeded the tiny garden Jesse had magically conjured out of our backyard. Jesse seldom came directly home after school because he functioned as the elementary school's only coach, as well as teaching seventh and eighth grade math and science and manual arts. Since Jesse's athletic expertise was mainly confined to track, he made everyone run a lot, no matter what time of year or what sport happened to be in season.

Running around the schoolyard track, you got a feeling for the compact variety of Healdsburg. The first quarter mile took you past some homes and a glimpse of the first hole of the golf course. The second quarter passed by a prune orchard. The third quarter adjoined the fairway of the golf course's second hole, the entry to Oak Mound Cemetery, and the school's bus garage. Entering the final quarter mile, you glimpsed a corner of the city baseball park grandstand, briefly crossed the paved surface of the outdoor basketball court, detoured around the auditorium-gym, and sprinted for home. I was not blessed with blazing speed so it took me a long time to run around the track. In fact, Jesse's professional appraisal was that I was "slower than molasses in January."

At Thanksgiving my parents bought a live turkey and housed it on the back porch for fattening-up. The turkey and I became great friends, and I named it Tom. I thought I could save Tom from execution and tried to tame it and teach it tricks. As the day grew near, I even vowed to my parents that I would not eat a bite of Tom if they killed him. I asked Mother if she would have eaten one of the animals in *The Jungle Book*, for Tom was more real to me than they were. But The Day inevitably arrived. I was shielded from the actual execution, which Jesse performed with an axe, and after moping about for a day, I dutifully ate Thanksgiving dinner.

We had a lot to be grateful for. Jesse was popular at school and he liked his classes, though he cautioned in letters that he was "the low man on the totem pole." Mother grew accustomed to our too-large house and her too-little garden. I was far from the Hartnell Street gang's influence, and shy little Margaret was making friends. It did not appear that the war would seriously affect us. Jesse was far too old for the draft and I was far too young.

Throughout the rest of Healdsburg, though, the enormity of World War II was finally becoming real. The draft board mailed out questionnaires to eighteen- and nineteen-year-old boys in anticipation of an Act of Congress that would establish a draft. Gas rationing became effective December 1, 1942. Dim-outs were mandated: whenever a light was turned on inside a house, the shades had to be drawn. Outdoor lights had to be shielded so that they didn't shine upward.

Taxes were raised for everyone who earned over $624 a year. The Victory Tax was raised from 4% to 6%, which meant that anyone making over $12 a week was taxed, and a ceiling was set at $25,000 yearly on individual incomes. Bars were required to postpone opening until 10:00 A.M. and had to close by midnight. No hard liquor was to be served after 8:00 P.M.

The news from the Pacific islands was not good. Fighting on Guadalcanal was described as "dogged," and the navy lost fourteen ships and the aircraft carrier *Wasp* in the Solomon Islands. Closer to home, four training planes from the Santa Rosa Naval Airbase crashed in one month, and Earl Warren was elected governor of California by a two-to-one margin.

But the mood in Healdsburg was optimistic. Bill Wolking, a popular local liquor salesman, arranged a "smoker" to help fund a servicemen's Hospitality House. The smoker featured "a talented corps of feminine hoofers" according to the local paper. The Healdsburg Footlighters produced *Ladies in Retirement*, and Italian-Americans were released from curfew restrictions. The city of Healdsburg supported this legislation since much of the local economy was based on Italian-American-owned farms and orchards.

Forty army men were Christmas dinner guests in eighteen Healdsburg homes, but my family celebrated Christmas alone. I received a mackinaw and a muffler with matching mittens that Mother had knit for me. I regularly stuffed the mittens into the pockets of my mackinaw before I walked into school because I had observed that American boys wore gloves, and mittens were for girls. Jesse bought Mother a new tea kettle. They still had their tea with lemon on weekend afternoons. During Christmas vacation we went to see *Mrs. Miniver*. Mother would always remember the picture for

Greer Garson's and Walter Pidgeon's cultured and stoic characters in wartime England. I identified with Helmut Dantine as the crashed German pilot. I so admired the cool, arrogant German officer he always portrayed that I wrote a motion picture studio for his autographed picture. Years later, when I was appearing in a Broadway play, he hosted a cocktail party for our cast. When I told him of my autographed picture, he seemed as distantly amused as one of his World War II officers would have been.

On the other hand, all the American boys and girls admired Van Johnson because he played courageous American officers. Johnson's characters always exuded a clean-cut, all-American sincerity. Mother thought he was a fine role model. At the time, none of us ever gave any thought to the reasons why Ronald Reagan, Van Johnson, John Wayne, and others were making movies rather than fighting in the war.

Jesse and Mother were drawn into Healdsburg's civic and social activities in 1943. Mother was a much-sought-after speaker on life in India. On PTA Founders Day, she gave an "interesting talk" and "displayed several souvenirs which she had collected while living in India." When she lectured at the Santa Rosa Saturday Afternoon Club, she "painted a vivid picture of India." At Mrs. Gibbs's urging, she also became a member of the Sew and Chatter Club (dedicated to sewing, darning, and chattering), though the club's name and avowed purpose must have galled Mother.

Because so many Healdsburg men were being drafted or were joining one of the armed services, new responsibilities and titles were heaped on Jesse. A Victory Book Campaign was organized, and Jesse was recruited to supervise elementary school students in collecting "good, readable books" for servicemen. A cub scout troop was organized, and Jesse accepted the position of cub scoutmaster. Jesse became a block warden too. He steadfastly refused to join any of the hastily formed Home Guard rifle units—there were now two: "The West Side Rangers" and "The Windsor Wolverines"—drilling under the command of Lt. Warren Richardson of the State Militia. (In real life, Lt. Richardson was a wealthy Windsor rancher.) A defense area for nine northern California counties was being established, and Lt. Richardson warned that the Japanese were going to attack San Francisco sooner or later. In January, Healdsburg held a full-scale defense drill with simulated casualties from bombs and fires. All wardens were ordered to be at their stations at 8:00 P.M. sharp and to arrest anyone who failed to observe the dimout ordinance.

Meanwhile, the Healdsburg *Tribune* called for more hunting knives to be donated for use by troops in the far Pacific theater "where jungle fighting makes use of such weapons necessary against the treacherous Japanese." The article went on to boast that "many local people have been sending hunting knives to Uncle Sam to help lick a Jap."

Mother volunteered to sew surgical dressings for the army at the Red Cross office, and so she was gone from home two evenings a week. She became a plane spotter and on Saturdays was posted to a tiny hilltop country school far out on Mill Creek. I often went along as her "assistant." Bill Wolking raised enough money from his smoker to open the Hospitality House and Mother promptly offered to serve as a dance chaperone.

At the elementary school a crisis developed. Mr. Gibbs announced that Russ Tanner, the school's most popular boy, was going to start a "Buy a Bomber" bond-selling campaign with the help of other elementary school students. A banner with a thermometer on it was placed in the plaza to record the campaign's progress. Elementary school students covered every block of Healdsburg selling bonds. They also collected and sold scrap metal and rubber and contributed their own allowances to the campaign to buy *Healdsburg Elementary School*, which was what the bomber was going to be named. Within two months, Russ Tanner and Lorelei Holbrook supervised the raising of $30,000 over the $75,000 quota necessary to buy the bomber, and Mr. Gibbs presented them each with $25 war bonds for their efforts.

The only hitch was that the chamber of commerce had not dreamed school children could raise such a sum and were distraught and embarrassed by the thought that a real bomber might be named after them. Local promoters moved quickly, and the next issue of the *Tribune* proclaimed that "with true community spirit the students have decided to change the name of the bomber which they won the privilege of naming to *City of Healdsburg* instead of *Healdsburg Elementary School* as planned."

The winter of 1943 was severe. High winds uprooted prune, oak, and other trees on several occasions. It was not unusual if three inches of rain fell in the span of two days. Jesse made his rounds as a block warden uncomplainingly, more often than not trudging the darkened streets in the rain. He would leave home wearing his white helmet and white arm band with red crosses on them. He was equipped with a shoulder bag containing a first-aid kit, a flashlight, and a pail full of sand to put out fires from air raids. These accouterments never impressed me. I always assumed that Jesse was the same age as most of the other kids' fathers. We never had discussed his age. I guessed he might be slightly old for the draft, but I would have been horrified then to learn that he was forty-five. So I didn't understand why he didn't buy a rifle, or have Uncle Bill send him one, and join the defense regiment. Even plane spotting seemed more glamorous than lugging around a bucket of sand and checking drawn blinds.

Perhaps I was feeling warlike because, through a circuitous set of circumstances, I was myself now a general. First, my family began attending St. Paul's Episcopal church. For a long time I believed that Mother instigated our move because she thought the Federated Church congregation had too much fun and not enough worshipping. In reality she missed the Lutheran services with which she'd grown up. Since there was no Lutheran church north of Santa Rosa, she had settled on the Church of England, which shared many Lutheran rituals. I once asked Mother why Lutheran, Episcopalian, and Roman Catholic ministers and priests wore such elaborate vestments and why their churches were so ornate. Why didn't these ministers and priests dress simply as Jesus had? Why didn't these churches give all of their money to the poor and to missionaries as Jesus and St. Paul had said they should and as the preachers were always exhorting us to do, instead of spending it on fancy robes and fancier churches? She replied that people needed pageantry—the implication being that if Jesus had been allowed to dress truly as the Son of God and not as the son of man, he would have appeared entirely differently. I asked, not insolently, if that meant that Jesus would have looked like the Archbishop of Canterbury.

The minister of St. Paul's, however, was not resplendent. In fact the church had no regular minister at all when we first began attending services there. Instead, various preachers from larger cities rotated in the St. Paul pulpit from Sunday to Sunday. The church building itself was small, rustic, and gloomy. The congregation numbered no more than twenty except at Easter and Christmas. The organist, Mrs. Izzett, played at a dirgelike tempo, contributing to the overall melancholy, and there was far too much kneeling for me. To add to the discomfort, neither pews nor kneelers were padded. Margaret and I were enrolled in Mrs. Brookins's Sunday School class, and it was there that I began recruiting for my own army. My first recruits were Mrs. Brookins's sons, Lynn and Doug. The boys' father, one of Healdsburg's two postmen, had joined the army and at the age of thirty-eight had won a boxing championship. Lynn and Doug were so proud of their father that instilling a martial spirit in them was easy. I made Lynn my second-in-command and I commissioned Doug, who was younger, a master sergeant.

Mrs. Brookins was a bustling, no-nonsense Christian and Mother had no objections to my playing with Lynn and Doug. We used Mr. Brookins's now abandoned toolshed for strategic planning. First of all I determined that our army would not practice any marching drills or fancy formations. Instead we would be like British commandos—experts at crawling, climbing, and sneak attacks. I recruited more commandos from Lynn's neighborhood, and we crawled with cork-blackened faces all over the Brookins's two acres. One day Mrs. Brookins caught us practicing rope climbing in her fig tree and canceled our maneuvers for awhile. But my little army grew and we began exploring terrain farther afield.

Families from Oklahoma and Arkansas began trickling into the Healdsburg area. Most of them moved slightly to the south of our house, where University Street became Front Street and angled on down to the railroad and automobile bridges. Old resort cabins along Front Street and the Merryland Auto Court across the river at Merryland beach became permanent dwellings for the new immigrants whom everyone called "Okies" and "Arkies." Whole families squeezed into one-room shanties and waited for the summer harvests. They were watched suspiciously by Healdsburg natives, and any aberrant behavior merited a full report in the *Tribune*: "Lonnie Jenkins, formerly of Oklahoma, stole a carton of eggs from Nelligan's store and is on trial. His brother, Ellis Jenkins, twenty, was arrested in Sacramento while trying to escape to Reno with a Healdsburg girl."

Many of these folks came from Texas or Tennessee, but all were called Okies or Arkies nevertheless. The one black family in town were politely called "Negroes." Smith Robinson, the family's only son, had been a high school sports star and was now a respected member of the community (though he never rose above working as a janitor at the hospital). Black transients in Healdsburg were unfailingly referred to by the newspaper as "colored." The only other local minority, the Pomo tribe of American Indians, were indigenous to Sonoma and Lake counties but were demeaned as lazy and slow. Pomo men were often called "Chief."

The newest immigrants were accused of fouling the river by bathing and washing clothes in it. Rumors circulated that they had been seen relieving themselves at Merryland, where summer swimming classes and annual Fourth of July races were held. Chris Jennings, who organized the classes and races and considered himself to be the premier athletic expert in Healdsburg, was especially outraged. He attempted to persuade the city council to detail militiamen from civil defense to patrol the river, and the mistrusted Okies grew understandably sullen.

Chris Jennings was himself a study. He ran the men's and boys' department at Rosenberg's, the largest, most expensive department store in Healdsburg. He was a big, gray-headed man who had lost his right hand in World War I. The hand had been replaced with an artificial fist made of dark hardwood, so that it always looked like his right hand was clenched, and covered with a black glove. He had a nephew (who was also his ward) named Jimmie, of whom he expected nothing short of sports fame. In the meantime, while Jimmie was growing up, Chris trained other Healdsburg athletes.

Chris had also somehow gotten himself appointed Pacific Athletic Association Commissioner for Sonoma and Mendocino counties, so the races he sponsored and at which he officiated produced lots of publicity. And since he tended to load the field for his trainees, his meets produced questionable records. Chris trained "Clipper" Smith, a local runner who under Chris's aegis, ran a race against the clock around Fitch Mountain's six-and-a-half miles for an official record. (Chris said the old record was held by an Austrian.) To Chris's credit, he organized marathons, which were very rare in those days. In the spring of 1943, Chris's Petaluma marathon was the only marathon besides Boston's held in the United States. Clipper Smith set another record for the twenty-six mile, three hundred and eighty-five-yard race, "blistering" the course in two hours, forty-seven minutes, twenty seconds.

In February an event occurred that may have borne the seed that blossomed into my adult occupation. At the time it seemed too good to be true. The elementary school decided to stage the operetta *Rip Van Winkle* as a special spring treat. Russ Tanner would play Rip, the scenery would be designed by Jesse, and over 100 pupils would participate. By now I had earned a solid reputation playing keep-away. I played with reckless abandon, diving, scrambling, punching, and fighting for loose balls all over the yard without regard for my clothing or skin. I was often sent to the boys' restroom or to nurse Nichol's small office after recess to wash off the dirt, comb my hair, and straighten my clothes, or to have Miss Nichols tend to my abrasions.

Because of my prowess—"you don't mind getting dirty," the operetta director said—I was cast as Rip Van Winkle's dog. My costume was a well-worn, sour-smelling shaggy dog suit rented from a San Francisco theatrical company, and I followed faithfully in Rip's footsteps throughout the operetta—even barking once or twice. The elementary school band played, choruses sang, and the 100 participants marched around in pilgrim suits cheering and waving flags at every patriotic reference in the operetta. Although my performance was not singled out for praise, the *Tribune* critic wrote that the show was "brimming with excitement."

Musical shows were very popular, and the Plaza Theatre presented a steady diet of musicals as well as war movies. Records for dancing were donated to the Hospitality House, and local girls were driven to dances at the Fulton Army Air Base. At one such dance a Healdsburg girl won a jitterbug contest over forty other girls.

Married men with children were now being drafted, and Doctor Holbrook left for the war as a captain. The Japanese armada was defeated off New Guinea, Guadalcanal was retaken, Flying Fortresses were pounding Italy, and F.D.R.—whose proposed $109 billion budget was being criticized in the press as "colossal"—met with Churchill. The press raked John L. Lewis over the coals for taking his coal miners out on strike for higher wages.

To the north of Healdsburg, Gustav Raube, German owner of the "Duck Inn," was ordered to immediately leave the coastal frontiers of the United States because of neighbors' complaints. The Healdsburg-Windsor Rifles became a state guard reserve unit. They were issued uniforms and shotguns and began drilling at the baseball park. Lt. Richardson described the unit's duties as guarding bridges, power plants, and other vital points in case of invasion. There was nothing in their orders about patrolling Merryland.

In June, a combined total of forty-seven students graduated from the high school and elementary schools. I was to begin Red Cross swimming lessons, and after July fourth I would go to work picking prunes. Neither of these prospects excited me, but the news that my application for a V-bike had been approved did. Since I had to walk four blocks to the prune dehydrator in order to catch a truck out to the prune orchard, I qualified for a bike. Mr. Lowrey, the bicycle shop owner, filled out my application and he may have stretched the distance I had to walk and the importance of my prune picking to the war effort.

One June evening I heard on our radio that Helmut Dantine had signed a new contract. After the release of *Mrs. Miniver* his fan mail had risen by 300%.

In June 1943, Mother wrote to Aunt Idylla:

Vacation time is surely holiday time for everyone but Mother. My regular schedule has been shot to the wind. Especially because this week and next the kids are taking swimming lessons, and I won't let them go down alone. I think Davy is really going to learn to swim this year, he seems to have the feel of it. In fact, if they had their way I'd sit by the river all day long!

My sister has embarked on her way to India. I don't know much about her trip, and what I know of course I must keep quiet about. I had two airgraphs from Father last week. The airgraph, in case you don't know, is like the V-Mail, but it is British and open to civilians. They are fine out there, suffering high prices as we are. How are you getting along with ration points? We have ample. I haven't been using mine up, but since fruit is so high, I shall use them up on canned fruit.

Jess got a raise for next year. Quite a good one too. He shouldn't have had such a big one for several years—I mean it should have come in gradations—but the school board—bless them!—thought we could use it now. We do like it here, and best of all, Jess is very happy.

The kids are fine. When Jess's brother Bert was here to visit, he remarked that Margaret looked just like Jess's mother. She has heard that so often that she asked to see a picture of her grandma. I sent her upstairs to look at the one by the bed. It's one taken long, long ago, when Grandpa's face was concealed in fashionable whiskers. Margaret came down and said, "Yes, Daddy's mother was pretty, but gosh his dad looks funny."

Have you done much canning? I've only done cherries and youngberries and yellow plums. And made some plum jam. Our garden is wonderful— but then Jess is a wonderful gardener. Much love to you all, Ernestine.

Once I learned to swim it was difficult to keep me on dry land. The beach at Merryland where we took our lessons was a long strip of sand about twenty yards wide that ran from under the automobile bridge to a temporary gravel dam some 200 yards downriver. The water deepened gradually going out from the beach but was easily twenty feet deep at midriver; the river itself, between bridge and dam, was more than seventy-five yards wide. Beyond the beach was a field of cropped dry grass, an abandoned and disintegrating roller rink, and a row of squat cabins among a thin grove of trees where the Okies and Arkies had moved in.

There were no amenities at Merryland—no refreshment stands, lifeguards, diving boards, or even a pier—just the narrow beach and the broad, deep river. Grandfather Neudoerffer's only son, my mother's only brother, had drowned while Grandfather was teaching in America. So, to my embarrassment, Mother always accompanied me when I swam. She would spread a colorful Indian blanket on the grass behind the beach and read or knit with one eye while keeping the other one on me and Margaret. As if this were not bad enough, sitting there in full view of my friends, Mother always wore her straw coolie hat and dark glasses, and she chain-smoked nervously for hours while we splashed and played.

We were lucky to have the Red Cross swim classes at all that year. A polio epidemic broke out all along the river, and although swimming classes were allowed to conclude, the traditional Fourth of July Water Carnival was canceled. Dr. Oakleaf, a prominent local physician, was appointed City Health Officer after three cases were diagnosed in Healdsburg, and he immediately recommended that Sunday Schools at local churches be suspended and that children avoid getting together in groups. Adults were also cautioned to avoid crowds because Dr. Oakleaf feared the disease would spread rapidly. Healdsburg residents were terrified because infantile paralysis was the most feared disease in the world. The new Sister Kenny treatment was being used in San Francisco, but Healdsburg Hospital did not have a practitioner yet.

Hundreds of Mexican farmworkers arrived to work in the hop fields and to help harvest prunes, apples, and grapes. An editorial welcomed these "Mexican gentlemen." My V-bike also arrived. It was delivered unassembled in a big box, and Mr. Lowery put it together for me at no extra charge. My slim, sleek, red, V-bike resembled nothing more than a racing bicycle of today, though it was not built with modern alloys and so it bent and crumpled easily. But it was easily bent back into shape. My sleek, lightweight V-bike was scorned by the more affluent children of Healdsburg, who all owned heavy-framed, balloon-tired Schwinns, but before long I could outrace and outmaneuver them all. At five in the morning I rode my bicycle to the dehydrator, parked it there, and jumped on a truck with ten or so other workers for the ride to the orchard. I was an insignificant member of the crew—most were Mexicans and lived in tents or cabins at the ranch for the summer—but every hand, even small boys' hands, were needed and accepted during the war.

******

In the early morning our truck traveled northeast into orchard-filled Alexander Valley. A mountain man, Cyrus Alexander, came into this valley and claimed it in the early 1800s and the valley had been named after him. Surrounding the valley were three mountains: Cobb Mountain to the north, Mount St. Helena to the southeast, and Fitch Mountain to the south. It was very quiet and beautiful in the valley. Our truck angled off on a dirt road for several miles to Syd Grove's ranch. We pickers got off the truck at a preselected part of the orchard and each picker took a fistful of tickets with a number on them. Each picker also received a metal pail. A tree shaker, using a long wooden pole with a metal hook on the end to catch the tree limbs, would have already passed through this portion of the orchard, and the fruit lay under the trees. Empty boxes too would have been scattered about by the tractor driver and his helper. We were each assigned a row of trees as our own personal picking territory, and then we would fall on our knees and begin putting the purple plums in our pails as fast as we could. Some of the pickers wore knee pads, but most disdained them because they kept slipping down onto the shins and slowing the work. Crawling speed and hand dexterity was everything in prune picking. If it was a first picking, the prunes lay thickly under the trees, but if it were a second or third picking, the prunes were fewer and of inferior quality. Then too there were different varieties of prunes: large Burtons, medium-sized Imperials, and the most common variety, small French prunes.

Prune picking was not so simple as merely stuffing prunes into your bucket by the handful. Although good shakers used a delicate touch to down only ripened fruit, pickers were admonished not to choose overripe, underripe, bird-chewed, or sunburned prunes for their buckets. If the rancher found too many inferior prunes in your boxes at the end of the day, you would be penalized. Prune picking was worse than kneeling in St. Paul's; a picker had to be on the move constantly and the sun-baked sharp-edged clods were full of stones. When you filled your bucket, you emptied it into a box. It took five or six buckets to fill a box to the brim; short boxes—boxes with leaves, twigs, or small clods in them along with the prunes—were not acceptable.

When a box was filled, you inserted one of your tickets in a corner of it, stacked a fresh empty box on top of it, and began working on the next one. I never finished my own row before the whole crew was ready to move on, and I always needed assistance. In fact at the rate we were paid (twenty cents a box) only entire families made any money by picking prunes. Several boys showed me how they would take prunes out of other pickers' boxes, put them in their own, and replace the victim's stolen fruit with a layer of clods. They also took tickets off other pickers' boxes, replacing them with their own numbers if they could get away with it. So I guarded my own boxes, few that they were.

The temperature regularly topped 110° that summer, and the trees offered little shade because the prunes fell outwardly and not at the base of the tree where the good shade was. In an attempt to motivate me, Mother offered to buy me a new jacket if I could pick fifteen boxes in one day. I picked as hard as I could, even skipping lunch, but I couldn't manage it. At dusk, when the truck was ready to leave, the whole Mexican crew chipped in and picked the last two boxes for me. Fifteen boxes was the most I ever picked in one day. Syd Grove, who owned the ranch, was also the manager of the growers' cooperative prune dryer where the prunes were taken after picking. Jesse worked at the dehydrator. He tallied the boxes from each ranch as they were unloaded from the trucks. It was a miserable summer, but I got to keep what I earned to pay for school clothes and—best of all—I got to pick my own clothes.

During the summer a new fighter plane, the P-39 Bell Aircobra was introduced at the Fulton Army Air Base. Aircobras turned out to be tricky planes to fly and they began crashing all over the county. Almost all of the pilots were killed because the planes' canopies jammed so that the pilots could not bail out. Many pilots never had a chance to try bailing out because the Army Air Force said that flying low was necessary for training. Working in the orchards, we would often look up apprehensively when we heard a low-flying Aircobra speeding in our direction. One evening a P-39 crashed into the side of Fitch Mountain. We heard the collision from our house and looked out to see a pillar of smoke and flame rising from just below the summit. The *Tribune* said that "the pilot was killed and the Army took such plane parts as they wished. Souvenir hunters made short work of the balance."

My cousin Mary, Bill and Ide's daughter, came to visit us late that summer. Shortly after her visit, Mother wrote to the Hillsborians, as Jesse called them:

Excuse the long silence, but time goes by and I hate to look at the date of your last letter. We very much enjoyed having Mary with us, even for such a brief visit.

I've been down at the Hospitality House and the air base since Mary was here. When I told Davy I had been asked to go to the base as senior hostess, he looked and looked at me, then said, "I don't know what boys would want to dance with old ladies!" Honesty begins at home, no doubt.

Has Mary's school opened? Jess's doesn't until the twenty-seventh. Poor guy, he is awfully tired. Working ten and eleven hours a day, at his age (as he would say!). Davy has been out picking prunes almost ever since Mary was here. He got his bike, too. And is he a happy boy! But prune picking is hard work, and he comes home so tired and dirty. He picks about ten boxes a day. That's $2 a day, which isn't bad for a nine-year-old. But when Sunday rolls around he is so tired he can't do a *thing! I want him to quit on Friday, and have a week to just play and rest. Jess is quitting this week, so he can get his school room and manual training room in order. It must be just so for his highness!*

Margaret just came in and gasped at my stack of letters to be answered! Guess there will always be a stack. But its time to write a few Christmas ones to India—and hope they will get there in time! Much love to you all from all of us.

The truest friend to Healdsburg servicemen and women was Smith Robinson, the black janitor. "Smitty" was confined to the hospital with a mild heart ailment, but he vowed to continue writing his weekly letters to every Healdsburg serviceman and woman from his bed. The same week that Smitty pledged this, City Judge Edward Quinn fined Bessie Harris, described as "colored," $10 for public drunkenness and fined Paul Masatini, "of Italian descent," $4 for the same infraction on the same day. On September twenty-fourth, some 300 local farmworkers returned to Mexico.

Shortly after school opened in October, Jesse supervised a Halloween party. He built a tunnel of wood and butcher paper that snaked around the entire elementary school auditorium. Jesse performed the costume and makeup jobs on the ghosts and goblins who popped out at the children and adults as they walked through the dark tunnel. Jesse was also called upon to do more coaching. He hastily assembled a touch football team that beat Windsor Elementary School 12-0, mostly on account of "Squirt" Moore's running ability. Squirt was one of the new students from Oklahoma whose family lived down from us on Front Street. I was not allowed to play on Dad's team because of my age, but as far as I was concerned touch football was not nearly as rough as a recess game of keep-away anyway.

Six

SUNDAY SCHOOL RESUMED, and I was reunited with my army. Our mothers stitched together backpacks for us made out of flour sacks when we began to range farther afield. One day we chanced upon perfect commando terrain in the cemetery behind the elementary school.

After climbing a short, steep hill and entering under the arch that said "Oak Mound Cemetery," you were confronted with the large headstones and mausoleums of the founders and old families of Healdsburg. Some of these plots were bigger than the cabins the Okies lived in at Merryland. The graveyard spread out from these plots to follow the second fairway of the golf course and up onto a high, wooded hill. A trail wound around the hill following a creek upstream and on the hill's far side lay the graves of the less affluent. Beyond this was Potters' Field.

At the far end of Potters' Field, where the gravesites were overgrown and marked with wooden boards, a little creek entered the cemetery. Runoff from Fitch Mountain was the creek's source, and the rivulet meandered through the golf course forming a natural hazard between the fourth and fifth holes. The creek circled the cemetery's western flank before emptying into a large drain pipe. The drain pipe ran under the ballpark, became part of the city's sewer system, and emptied finally in the Russian River. Unless heavy rains came, the creek seldom had more than a trickle of water in it, and so it was perfect for commando maneuvers. The creek bed itself was rocky, with sudden twists and deep gouges. The banks were overgrown and trees and boulders hung out over the creek, shrouding it from view in many places. Smith Robinson's father and Earl "Cocky" Lodge were the cemetery groundskeepers. Smith's father was a very old, very dignified black man, and Cocky was so called because he was cockeyed and thought to be as crazy as a loon. Neither of them paid us the slightest attention as we commandos studied and mapped every inch of the rugged creek.

When we had memorized the terrain, I challenged Jere Holbrook's army to a war. That is how the Great Clod Wars began. Sun-baked dirt clods could do real damage—you could see the enemy flinch or hear him cry out with a well-aimed missile, and selecting a lethal dirt clod was an art. War clods had to be firm, not crumbly, and it was a plus if they had jagged edges for a good grip. We really thought of them as grenades, and we selected lime-sized clods for both speed and accuracy in hurling them. You seldom wasted a really fine clod in target practice. Great clods (like great stickers in marbles) were collected in our floursack packs for use in the heat of real battle. We practiced throwing clods from every conceivable angle for hours.

Jere accepted our challenge to do battle. I went to his fort and we signed a declaration of war. We also laid out ground rules: No fistfights, no rock throwing, and a truce would be called whenever either side ran out of clods. I insisted that each day's hostilities cease by four-thirty in the afternoon because I knew I would be in trouble if I wasn't home by five. These were my orders from Mother.

We agreed that Jere's army would gather in Potters' Field and march south along the creek bed. My commandos would advance from the drain pipe north. That Saturday we routed Jere's troops. We knew the creek so thoroughly that we caught the enemy in an enfilade coming around a sharp bend where there were many boulders and trees to use for cover.

We had some great battles in the creek until Jere lost interest. One Saturday we arrived at the cemetery to find Jere's brother Bruce leading an army that consisted mostly of mercenaries from Oklahoma—among them was a bully named "Ace" Lingo and some of his siblings. We were taken by surprise and completely surrounded. Bruce's troops hurled rocks at us from the banks and we fell like tenpins. Cowering, and scurrying along the creek bed, we tried to protect our heads. Our yells alerted Cocky Lodge, who rushed down toward the creek raving and waving his arms. Cocky's crazy tirade caused a moment's hesitation in the rock-throwers, and most of us were able to scramble up the bank and scatter toward the ballpark and the safety of the street.

My face was bloodied and one knee was skinned, and as I skulked home I passed Jere's fort where two of my captured commandos were tied to a tree. It was late when I arrived at our house and my punishment would have been more severe had I not been weeping with anger and humiliation.

To my surprise, Jere saw his troops' actions (rocks were banned weapons) as dishonoring him personally. We disbanded our armies and the Great Clod Wars ended.

A serviceman came to our house at Thanksgiving. We had many more during the course of the war, but Art, our first guest, became almost a part of our family. Art was not a war hero. In fact, he was not even a pilot, a gunner, or a bombardier at the air base, but a mechanic. He had a big nose and a pimply face. Though he seemed terribly old to me, Art probably wasn't more than twenty. On his first visit he brought Mother flowers and Jesse a big picture book on the history of aircraft engines. For me he had a genuine Eighth Air Force cap with braid and insignia. Art became like a second son to my folks and came to see us whenever he could from then on.

At Christmas, Art gave me a genuine pair of silver wings. And Jesse's gift was no less remarkable. He had bought a fine-grained, flawless length of redwood, probably an eight-foot 4x4 and shaped it in the garage workshop. He chiseled, carved, planed, and sanded it until he produced an exact replica of the army's newest rifle, the M-1 Garand. Other children owned roughly cut model weapons, but no one had seen anything like Jesse's Garand. Even Art, turning it over and over in his hands, was amazed. It was perfect in every detail, down to the bolt action, the adjustable sight, the barrel strapping, and the carved screw heads in the simulated stock. Again, it was much too fine a gift for a small roughneck of a boy. Being made out of redwood, it was fragile. I used it to practice bayonet thrusts and to club imaginary enemies, and the beautiful redwood rifle didn't last long.

Early in January a Cub Scout troop was organized at the elementary school, and Jesse was recruited to be the first Cub scoutmaster. The Healdsburg Red Cross chapter announced that it produced 50,537 surgical dressings for the war effort in 1943, and Mother, who was the supervisor, had put in the highest number of "man hours" at 396. At about the same time, Mother received a red ribbon for being a fifth-time blood donor. Poor Jesse—he fainted the first time he tried to give blood.

Mother also took over the leadership of an older group of Camp Fire Girls—a chore that greatly distressed me. I was given a pair of roller skates for my ninth birthday and I requisitioned our huge second-story screened porch for my own personal roller rink. When Mother's Camp Fire Girls took over the porch for their meetings, I was displaced. If this wasn't bad enough, the Okizu troop, as they were called, filled the porch with pennants and posters and projects. Too, the stairway in our house led up to my bedroom and only from there was the porch accessed. So once or twice a week all of these girls would come trooping up the stairs and through my room, giggling and whispering.

Not that I was oblivious to the differences between boys and girls by this time. One afternoon when I was swinging in our backyard, a slightly older dark-eyed girl cruised down the alley on her bike. She stopped and said frankly: "You're not bad looking. How about taking me to a movie sometime?" I turned crimson, hurled myself out of the swing and rushed into the house—the screen door banging behind me. I stood there, my heart pounding, and perhaps it was then that my fascination with femmes fatales began. I clearly remember one of Squirt Moore's older sisters. I used to ride by Squirt's house on my bike—ostensibly to talk to Squirt—but actually to wonder at his sister Alice. She wore thin cotton dresses and flounced about haughtily, thrusting her small breasts forward.

In spring the city council hired Dad to direct a school playground program on weekday afternoons. About forty boys attended regularly and keep-away was not allowed. No matter, Okie boys and girls never came to the playground. It was Mr. Gibbs who had made the pitch for the playground before the city council, saying it was necessary to "keep the kids off the street." Whatever the after-school program's real intent was, it helped to segregate local children even further.

Boys did not spend all of their time playing. I mowed neighbors' lawns for a nickel, and I washed windows too. Most of us scoured our neighborhoods for scrap metal because we were admitted into the Saturday afternoon matinee at the Plaza Theatre for free when we had collected twenty-five pounds.

One day I hauled my wagonload of scrap to the movie house to see what was billed as "Lover—Fighter—War Correspondent—Pirate—Prospector! WHAT A MAN!—Michael O'Shea and Susan Hayward in *JACK LONDON*." While my wagonload of scrap was being weighed, I checked out the coming attractions posters. Suddenly I was aware that standing next to me checking out the same poster was Buck Butler, a friend of Ace Lingo's, who was reputed to be the toughest boy of all the Okies. Buck was very big—he must have been at least eighteen—and he turned to squint down at me. "What are you looking at, kid?" he growled. I gulped and said, "You." And Buck Butler decked me with one punch, right in front of everyone in the Saturday afternoon matinee box office line. At least I didn't cry. I got up and went into the movie after Buck sauntered off down West Street. I decided I would become tough like a merchant seaman—like Jack London had. I began to check sea stories like *Wind in the Rigging* and *The Tattooed Man* out of the Carnegie Public Library.

St. Paul's was assigned a real vicar on a trial basis. It was agreed that if the congregation grew, the new vicar would stay permanently. Maybe we got the vicar because, for one day that spring, St. Paul's was packed to overflowing. John Grant, scion of one of Healdsburg's pioneer families, died suddenly and his funeral was held at St. Paul's. The three most powerful families in Healdsburg's history were the Grants, the Powells and the Fitches. Like the Southern aristocracy after the Civil War, these families' fortunes fell on hard times, but John had been an influential man in his day. He developed the large gravel extraction company south of Merryland that was now Basalt Rock Company and another, smaller operation near the Dry Creek bridge on Westside Road. More important, John owned thousands of acres that contained geysers in the mountains of Lake County. There he developed one of the most written-about health resorts in the world. Visitors came from far and wide to see the "Devil's Cauldron," as one journalist had called the area. Robert Louis Stevenson himself made the arduous journey by stagecoach to these sulphurous fountains of youth and wrote about them in *Silverado Squatters*.

John's big house on the Camino Real one mile south of town was called "Grant's Station," though John had long since removed himself to the desert of Southern California. His body was brought all the way from Palm Springs by special limousine for the funeral.

John's only son Delano, or "Del" as he was called, started out well enough. While attending Stanford Medical School, Del married Faith Powell—the youngest and prettiest daughter of the Powell clan. But Del discovered alcohol before he graduated from Stanford. He subsequently sold, piece by piece, what little land John had given him, and at the time of his father's death Del was running a roadside vegetable stand in front of the old mansion. The mansion itself had been leased out to the Seventh Day Adventists as an academy for girls, and Del was allowed to stay on, living in a small shack on the property.

Faith Grant, his wife, had left for Los Angeles long ago, taking with her as much money as she had been able to salvage. She took their oldest son, Powell, with her. Faith left her old mother, Minerva Powell, to raise their youngest son, Billy, on a small farm in Alexander Valley.

Neither Del nor Faith attended John's funeral. But Minerva Powell and Billy were there among the pews full of prosperous, powerful people. The turnout must have warmed the heart of the new vicar, and he was no doubt counting sheep to add to St Paul's tiny flock. Our family was not invited, but one of my jobs was cleaning up the church grounds on Saturdays and the vicar proudly told me about it. John Grant was buried in style near the entrance to Oak Mound Cemetery.

******

Experts predicted that 1944 would be the driest winter in seven years. In April only two-and-a-half inches of rain fell, and brown rot began to eat away at the trees in the prune orchards. On the other hand, a profitable hop harvest was assured because hops had been declared an "essential industry" by the Office of Price Administration and ceiling prices were fixed. Every hop grower in the county signed contracts with the government to buy their crop. Forecasters thought the wine shortage would last another year even though Sonoma County led all of California in the production of table wines. Mexican laborers were being sought by dairy farmers as a milk crisis was deemed imminent.

Spring in Healdsburg was a season of concerts, musicales, and dances. The Fulton Army Air Base orchestra played an afternoon concert at the plaza and followed it up by playing for a dance at the Hospitality House. Mother chaperoned the dance. I began taking trombone lessons, but was not even good enough to make the elementary school orchestra.

The traffic brigade at the elementary school—made up of eighth-grade students who stood on nearby corners and guided younger children safely across streets—held their annual dance. Mr. Gibbs gave a speech and handed out certificates of merit.

Jimmie Jennings and his uncle Chris attended the spring AAU women's swimming and diving meet in Oakland. On his return, Chris reported that Neil Moran, a championship diver and son of Tom Moran—one of Fitch Mountain's most prominent summer residents—had given a diving exhibition. Chris added that he took time off from training Clipper Smith for the Boston Marathon to attend the Oakland swimming meet.

On June ninth, news of D-Day shared front page space with a formula for earwig control: "Mix Your Own: 1 2/3 qts. dark Karo, 1 2/3 lbs. flu si dust (sodium fluosicate), 10 lbs. bran, 1 gal. water. Mix well and apply damp."

Mr. Gibbs announced that the city would continue to employ Jesse as director of the elementary school playground project at a salary of $55 for June and $65 for July. He also announced the hiring of a young assistant director.

Then, as Healdsburg's First Aid and Water Safety Chairman, Mr. Gibbs gave out the bad news that all swimming and lifesaving classes for the summer would be canceled due to lack of sufficient water and unclean beach conditions. For the first time, a gravel-fill dam like the one at Merryland was to be erected around Fitch Mountain at Del Rio Woods, but there would be no classes there either.

Jesse and Mr. Gibbs were both scheduled to attend summer school at San Jose State College right after school closed, but before they left, Dad and Mother supervised a picnic for the Cub Scouts and Camp Fire Girls at Merryland. Jesse and Mother dispensed awards to the boys and girls. Lorelei Holbrook achieved "firemaker" rank that day. I didn't enjoy myself very much. I hadn't taken to Cub Scouting at all. Even with Jesse's help I couldn't master knot-tying or signaling, and I didn't take much to my fellow Cubs either—they were beginning to seem too obedient, docile, and clean-cut for me. My parents sensed my depression and after the picnic they let me spend a weekend in Petaluma with a classmate whose aunt had an apartment there.

My classmate's father drove us down 101. We rode over the automobile bridge and past Merryland on our way south, where a billboard in front of Basalt Rock Company said:

IF YOU LOVE THE JAPS
this message is not for you
But If You Have
GOOD AMERICAN BLOOD
that boils at the news of
Jap Atrocities
BUY WAR BONDS

******

I delivered the San Francisco *Chronicle* and *Examiner* that summer. I had to get up at 4:30 A.M. but it beat picking prunes. There were three of us who delivered the morning papers—two handled the *Chronicle/Examiner* and the other the Santa Rosa *Press Democrat*. Mother made me eat breakfast before I left the house and when I arrived at the shed behind Brown-Wolfe's drugstore it was a little after 5:00 A.M. The three of us would spend about a half-hour folding our papers. Then we stuffed them into our canvas saddlebags, hooked them on our bikes, and took off on our routes. Each of us had a different method of attaching the bags to our bicycles. One of the boys slung his bags over his handlebars, the other boy hung them on the frame in front of his seat, but I preferred to fix my saddlebags with snaps on a frame mounted over the rear fender.

Bicycle racers nowadays put their handlebars on upside down so that they hunch over and clasp the grips. In 1944, handlebars were modified in one of two ways: either you loosened a bolt and turned them under so that the black grips stuck out in front—away from the rider—to achieve a non-chalant look, or you loosened the same bolt and cranked the bars upward so that the grips stood straight up like steer horns. That is the way I rode—and with my seat raised up to the highest notch, so that when I rode I almost stood in the stirrups like a cowboy. I'd pack *Chronicles* in the right-hand bag and *Examiners* in the left- and take off in the cold, quiet mornings. I was lucky that summer. Because I was new, the boss, who was the assistant pharmacist at the drugstore, gave me the easiest route. I covered the central and north part of town where most of the homes were big, the lawns were large, and the porches were broad. One of the other boys got the route that covered Front Street, the river cabins, and homes down near the tracks where the streets weren't even paved and where he got pelted a lot by the Okie boys.

Our newspapers were as intricately folded as paper party hats. They had to be flat and sail true. As a boy got better he could arc a paper behind his back, fling it from under the bike's chassis in the same way that we saw movie Indians shoot arrows from under their horses' bellies, or even curve the paper softly around obstacles like trees and shrubs so that it would plop perfectly before a front door.

One late evening in July I was almost blown off my bike. An ammunition dump at Port Chicago—sixty miles away in the Carquinez Straight—blew up, killing over 300 people ("blown to atoms" the *Tribune* said) and injuring a thousand more. Some 220 of the seamen who were killed were blacks. After the explosion, fifty black seamen refused to load any more ships and were convicted of mutiny by a Navy court. By the end of November the fifty men were incarcerated at the Terminal Island Prison in San Pedro, according to the *Chronicle*. When I read the story about the rebellious ammunition loaders, I knew that Mother and I had really been imprisoned when we docked in America.

Most summer days, since Merryland was closed to swimming, I went to the elementary school playground after I finished my paper route. Dad's new assistant, Morris Ruby, was now in charge of the baseball diamonds and that was the game most of us went there to play. Jesse was, first and foremost, a teacher in all things—including athletics. He would go into minute detail showing children how to pass a baton in a relay race, how to throw a football with their fingers over the laces, and how to tuck the ball solidly under an arm when running with it. He demonstrated how to properly grip a baseball bat and how to pitch a softball—and then he would content himself with refereeing football games, timing and measuring track and field events, or umpiring a baseball game. When not instructing, Jesse stayed in the background. Not so his new assistant, Morris Ruby. Mr. Ruby, as we were directed to call him, was about twenty-two years old. He had recently graduated from Pepperdine, a Christian college in Los Angeles, where he had excelled in sports. Although Mr. Ruby had not been ordained, he aspired to the ministry and hoped to somehow combine athletics and preaching. Mr. Ruby was admired but not liked among the children, though it was his overzealousness rather than his lack of ability that affected his popularity. He played in our games with us, and the best way to describe him is "peppery" in everything that he did. He was a short, sandy-haired, tightly muscled young man and he chattered constantly. "Praise Gods" were interspersed with "Atta boys" and he tore madly after every fly ball whether it was hit to his field or not with his short legs pumping like pistons while he screamed out: "I've got it, I've got it," or "Mine, mine, mine!" We children stood around in dumb amazement while he whizzed between us picking off flies out of the air and scooping up grounders from the dirt, chattering all the while. At the plate, he would crouch and wave his bat around in circles, begging the pitcher from between clenched teeth to "put one over the plate; just put one over."

When Mr. Ruby got a hit, which he generally did off our ten- or eleven-year-old pitcher, he raced madly around the bags—stretching his hit as far as he could—and sliding recklessly in a great cloud of dust. Mr. Ruby played ball like a whirling dervish—he seemed to be everywhere at once. You might imagine that I would have admired Mr. Ruby after my own abandoned style of play in keep-away. But fashions change. It was now much more in fashion to be nonchalant than to be "crazed," which is as good a word as any. But in due respect, part of Mr. Ruby's plan was to convert us all to his own fiery brand of Christianity through his daring play. The only quirk of Mr. Ruby's that was widely copied was his method of molding his baseball glove. His was an old glove—the color of mahogany from soaking it in dark oils—and he had stitched all the fingers of the glove together. At night he soaked his glove, placed a ball in the pocket, and tied the whole thing up tightly with string to properly mold it.

Jesse and Mother were now involved in civic volunteering, and they debated local issues at our dinnertime discussions. We discussed crops because we all worked the harvests in one way or another, and in the summer of 1944 we talked about the new prisoner-of-war camp in Windsor. Both Mother and Dad thought local fears that some German POWs might escape and terrorize the countryside were without justification since the Germans were so far away from home. I wondered what Mother wrote to Grandfather about the camp.

Between the summer heat and the spring brown rot, prune growers did not have a good harvest that year. Ranchers who had switched to growing hops, however, couldn't hire enough workers to harvest them. In the Healdsburg area 2,500 acres of hops were ready to be harvested and 1,200 Mexican nationals proved insufficient for the job. Since hops enjoyed priority status, the government established a German prisoner-of-war camp downriver from Healdsburg at Windsor. Several hundred POWs were put to work harvesting the "beer buds," as they were called, under military police guards. Because it was against Geneva Convention rules to work the POWs as part of their sentences, they were paid prevailing wages.

One hot day while the prisoners were stripping vines in the fields of a farmer named Whilton, a Bell Aircobra, on fire and trailing smoke, plowed into the field. Snapping posts and clipping wires, it crashed through the lattice-like network of hops and exploded in a ball of flame. We wondered what the Germans made of that. I knew from one of my classmates, whose parents owned the adjoining property, that attempts to teach the Germans to play American football were a dismal failure. There had been a notice in the *Tribune* that guards at the camp were in need of old tennis shoes, as their own rubber-soled GI boots were inadequate for engaging in sports activities that were part of a physical fitness program being instituted at the camp. According to my classmate, who knew some of the military policemen, the German prisoners were taught the rudiments of football, but they played it so recklessly that bones were broken. The guards, who were probably teaching the Germans football so that they could get up a game with them, were so discouraged by the mayhem the prisoners worked on each other that they gave up the project.

In the meantime, an allied victory in Europe was clearly approaching and the city council was planning a big celebration. It seemed odd that the war was being won, because more and more local servicemen's obituaries were appearing in the paper. I had lived in Healdsburg long enough now so that I knew most of the family names—if not the servicemen themselves—and war games lost their luster for me then.

Hatred of the Germans and the Japanese was not new. But now, traveling shows began to appear in Healdsburg. A captured Japanese two-man submarine was put on display in the plaza one weekend, and for fifty cents an interested townsperson could squeeze through the sub's tiny conning tower and inspect its crude interior by crawling through it. Another time the hardware store's warehouse was cleaned out so that a photographic display of Japanese atrocities could be hung on the walls. Instruments of torture were also exhibited in order to illustrate the brutality and barbarity of the "buck-toothed fiends."

At an August meeting of the Kiwanis Club, the chief of the State Narcotics Bureau told club members that the Japanese were using opium in China for fifth column activities. Chiang Kai-Shek had cleaned China of its opium habits, according to the chief, but the arrival of the "Japs" had "made the curse more widespread than ever before."

Because of the unusually hot, dry weather, police and fire departments were overburdened. Fourteen hundred acres of rangeland were burned at the geysers, and several other fires were blazing out of control in the vicinity of Healdsburg. Residents of our town seemed to be drinking more in the unrelieved heat, and there were often several people sobering up in the courthouse's single-cell jail. The authorities were running out of patience. Chris Feeney—often described as the harmless town drunk—had been arrested many times and hauled before Judge Quinn. Chris always received a stern lecture and sixty days' probation from the judge, but in the summer of 1944 Judge Quinn sentenced Chris to thirty days on the county jail farm.

The owner of the Healdsburg *Tribune* irritably joined the fray. In a heated editorial he said that the Healdsburg Police Department spent entirely too much time "riding herd on drunks." The writer suggested that "dispensers of liquor should be made to halt the sale of liquor to sots and to those who don't know the meaning of 'refreshments.'" Following this blistering editorial the chief was fired by the city council, and his deputy was hired to take his place.

Jesse returned from summer school and was rehired by the elementary school to teach mathematics, science, manual training, and boy's physical training. He was also rehired as playground director, and the newly ordained Reverend Morris Ruby was retained to assist him. They were to be paid $40 between them monthly to "share to their own satisfaction." While

Jesse was away at summer school the playground program had closed and the entire school yard was levelled, spread with hot asphalt, graveled, and rolled to a shiny black surface. The surface did not dry properly and for several months boys and girls tracked tar and gravel through the hallways of the school.

Just before school opened, the University Street house we'd lived in for two years was sold and we had to move. In the original town platte, University Street was the last, easternmost city street, with only the Healdsburg Institute and farmland between the street and Fitch Mountain. The land was meant to remain agricultural, but no housing provisions were made for the carpenters, bricklayers, and other workmen who built the landowners' homes, and so the city limits were extended two blocks further east from University Street. Here, on First and Second streets, craftsmen built their own houses.

We moved to one of these houses on two-block-long Second Street, whose north end culminated at the elementary school playground. The south end of the street dead-ended at the small estate of a wealthy lumberman. The lumberman bought the lots surrounding his estate, and he kept them undeveloped. He grew high hedges all around his property, which enclosed the only swimming pool in town. On one adjacent lot stood an old mansion—abandoned now and unsafe, its stone portico cracked and its pillars peeling. A small, fenced orchard abutted the lumberman's house on the other side, and diagonally across from the estate was a grove filled with oak and madrone trees. Our house faced the old mansion and was separated from the grove by a narrow alley.

Our new house was small, but shady and cool. There were two small fir trees growing in front of the house, an apple tree and flower garden on the north side, and a long, wide backyard was dominated by an apricot tree. Two front bedrooms flanked a living room. Behind them were the dining room, the kitchen, and a utility porch with the house's only bathroom attached to it. A small screened porch looking out at the apple tree and garden became my bedroom. There was a private bedroom for my sister, an attic for storage, and a root cellar for canned goods. Since the house was rectangular, the kitchen was the same size as the living room and dining room, and could accommodate a sewing area and a pantry. Jesse had a large woodshed too, and a smaller structure suitable for a shop. At the far end of the yard there was a ramshackle old chicken house next to the garage. Low hedges separated us on the one side from our nearest neighbor, and on the other side, beyond a narrow alley, was the grove.

Jesse curtained off part of my screened porch bedroom and strung a pole across its width so that I could hang up my clothes. There was just enough room left for a double bed, a night stand, and my bureau. But over the years I managed to get the maximum use out of my porch. Though it was always referred to as the "screened" porch, glass covered the walls up to a height of six feet or so and only the remaining two feet up to the eaves were screens. But it was open to the elements. The seasons were distinct: the glass frosted over in late fall, it was almost like being out in the rain in winter, in spring the smell of the garden just outside filled the porch, and in summer I sweltered.

School registration broke the all-time record in the fall of 1944. Some 325 students were enrolled at the high school and 440 at the elementary school. Many of the newcomers were children of the emigrants from Oklahoma and Arkansas, and they were integrated into the old group of classmates I'd had since the fifth grade. Generally the Okies, Arkies, and Texans who comprised most of the new students were older than the rest of us, but less educated. They were polite in class, but rough in the school yard. Our games must have seemed infantile to them.

The seventh and eighth grades at the elementary school were divided into three groups. Jesse was the homeroom teacher for the brighter students, and Mrs. Luce, whose primary subjects were English, literature, and sewing, had homeroom responsibilities for students with less aptitude or less ambition. The third teacher was Miss Shanahan, who taught U.S. history and social studies. We all suspected that Miss Shanahan had a drinking problem. She was very surly and ill-tempered on Mondays, by midweek she was reasonably coherent and good-humored, but by Friday she was a nervous wreck and couldn't seem to keep her mind on any subject. She had been observed buying bottles of whiskey in a Santa Rosa liquor store, and she often slipped out of class and into the supply room during tests. Rumors circulated about Miss Shanahan's sexual preferences too, because she shared her house above the golf course with Miss Nichols, the school nurse. Since Jesse was my father, Mr. Gibbs initially placed me in Mrs. Luce's room. But after several weeks, he decided I was not being sufficiently challenged and moved me into my father's section. This decision affected both my father and me. He could not very well give me preferred treatment in his classes and so he became, to my way of thinking, stricter and more demanding of me than of anyone else. I did not even know how to address him in class. I couldn't call him "Mr. Manley," and "Dad" was too familiar—so I didn't call him anything at all unless I had to. I did not want to appear to be too smart in front of my peers, nor did I want them to think I was being coached at home, so I didn't study hard. As a result, my growth in the subjects my father taught was stunted from the start.

Jesse was a fine teacher, full of wit and compassion, and all of the other students loved him. The newcomers particularly took to him and he to them. They politely called him "Sir" in class and he took special pains to make them feel included.

Jesse, as P.E. teacher, would not field a regular football team, thinking the sport too rough for elementary school children. Besides, the new asphalt playing surface was still gummy with tar. For a while we revived a sort of modified keep-away at recess but that came to an end shortly. One of the new boys from Oklahoma was a hulking fourteen-year-old named Charlie Hulburt. The first time Charlie invited himself into one of our keep-away games, he cold-cocked the boy holding the ball. Then he took the ball, stuck it under his arm, and dared anyone to come and take it away from him. Several boys tried, and Charlie swatted them away like Gulliver dispersing Lilliputians. Our keep-away games were finished for good after that, as were many of our other games. Charlie and his friends—Ace Lingo among them—would scatter marbles like chaff, scuff out chalk marks on hopscotch games, grab yo-yos and tops from children and stick them in their pockets, daring their owners to retrieve them. If a boy opened his mouth, he would usually get a fist in it. We took to cowering in groups in corners of the yard—these older strangers seemed like the Mongol horde to us, so alien and ferocious were they.

School policy was that Mr. Gibbs handled classroom discipline problems, and yard duty teachers handled problems that occurred during recess. Since the boys were almost always polite in class, the principal did not have to take them to his office for a few swats from his large paddle. All of us locals would have given a month's allowance to witness Mr. Gibbs disciplining Charlie or Ace, but it seemed like good fortune always smiled on Mr. Gibbs. The only teacher who dared to intervene in their school yard fights—and they often brawled among themselves—was Jesse. A quiet "OK, boys, break it up," from him was usually enough to get the fighters shuffling to their feet peaceably. I couldn't understand how he did it. They were generally twice Jesse's size, but they meekly submitted to him. It is a fact, though, that I never saw Jesse punish Charlie or Ace.

Charlie Hulburt's sister, Laviva, caused as much of a sensation among the girls as Charlie did among the boys. She was a year younger than Charlie, and was very sensual. Laviva was a little horse-faced, but had a ripe young body that put even Squirt Moore's sister's to shame. Laviva would sidle up to a boy boldly and even touch his body with hers. This was a far cry from a local girl's method of letting a boy know she liked him: she might pass him an unsigned note or take part in a popular recess game of "Ring around the Rosey" in which losing girls had to loudly disclose the object of their affection.

Seven

THAT FALL, WHILE B-29S BOMBED TOKYO, the students at Healdsburg Elementary School received a Treasury Department award for "exceptional activities" in the sixth war loan drive and were mentioned by Sam Hayes, a famous radio broadcaster, as one of the ten outstanding schools in the far western states. Dick Bong, the American ace fighter pilot, shot down his 25th plane; and it seemed like every issue of the *Tribune* had a headline now that read: "Healdsburg Has Lost Another One of Its Fine Young Men." My classmate Jennie Pearl Hicks's brother, Ovid, was killed in action. He was the seventh member of her family to be killed in the war. A gold star went up in the Hicks's front window. The paper announced that no outdoor Christmas tree lights would be allowed this year even though dimout restrictions had been removed.

Almost everyone in the elementary school tried out for the new basketball team. The team was Morris Ruby's idea and he persuaded Jesse to go along with it and to let him coach it. I was not very big or very fast, but I found that I had some talent for basketball. In our opening game we beat a team from Lytton Home—a Salvation Army facility for "troubled" boys and girls from the Bay Area—that was located near Geyserville. The *Tribune* said they were "drubbed by a decisive score" of 30-10.

Since Jesse was not coaching basketball, it gave him time to do something he really enjoyed, playing billiards. There were only two billiard tables in town where "respectable" people could play. One was at the Masonic Hall and the other was in the Oddfellows Temple. Jesse never had any inclination to become a Mason—they were a little too "high falutin'" for him—and the Oddfellows were a little too boisterous for his tastes. But the Knights of Pythias shared the Oddfellows meeting hall, and Jesse fit in well enough with them. Besides, he said, the best billiards players in town belonged to that fraternal order. Mostly they were older, quiet men who enjoyed the easy pace of billiards and never, never called it "shooting pool." So once or twice a week now he would mosey down to the Temple for a game or two with Harry Pitts, who owned the nursery, or with Hugo Hadrich, our new neighbor.

On the Sunday before Christmas, Mr. Hadrich's house caught fire. He had started the heater for his wife when he went out early to work at the city pumping plant. Jesse and another neighbor fought the blaze with garden hoses until the fire department arrived, and they were credited with saving the Hadrich's house. So my father's warden's training paid off after all.

St. Paul's new vicar decided to beef up the choir and to recruit a couple of altar boys. As it stood, the choir was made up of an elderly soprano with a wobbly voice, her daughter, and a plump, angelic-looking boy who sang a thin, but accurate tenor. George Izzett, the organist's son, and I were nominated by our mothers to become the new altar boys and to fill out the choir. The vicar found cassocks and surplices for us and at the Christmas service George, the tenor, and I sang "We Three Kings of Orient Are."

Mother wrote a Christmas letter to Uncle Bill and Aunt Idylla just before the holiday. In an addendum to Mother's letter, Jesse refers to her as "Ernie." My father's relatives had given Mother that nickname and addressed their letters to "Jake and Ernie." Mother did not like the nickname at all:

In July Jess went to summer school at San Jose State. Then he worked all summer at the prune dryer again. Made better money than he does teaching school! And the week before school opened we moved.

The house we were in was sold in July, and we had about given up hope of finding another one—we were definitely not in the market to buy. Then, a friend called and said if we hadn't found a house, they had bought one the day before and were we interested in renting! It is so much superior to the other, and we felt most fortunate indeed. Jess—or the farmer in him—is thrilled with the yard and its possibilities. There are two chicken houses at the back, and Davy is going to raise chickens as a Cub Scout project. It's to be all his job. Only, even now, before the chickens have arrived, I hear him offering Margaret certain jobs! Jess went out to clean out the tangled growth on the side and discovered, too late, it was poison oak. So he spent the Thanksgiving vacation itching. Then I went at it—I'm immune to the vile stuff (too much bad in me for there to be room for any more!)—and cut all the rest out. And this last weekend he put new roofing on it, and he and Davy are now planning a white-washing orgy. Then the chickens. I hope they enjoy the house!

We had a fire next door on Sunday. It was fortunate there was neither rain or wind, and everything was gotten out. But the house is a wreck. I hate fires.

Howdy. "Ernie" has rationed me to just this much paper, so I'll have to be brief! We are now in our new place; new in the sense that we moved in about two months ago. We like it very much and I'll be happy if we don't move again for a long, long time. We now have some garden space, fruit trees, a grape arbor and a chicken house. I like to have room to get out and dig in the dirt and raise a few vegetables and flowers. David says he'd like to have a few chickens, so I put a new roof on the chicken house. It will be a good experience for him to have a little responsibility, and he doesn't realize that a dozen hens can be any care! Our neighbors got burned out last Sunday. Fortunately it was on a day when the men folks were at home, for we got everything out in time.

We received a letter from Art that Christmas. He was stationed at an unnamed air base in England repairing bombers that returned from the Berlin run. Another air force sergeant was our guest for Christmas dinner. The sergeant spent the afternoon sitting at Mother's pantry table in the winter sunlight reading the Sunday papers. When the sergeant wasn't reading, he would smoke a pipe and stare off into the grove of trees—lost in thought. Mother had made a pair of mittens for him as a Christmas gift and they sat on the table in front him. Every so often, he would touch them, as if he was remembering something.

I remember the warmth of our Christmases: sitting around the tree on Christmas Eve with a glass of hot cider, then walking down Matheson Street to admire the decorations through the windows of the big homes. On Christmas morning Margaret and I were always up first, begging Mom and Dad to get out of bed. We sat around the tree in our pajamas while Jesse and Mother drank coffee, and Mother read Luke's version of the first Christmas.

Mother kept all our schedules organized. She insisted that we be home for meals so that we could all be together as a family at least three times a day. On a normal day she cleaned the house and washed clothes in the morning. After she cooked and fed us lunch, she gardened, shopped, cooked dinner, and worked at the Red Cross or another volunteer agency in the evening. Since eggs were rationed, we ate a bowl of oatmeal or cream of wheat with honey and wheat germ on it every morning. Jesse, Margaret, and I walked home from school at noon for homemade soup. Dinner usually featured pot roast, swiss steak, stew, or leg of lamb and vegetables from the garden. Mother always said "remember the starving children in India" to get us to eat all of our food. We had a lot of tapioca pudding and custards for dessert, and on Fridays we ate fish because Roman Catholics did and fish could be bought cheaply then at any of several Italian markets in town.

After dinner, Mother washed the dishes, and Dad corrected papers. Margaret and I were supposed to alternate drying the dishes, but I never held up my end of the bargain. One of Jesse's nicknames for me was "King Tut," as in "Who do you think you are?" Mother often reminded me that "procrastination is the thief of time."

Mother decorated our living room with pictures and mementos of India. There were photographs on the walls of the mountains near Kotagiri and several paintings of Indian architecture, including a moonlit Taj Majal. Two Javanese batiks hung near the front door, and small ivory carvings rested on teak tables that had elephant heads for legs (I was always tripping on the tusks that protruded from the legs). These Far Eastern trappings were interspersed with a second-hand sofa, two overstuffed chairs, and a coffee table that Jesse built in his shop. Mother sewed furniture coverings and window curtains from colorful Indian cloth.

In the evenings our family gathered in the dining room. A gas heater sat between the windows that looked out into the grove. We acquired a large wooden Atwater-Kent radio that was about four feet high and rested against one wall. Dad's and Mom's stuffed chairs flanked the heater. A wicker armchair was placed across the room for guests. When the dishes were done we usually listened to approved radio programs: "Corliss Archer," "Mr. District Attorney," "Henry Aldrich," "The Great Gildersleeve," "Fibber McGee and Molly," "Fred Allen." Dad's favorite was "Amos 'n Andy." Mother's was "Jack Benny." We also tuned in every Saturday evening to "Your Hit Parade." Most popular singers were away at war, so "Your Hit Parade" replaced them with opera singers who performed the top songs of the week. Laurence Tibbett or Lauritz Melchior of the Metropolitan Opera Company sang "Mairzy Doats and Doazy Doats" and "Praise the Lord and Pass the Ammunition," and Helen Traubel warbled "Don't Sit Under the Apple Tree with Anyone Else but Me." Mother rather liked their Wagnerian renditions. In fact, my father and I often argued with her on Saturday afternoons over whether we would listen to a Stanford football game (my father was still a fan even after Stanford had treated him so shabbily) or to the weekly opera.

Mother normally controlled our radio listening—in terms of time and quality. Shows that were definitely not allowed were mysteries like "Inner

Sanctum," or "Lights Out." Mother said they would scare Margaret and me so badly that we wouldn't sleep.

Though she seemed very old to me, Mother was only thirty-four. In winter, she rose first and turned on the dining room heater. Then she turned on the radio for her fifteen-minute exercise program. Mother switched the dial to "The Sons of the Pioneers" at 6:30 A.M., and during breakfast, at a quarter to seven, she changed stations again in order to hear "Fred Waring and his Pennsylvanians." After Fred Waring we left for school, and Mother usually caught up on her correspondence before beginning the housework.

Despite my parents' high hopes for me as a chicken farmer, I quickly lost interest in my flock. I liked them when they were chicks and I liked collecting the eggs when the chicks were grown, but I soon lost interest in cleaning the chicken house. If I owed my sister for a year's worth of drying dishes, I must have owed her for another six months' worth of cleaning chicken houses. Luckily for me, but not the chickens, a weasel killed them all and I was off the hook.

I made the grammar school basketball team. I was only a substitute, but I began practicing basketball at the expense of chicken farming and trombone playing. Jesse mounted a basketball hoop for me on our garage door and I dribbled and shot by the hour. For indoor practices, I twisted a black metal coat hanger into a miniature hoop and attached it to the inner wall on my screened porch bedroom. Then I shot a tennis ball at it, leaping over, onto, and around my bed for rebounds.

The *Tribune's* front page story in early January 1945 concerned the Healdsburg City Council. In their first action of the year the council hired Pestaway Service of Santa Rosa to exterminate an infestation of rats in the local sewage system. Besides the rat problem, council members said the system itself needed modernizing as it was old and not sufficient for the new growth Healdsburg was experiencing. Our family laughed about the sewage problems and the rats. Jesse would joke that maybe Healdsburg could dump its sewage in the river like the East Indians did in their rivers, and Mother suggested maybe a Pied Piper could be hired to lure the rats up onto Fitch Mountain. In a companion statement, the council said that "the water supply is of great concern due to increasing demand and lowering of the river water level by gravel extraction operations."

Minor news items included an announcement that the Frost and Calhoun ranches were employing POWs in the off-season at their ranches. A local swimming star married a serviceman from Brooklyn whom she met at a Hospitality House dance. Our basketball team continued to win games.

Chris Jennings, who was now covering sports for the paper, wrote that "Jimmie Jennings is a consistent scorer."

A curious bit of news appeared on the paper's second page: it was noted that the first Kiwanis speaker under Mr. Gibbs' incumbency was John Kuropatkin Chappeel—commentator at an Oakland radio station—who told the assembled Kiwanians that Josef Stalin was not really Russian, but Mongolian, and that his ambition was to rival Genghis Khan.

About this time, across the road from Squirt Moore's big old house, an Eskimo family with two sons and an exotic daughter named Rita moved into a cabin by the river.

Squirt and I were friends, and through him I became friendly with Jack Butler, Buck's younger brother. Jack did not run with Charlie Hulburt and Ace Lingo. The reason I gained Jack's confidence was because I agreed to spar with him when few other boys would. I had been going to a new boxing club in the elementary school gym on Saturdays and was confident I could hold my own with Jack. So one day Jack and I went to a corner of the schoolyard and I ventured to put some slick boxing moves on him. He ignored my feints and kept knocking me down.

It was through Jack that I learned about the "birds and the bees." One day after school we were walking down Matheson Street on our way to town. I was headed for a lemon coke at Tomasco's drugstore and I asked Jack where he was going. Jack said, "I believe I'll go and fuck Laviva Hulburt." I asked, "Do you want to have a baby, Jack?" Jack had a terrific smile when he chose to smile, and he really grinned when he replied, "Hell no, it's fun." I didn't know that. We stopped right there under a Hawthorn tree and I questioned him closely, and that is how I learned about sex.

One day Jack asked me if I would go on a double date to the movies with him. He had asked Doctor Oakleaf's daughter Ruth Elaine to a matinee and she accepted on condition that I go along with her girlfriend. Ruth Elaine Oakleaf was far beyond even my romantic aspirations. Her parents moved in the same sort of company as Tom Moran, the rich Irishman from Fitch Mountain. I can only surmise that Jack, in a moment of fierce pride, decided to go for broke and that Ruth Elaine figured that an afternoon of slumming might be fun.

When the day of the matinee arrived, Jack looked far better than I did. Dressed up, Jack was just about the best-looking boy in Healdsburg. He was muscular and with his blond hair slicked back with Rose Hair Oil, he was as good a date as any girl could have wanted.

We went to the show, each of us sitting with our respective dates, and I peeked over once in awhile to see if Jack and Ruth Elaine were holding hands. At intermission, I went to buy popcorn and returned to find that the girls had switched seats. Ruth Elaine said gaily, "I have decided to sit next to you, David, for the next show. Jack says it's all right with him." I was puzzled, and I looked at Jack questioningly. He glowered but didn't offer any opposition to the idea. I meekly acquiesced.

We went our separate ways after the movie. Later that afternoon, I rode my bike past Jack's small house looking for him. But only his brother Buck was there, so I rode off quickly. Jack never held that afternoon against me, but we were never chums, as my father would have called it, after that. I had only double-dated with Jack as a favor anyway. By now, I had my eyes fixed on Rita Rose.

Our basketball team had won a sort of unofficial championship. Mr. Ruby was hot stuff around town after that, and Jesse made a popular decision to let him coach the baseball team too. In February, the school gave block "H's" to those who had played on the team. The large felt blocks were gold, and Mother knit me a dark blue sweater to sew my "H" on. At an assembly in the gym, Jesse handed out the blocks with Jimmie Jennings, as president of the Block "H" Club, standing by. We initiates had gone through a ceremony in the morning that included being dressed up as bums or girls and having foul-smelling garbage dumped all over us. We had to obey the older Block "H" members and call them all "Mister." The Okies couldn't believe their eyes. They had never seen anyone undergo such abject humiliation without fighting back, and they were stunned speechless.

At the awards assembly, Bill Wolking—who had produced the American Legion Smoker—presented the student body with a real Wurlitzer juke box. The Block "H" Club scheduled a celebration dance for that Friday night.

I was very proud of my block "H". The evening after the assembly, Mom sewed it on the front of my new blue sweater. The next afternoon I rode down to the cabins near the river and asked Rita Rose to go to the dance with me. She surprised me by saying she'd have to ask her parents, but I couldn't really see how she could turn me down.

That evening at dinner I asked Mother—for it was she, not Jesse, who was in charge of things like this—if I could go to the dance. She paused, fork poised in mid-air, and considered it.

"Since your father is going to be a chaperonee, I think it might be all right," she agreed hesitantly. "You would have to walk back and forth from the school with him, of course."

"Well, I was thinking about taking a girl," I replied.

"What girl?" Mother asked suspiciously.

"Rita Rose," I said nonchalantly.

My mother's jaw dropped and so did her fork. "Absolutely not. Under no conditions. In no uncertain terms. No. What is the matter with you anyway, thinking of asking a girl like that when there are so many nice girls in your class?"

I tried to say that I thought Rita was a nice girl.

Mother ignored me. "As a matter of fact, I have been thinking that Lucille Peterson might make a fine first date for you, and if you really want to take a girl to the dance, Lucille would be a wonderful choice."

"But, Mom," I protested, "I really like Rita."

"Young man, it will be Lucille or no one and that is that."

When Mother said, "that is that," she meant it. I gave up the argument and finished my dinner in surly silence.

Lucille Peterson was a fine girl. Her parents owned a small farm and her mother sewed dressings down at the Red Cross with Mother. She possessed a fine singing voice in an operatic sort of way and was asked to sing at a lot of teas and ladies' club functions. She was also very big—a hearty, hefty girl who most of us considered a "buddy" rather than romantic material. In fact, everyone called her "Pete."

I didn't get any help in my date predicament from Jesse or Margaret. Jesse kept eating away quietly with a "leave me out of this" look about him. Margaret kept her head down as if to avoid blows whenever Mother became stern with me. I got as far as "Aw, Mom..." in protest before Mother indicated the case was closed.

So the next afternoon I bicycled back to Rita's cabin. When I pulled up, she was holding hands with an Oklahoman. She said she'd completely forgotten about my invitation. I told her I didn't think I'd be able to go anyway and so we broke the date we never had. But I wanted to show off my new block sweater so badly that I dutifully went to the dance with "Pete."

In their pre-Easter Issue the *Tribune* reported that the federal government was contemplating construction of a 175-foot-high dam at Del Rio Woods around Fitch Mountain. The dam would be built after the war, and the lake created behind its spillway would flood the entire river gorge and all of Alexander Valley north of Healdsburg. Ranchers were outraged over this possibility. Other stories reported that draft evaders were being picked up on local ranches. Golf rates at Tayman Park, the local golf course, were raised to $.75 daily and $1 on Saturday and Sunday, and the monthly rate rose from $3 to $4.

Major Taylor, Superintendent of Lytton Home, announced their annual Easter Sunrise Service would be held at 6:45 A.M. at the site of the home's twenty-foot-high lighted cross. The public was invited to attend. Reverend Morris Ruby chose "Resurrection Rays" as the topic for his Easter sermon at the Church of Christ.

I must have learned a thing or two about baseball from Rusty and the Hartnell Street gang because I was assigned to play right field for the elementary school team. But our grammar school softball team was small potatoes compared to all the other baseball teams in town. The high school team, the Junior American Legion team, and the summer softball league teams all played at the old city ballpark with its gracefully curved, covered grandstand and its high wooden outfield fences plastered with local merchants' advertisements. People always voted for ballpark improvements at election time. This year the ballpark was getting another facelift. Our neighbor, the wealthy lumberman, donated lumber and materials for a new "big-league" scoreboard. Another prominent citizen donated four brand-new loudspeakers. "Slim" Price, the newly elected Mayor of Healdsburg, would throw out the first ball at the first game of summer and Judge Quinn would attempt to hit it.

This act alone should have been worth the price of admission. Judge Edward Quinn was over seventy years old, and was not known as a mirthful or game-playing man. "Sour" was the adjective most often applied to the judge, and "senile" was the second most commonly used descriptor. People often found themselves responding to a comment of Judge Quinn's only to realize that he was talking to himself. Then they were fixed with a sort of crazed stare in reproach for interrupting him. Healdsburg legend had it that Judge Quinn started to become mean and deranged shortly after Cocky Lodge began an affair with the judge's wife. The affair took place long ago, everyone agreed, but that was about all they agreed on.

According to the legend, Cocky had been caught *in flagrante* by the judge in the judge's own home. It was suggested that his wife's infidelity bothered the judge less than the fact that her lover was a lunatic. And it was true that, even in 1945, the mere sight of Cocky would drive the judge into a frenzy, and he would reel up the street after him, cursing and shaking his cane. On those occasions, Cocky would cackle crazily and ride off on his "wheel" as he called his bicycle, although once he had

119

tried to run the judge down. The story was that cuckoldry had driven Quinn queer in the head and Cocky crazy as a loon.

Jesse only had one run-in with Earl Lodge that I know of. A group of us were standing with my dad near the outdoor basketball court at the edge of the school one afternoon when he came whizzing down out of the graveyard on his bike. He screeched to a stop near us and looked us over with a curious stare as if he had never seen schoolchildren before. Then, in his strange, glottal voice, he said, "Hullo." My father, never having seen this apparition before, asked very quietly—for all of us were transfixed—"Who is this?" Bruce Holbrook whispered, "That's Earl Lodge, but he likes to be called Cocky." My father dutifully said in a soothing voice, "Hello, Cocky," and of course all hell broke loose. Cocky tried to ride Jesse down, all the while screaming that he was a "Lytton Home runaway bastard" (which is what he called everyone when he got angry), and just as quickly he tore off down the street like some latter-day Ichabod Crane being pursued by a headless horseman.

The news of President Roosevelt's death on April 14, 1945, shared front page space in the *Tribune* with a report that Clipper Smith finished second in the Petaluma marathon and that the city of Healdsburg had hired a dog catcher and opened the first dog pound in its history. Nearly 400 people attended the plaza memorial service for the president, and that same night the Cub Scouts celebrated their first anniversary at the Healdsburg Elementary School auditorium.

On May eighth, at three o'clock in the afternoon, the war in Europe ended. The official number of "gold star heroes from Healdsburg" was calculated by the newspaper at thirty-four. On May eighteenth, Healdsburg held another memorial service in the plaza to celebrate V-E Day. Most of the town turned out to hail the "capitulation of the Nazi monsters in Europe." The city council voted to honor President Truman's call for no "undue festivities, but rather a day of rededication and prayer," so the Healdsburg American Legion withdrew their sponsorship of the event. Ace Lingo's father was arrested for vehicular manslaughter when he killed a man while driving drunk on the night of the memorial service.

Because the community baseball park had been beautified, the city council decided to field a city team for the summer and call the team the "Prune Packers." The local flying club held a gas model plane contest, which was won easily by Jere Holbrook. Judge Quinn sentenced Ace Lingo's father to two years in the county jail, a fine of $250, and loss of his driver's license. The rat eradication program ended and the dog pound closed because, according to the paper, "dog owners made it so uncomfortable that the new dog catcher quit a month ago."

Jamaicans, recruited in Los Angeles, began to arrive to work in the harvests just as growers were pleading to the California Wage Board for wage ceilings for farm workers. There was a big debate over whether or not the city should buy a machine to chlorinate water. A news story declared that the head of the chemistry department at Oberlin College reported that large intakes of Vitamin C relieved hay fever, asthma, and "many other ills."

When summer vacation officially began, Bay Area families started migrating north to their Fitch Mountain cabins. Tom Moran was leading a fight to stop talk of a permanent government dam at Del Rio Woods.

The "Grand Reopening of Palomar Dance Hall in the Heart of Del Rio Woods on the Russian River" was announced along with news that Gary Nottingham and his trombone and orchestra would provide music for dancing. Farther downriver toward the coast, Bob Wills and his Texas Playboys were scheduled to appear at Mirabel Park. "Dance among beautiful redwoods in the new semi-outdoor dance pavilion," the Mirabel announcement read.

There were two county roads that accompanied the Russian River west out of Healdsburg. Eastside Road followed the river's eastern banks, and Westside Road meandered along to the west of the river. For five miles or so farms lay between roads and river, then the timbered coastal mountains pressed in, squeezing out the farmland. Both roads ran along the river, then through forests of fir, pine, and redwoods. Summer homes hung precariously out over the high river banks and were built in canyons that led up and away into the timber. Occasional beaches appeared along sharp veers of the river. Eastside Road bridged the river at Mirabel Park beach and dance pavilion. The two roads became one and ran straight beside the river toward several small summer communities: Rio Nido, with a large imitation-Swiss-chalet dance hall surrounded by little chalets that served as summer cabins; Guerneville, with its block-long dance hall called "The Grove" (The Grove had a jungle theme) and the best beach of the river resorts; and the last little community, Monte Rio. From Monte Rio westward the land flattened and became rocky and sandy, the river broadened, sheep ranches proliferated, and one could smell the ocean.

While most high school boys in Healdsburg might visit the Palomar Dance Hall once or twice a summer, Fitch Mountain was really the private domain of the mountain's Irish-Catholic summer residents. The beach at Del Rio Woods was strictly their territory, as to a lesser extent was another beach, Camp Rose. If a local boy were to wander around the mountain to either of these exclusive enclaves, he would feel as out of place as I had felt my first day at Gold Flat school.

The resorts downriver were less awesome to local youths. Crowds of teenagers from San Francisco would descend on Guerneville and Rio Nido every weekend, camping on the beaches or up in the canyons. One could easily remain anonymous on this stretch of river, mainly because everyone wore swimming suits morning, afternoon, and evening. So mode of dress never gave anyone's class away. Many older Healdsburg youths drove to the river resorts on weekends to check out the city girls—nudging and punching each other at the sight of them, rolling their eyes and groaning in unison with lust. This unmasked them, of course, for the Bay Area girls were always lofty and disdainful, while the true city boys—in the fashion of the day—pretended to ignore the girls in return. It was a strange sight to see.

The situation changed at the evening dances. Though Healdsburg youths who ventured downriver to jitterbug at Guerneville or Rio Nido, bragging that they were off to "pick up some city girls" seldom succeeded, local boys were very successful at whipping city boys in fights outside the dances. Rich, well-groomed young swimmers with their privately-taught boxing techniques were seldom a match for the hard fists of boys who worked in the fields all summer long.

At eleven years old all these tales came secondhand to me. They were filtered down through classmates who had older brothers or cousins. The river resorts seemed as unreal to me as was Camelot, and Fitch Mountain's Palomar Dance Hall appeared no nearer. The fact was that in those days most local boys seldom went anywhere outside the city limits of Healdsburg. But we often saw these golden girls from "around the mountain" shopping with their parents in town, and like every other Healdsburg boy I dreamed of the day when I would court one of them in spite of class differences.

It was considered a good sign that two Fitch Mountain resorts were sold at the beginning of the summer. It meant that important people thought the war was ending and good times were about to return. The Bellevue Villa, which had twenty cabins and catered to hikers and horseback riders, was bought by a Guerneville man who said he intended to restore it.

The Villa Chanticleer, the resort closest to the summit of the mountain, was also sold. Historically the Villa had catered to a French clientele from San Francisco, but now was collapsing into ruin. One of my classmates was the daughter of the resort's manager, and I had been invited up there for a birthday party once. The property was overgrown, the pools and ponds were empty and leaf filled, and the picnic tables were falling apart. But the new owners from San Francisco, who were described as "bar operators" by the *Tribune*, promised to change all that. They hired Bill Wolking to manage the new operation and big-time entertainment was pledged.

The city of Healdsburg had no jurisdiction around Fitch Mountain, and the county paid little attention to the area. Only when Fitch Mountain Road ran steeply down the north slope of the mountain, past the Bellevue Villa and the northern edge of the golf course, did the land become city governed again. So there was no law readily available except for a part-time constable who was supposed to patrol the mountain occasionally.

The Red Cross summer swim campaign at Merryland was reinstated in 1945. Chris Jennings, acting as chairman of lifesaving and swimming for the Red Cross, made the announcement. Volunteers built a fifty-foot pier for students and racers to dive from. I enrolled in the Intermediate swimming class, which started at 7:00 A.M., and had to rush on my paper route to get to my lessons on time.

One morning while I was delivering papers, a woman came out of a large brick house and hailed me. She said I looked to her like the sort of upstanding youth who could be trusted with a magnificent and rare young puppy she owned. He was a purebred Australian hunting dog, she told me, and although she could not keep him, he was too beautiful and valuable to just give away to anyone. He turned out to be a huge animal, as tall as my bicycle, with a mammoth head and lean, sleek lines. I wouldn't have known an Australian hunting dog from a Chinese bull-terrier, but he certainly looked like he could chase down big game. The puppy seemed to like me too, for he leaped and bounded with enthusiasm. When he tried to lick my face, he knocked me off my bike. When I recovered and got to my feet, he put his paws on my shoulders and we looked each other straight in the eye. He was magnificent. I fell in love with him straightaway.

I told the lady I would return that afternoon for my new puppy. At lunch I did not say anything to Dad or Mom about my new dog. We had never talked about owning animals, other than chickens, and I was apprehensive. But I knew for certain that once they laid eyes on my beautiful hunting dog they would be as enraptured with him as I was.

So I hurried through lunch and walked back to the lady's house. I did not think that the puppy would follow meekly, and it was with some difficulty that I led him to our house. He bounded and strained against the leash at the slightest rustle in a bush or the burst of wings from a tree and almost pulled me off my feet a couple of times.

When I got my dog home, Jesse was working in the garden. I led the puppy up to the fence and surprised Jesse, who upon looking up said, "What is that?"

"He's my new dog," I replied excitedly. "Actually, he's only a puppy. He's seven months old. He's a genuine Australian hunting dog."

"He's awfully big for a puppy," Jesse commented. "He resembles a Shetland pony more than anything I can think of."

Mother must have spied us from the kitchen window, for by now she was standing on the back stoop with her hands in her apron pockets.

"How would we feed him?" she asked perceptively.

"Where would we put him?" my father asked, equally perceptively.

"I've thought about that," I said, "and I figure we could keep him in the chicken house now that we don't have chickens anymore."

"No," Jesse said.

"Listen," I pleaded, "I know I wasn't very good with the chickens, but I promise to take care of my puppy and none of you will have to bother about him at all."

"No," my father repeated, and went back to his hoeing.

I argued and pleaded, but Jesse wouldn't budge. He was just too big a dog, he said, and there simply wasn't the room or money for food for him. "That dog would eat us out of house and home," I believe Jesse said—or maybe it was Mother, for she too was eyeing him apprehensively.

I walked round and round the grove with my puppy all afternoon, weeping. I did this in full sight of our house's windows. I paused from time to time to pat the puppy and sob loudly, "I don't care if nobody else wants you and you will have to go to the dog pound, I love you," and I would cry some more. It was all to no avail, though I knew my parents could not have been unmoved. In late afternoon, tearfully, I led my puppy back to the nice lady who did not seem at all surprised to find that my parents had forbidden me to keep him.

That evening at dinner Mother suggested that perhaps someday I might be permitted a very small puppy of my own if an opportunity to obtain one presented itself. Jesse was very quiet about the whole idea—no doubt remembering the chickens. But within a matter of weeks, I did get a puppy. He was a tiny, black, furry ball when we picked him up from one of the matriarchs of St. Paul's who owned a sheep ranch. He was a sheepdog, the matriarch said, and we thought she meant one of those small, energetic, disciplined dogs we had seen at Future Farmers of America fairs. As it turned out, he was a McNab shepherd and grew almost as large as the Australian hunting dog. His coat was black except for a tiny white spot on his tail and so I named him "Tippy." Jesse called him "Tippecanoe and Tyler Too."

Eight

THE SUMMER SWIM CAMPAIGN ended with a water carnival and races. I won a blue ribbon for finishing first in the twenty-five-yard freestyle for Intermediate swimmers.

After the swim campaign ended I quit my paper route in order to pick prunes again. Jesse was already working at the dehydrator, helping to get the machinery cleaned up and ready to run.

Before I started work, my family went out to the Fulton Army Air Base for the 1945 Army Air Force Day. It was the biggest celebration in the history of the Air Base. The *Tribune* said that the new P-59, the first American-made jet-propelled plane, drew expressions of wonder as the pilot flew the "jet job" at more than 500 miles per hour. There were also thirty-six P-38s performing mass maneuvers. Sitting at the controls of a B-17 Flying Fortress made the day for me.

I actually did a little better at picking prunes that summer than I had before. Pickers' pay was better too because the harvest was so big. Wages went clear up to twenty-two cents a box—a hike of two cents.

Work everywhere was interrupted the day the war ended. Japan surrendered a few minutes after 4:00 P.M. on Tuesday, August fourteenth. The fire bell and all of the church bells in town were rung. Cars raced around—those that had gas—with their horns blowing. Tuesday night West Street was roped off at the plaza. Mr. Lowery opened his bike and radio shop, set up his public address system and turntable, and cranked up long after dark for dancing on the street under chamber of commerce auspices. The chief of police reported that "there was no disorder or breaking of windows, no vandalism such as occurred in other cities." There was but one arrest, according to the chief: "Jess Murray, who was said to have hit a colored person during an argument Tuesday afternoon." Murray was given thirty days to cool off in the county jail by Judge Quinn.

Though the war was over, it took some time for emotions to cool down. The Santa Rosa *Press Democrat*, under a headline reading, "Anti-Jap Hotheads," reported that the county sheriff was warning people in the Sebastopol section of the county not to molest Japanese-American citizens who were being released from detention camps. The warning came following threats of violence by two men against one K. Morita.

Everyone believed that the rich prune harvest of 1945 would be repeated yearly forever. So, since a badly needed sewer extension would have to be placed where the Healdsburg Cooperative Prune Dryer wanted to expand, the new sewer line was scrapped. Crews in all of the county's orchards were working seven-day weeks in 102° temperatures to keep up with the abundance of fruit. Those of us who picked during that hot summer envied the city boys and girls who spent their days swimming and their evenings dancing. Jimmie Lunceford was appearing at Mirabel Park, Palomar Dance Pavilion was open, and there was now dancing with an orchestra every night at Villa Chanticleer. Manager Bill Wolking even sponsored a stag smoker for the members of the Healdsburg Boat Club and provided "entertainers from San Francisco."

Then on September fourteenth, the Villa Chanticleer mysteriously burned to the ground. The fire started, it was said, in the kitchen while 200 people danced in the Villa's ballroom. Bill Wolking could not save the office records, but a piano was recovered along with a slot machine that Bill was quick to point out did not belong to the resort. The new owners promised to replace the burned structure with a modern building and to continue improving the grounds and cabins.

It was not really surprising that the fire consumed the entire Villa. Since the mountain was under county jurisdiction, fire trucks had to be dispatched from Santa Rosa—fifteen miles away. The Healdsburg Fire Department pitched in, but they only had one truck and the fire fighters were not trained for rural blazes. To make matters worse, two weeks later a wildfire swept down the mountain's eastern slope, destroying eleven homes. All along our block for three evenings people sat on their front porches and watched the mountain burn. Fire fighters had immense difficulty with the steep terrain, and trees exploded so loudly and with such bright flashes that we could hear and see them all the way down in the town.

Polio took its toll that summer too. The postmaster's son died, and several other youths were struck less seriously by the disease. No one knew why the river was a breeding ground. No swimming hole was safe from infection.

126

Late in the summer I was struck with a case of strep throat that almost turned into scarlet fever. A new doctor who was recently discharged from the army treated me. Mother swore it was his use of the wonder drugs, sulfa and penicillin, that pulled me through. For many years Mother went out of her way to patronize veterans, from physicians to plumbers. When she became a PTA lobbyist and had to fly all over the state of California, she would only fly on a veteran-owned airline. On her recommendation I once flew that tiny airline on an awfully rocky flight from Los Angeles to San Francisco. When I asked Mother why she patronized them, she told me that "their pilots flew in the war and they know what they are doing."

Doc Robinson, the young veteran, remained our family doctor for as long as he practiced in Healdsburg. I could be lying in bed with strep throat or torn knee ligaments or a wounded arm, and he would always come into our house and greet me with "What's wrong with you this time, you big lug?"

And after my bout with strep throat, I actually became a big lug. No one, not even Doc Robinson, could figure out the reason for it, but during my illness I began to grow alarmingly. All in all, I grew six inches in three months. Suddenly, instead of being 5' 8" I was 6' 2" tall. My parents were flabbergasted; no one on either side of our family had ever reached this stature before. Doc Robinson checked me weekly to be sure my heartbeat was not erratic and for signs of rheumatic fever. I was forbidden to play at recess and came straight home from school every day to take a two-hour nap.

Actually elementary school started without me because I was still recuperating. At 535 children, enrollment was the highest in the school's history. A part-time physical education teacher was added to the faculty, and Jesse did not have to coach any more.

Jere Holbrook was elected student body president. I was chosen as my father's class representative. Part of the class representative's job was to try to keep the peace between students from different backgrounds and social levels. I had no sooner returned to school than a transfer student made my job difficult. He had a vocal hatred of blacks because he said they had invaded his hometown to work in the shipyards and forced the locals off the sidewalks and into the gutters. Most of these blacks were recruited in the South. They harassed his little sister, beat him up, and his family moved to escape them. Because of Smitty Robinson we defended blacks. But the Okies sided with the new boy and arguments turned into fistfights. Jesse said there wasn't much to be done about it; as we grew older we would learn to judge people as individuals and not by race, he said.

Smitty Robinson was presented with an inscribed Swiss watch by the city council for writing to local servicemen during the war. The Army closed the Fulton Air Base, but by popular demand dancing continued on Saturday nights at the American Legion Hall. Mom and Dad never attended these dances. Healdsburg teachers were never seen dancing except at school dances. They were never seen drinking either. If a teacher wanted to go out dancing or drinking, he or she went to Santa Rosa. But Jesse resisted dancing even at school affairs. Whenever a girl invited him to dance, he would begin limping and tell her he had been wounded in the charge up San Juan Hill during the Spanish-American War.

Over 500,000 California acres were burned by fires that summer, and the county board of supervisors considered purchasing huge incinerators to replace "unsightly sanitary refuse dumps."

Local servicemen began returning from the war. A former football hero, a classmate's brother who had led a bombing raid in Burma, was among them. And newcomers like Doc Robinson, who had "done a job for Uncle Sam," were settling in Healdsburg too. A new high school teacher was Lt. Bob Fletcher, who had won seven battle stars in the Pacific.

While I was recuperating I followed the fortunes of the high school football team's right halfback, Johnny Hassenzahl. Johnny had curly black hair, a dazzling smile, and a flashy running style. Swashbuckling was an apt description of Johnny. Ferndale, the Humboldt County champions, came south to play the Greyhounds—as the high school's athletic teams were named—and Johnny almost singlehandedly ran them into the ground. Johnny raced forty yards in thirty seconds for the winning touchdown.

By Thanksgiving I was tentatively playing basketball. I was very clumsy. Although 6' 2" does not seem uniquely tall now, in 1945 the average adult male was about 5' 10" in height. To be that big at twelve years old in the eighth grade was almost freakish. Fuzz began to grow on my upper lip too. One day after basketball practice a girl peered at me—I hoped in admiration—and said, "I knew it."

"Knew what?" I asked cautiously.

"Betty Hutchinson said it was only dirt," she answered, "but I knew you were growing a real mustache."

A *mustache*. I hurried home to check myself out in the mirror and, sure enough, the dark smudge on my upper lip could be seen as a mustache if one wasn't too particular about definitions. I smugly reported the incident at dinner that night. Jesse grinned and started to say something before Mother stopped him. Margaret giggled outright. The next morning I watched Dad shave. Without removing his glasses he lathered his face with his brush, stropped his razor, and began shaving rather hastily and self-consciously. I sat on the edge of the bathtub and watched carefully as he blew out his cheeks, tilted his head back, stretched his skin taut with his free hand, and seesawed his mouth back and forth to get every whisker.

"I'll sure be glad when I can shave," I said.

Jesse washed the lather off his razor and resumed shaving before he replied, between razor strokes. "Shaving is a terrible chore when you have to do it every morning over and over again. Frankly, I'm mighty tired of it. If I could pluck every hair out of my face like quills out of a chicken so they would never grow back, I would do it," he said. Then he added, "I wish the baldness on my head had extended to my whole face."

"I don't believe it," I said. I didn't, either. I still wished my fuzz was thick enough to shave. Jesse just grunted.

We lost our vicar at St. Paul's and had an unusual Christmas Eve service. Our lay reader, Mr. Kent, led us all in singing carols from eleven to midnight "in the old English manner," whatever that meant. Mother and Jesse said they didn't know what it meant, and we had come the closest to standing on English soil, having lived in Colonial India. It is a fact that Mr. Kent knew nothing of carols sung "in the old English manner," though he had a fine English name.

In reality Frank B. Kent was a retired railroad man who prided himself not on his singing, but on his sermons, which he delivered without benefit of forethought and depending on God's presence to inspire him. Railroading was the only thing he knew, and so his sermons mostly had to do with that profession and the many characters and situations he had encountered. He could, for example, take the parable of the Prodigal Son and apply it to a wastrel of a brakeman he had once known; the Woman at the Well became a sort of railroad groupie; and God, of course, was the engineer. Although Mr. Kent was himself a charitable, kindly man, his sermons were puzzling, and in the matter of singing he was tone deaf.

Our small choir had not improved much even though George Izzett and I had been added to sing bass. The lead soprano only sang more loudly trying to drown us out, and the other boy's thin tenor was lost altogether in the new arrangement. George's mother pedaled the organ mushily and played "Adeste Fideles" at the same funereal pace as "Away in a Manger."

There was always something special about a Christmas Eve service though. The church would be full with rural Episcopalians who otherwise only showed up once or twice a year. There was plenty of good will to go around, and St. Paul's glowed and gleamed in the candlelight with its polished wood, brass, and colorful lineaments. On Christmas Eve our little church could easily have been dropped down into a small English shire—and perhaps that was enough.

Most of the rural members of the congregation returned for services on Christmas day. Part of my job as church cleaner was to get to St. Paul's early and tie Christmas foliage to each of the pews. The congregation wore their finery and Jesse loved to comment on the women's hats—especially the plumed ones. His observations would make me laugh, and I would get a jab in the ribs from Mother. If the church was very crowded our family would have to sit in separate pews. If this was the case, Jesse always tried to sit in front of Margaret so he could wiggle his ears—this always collapsed Margaret and dismayed Mother.

About every seventh winter the Russian River would flood. Swollen, it swept wide and strong around Fitch Mountain and roiled full-tilt through Merryland. In January 1946, heavy rains swelled the river so that it rushed two feet below the railroad and passenger bridges. It rocketed beneath the bridges bearing trees and boulders stripped from banks as if the channel were a logging chute. Waterborne debris smashed and banged off the bridge's pilings so that both structures shuddered and shook, making them hazardous to cross. On the west side of town toward Dry Creek the lowlands flooded, isolating the ranchers' families; farther down, the river bed summer cabins were swept away entirely or uprooted by the river. Cabins were often flung clear over Westside and Eastside roads and deposited on the hillsides. And every year that this happened, the owners would haul their cabins back to the river's edge, repair them, prop them up so that their decks hung out over the water again, and leave them there for another six years. Although entire villages downstream would be seriously damaged during these winters, Healdsburg itself was never threatened. The city was on fairly high ground, and the heavy rains drained away to the river and surrounding creeks. People stayed home on those rainy evenings, listening to their radios or playing board games. I would lie daydreaming on my porch while the rain drummed on the roof overhead and ran loudly along the gutters and down the drain pipe.

There would be rainy-day sessions at school, and recesses would be spent in the students' homeroom. Jesse would organize games to play in our steamy classroom. It was during this rainy winter that I took up boxing. The playground was closed and after-school activities were limited to the auditorium, which doubled as the gym. Lots of boys were sent to the gym on rainy afternoons because fears of juvenile delinquency were widespread after the war. Though it was not true in my case, many parents required their sons to appear at the gym after school for calisthenics and tumbling so that they would be physically able to confront a juvenile delinquent if they ever ran into one. In fact a "Crime Wave" editorial in the *Tribune* reported that FBI Chief J. Edgar Hoover was predicting a post-war crime wave—not perpetrated by returning vets, but because of "juvenile waywardness." The editorial sternly recommended that Healdsburg parents and citizens meet the problem squarely. It opposed canteens, YMCAs, and clubs for youths and urged parents to take a firmer hand during this "crisis." The message went on to applaud Reverend Brink, pastor of the Christian Church (and a member of the Kiwanis Club), for blaming juvenile delinquency on the "isms": "communism, naziism, and fascism."

As if to prove the validity of the *Tribune* editorial, our old nemesis from the seventh grade, Charlie Hulburt, was discovered hiding out on a local ranch. He was arrested by the military police as a deserter from the Army. This news confirmed our belief that he had been eighteen when he was in our seventh grade class.

It was Al Barbieri who started the boxing club at the grammar school gym. Al had been an amateur boxer, and with his younger brother Elmo he had recently opened a furniture and appliance store in town. Boxing did not have a sordid reputation then. Joe Louis, Billy Conn, Tony Zale, and Rocky Graziano were role models. It was generally agreed that a boy should know how to "handle himself." Although boxing was considered a just way of settling quarrels, picking on someone smaller than you was cowardly, so we were all separated into age and weight groups and matched with a suitable sparring partner. Al wandered among us offering professional coaching that very few of us could follow. He would advise: "Jab him quickly three times with your left, hook him fast off the jab to the body and then to the head. Follow with a right cross and an uppercut." We all staggered around obediently, poking and probing, mostly swinging roundhouses. We must have looked very funny—small boys in huge padded headgear and gigantic gloves, circling and pawing and trying to follow Al's pleas to "stay up on your toes, stay up on your toes."

One day Al decided we needed to witness an exhibition of how to box properly—or perhaps he had talked so much about his own accomplishments that we begged for an exhibition of his skills. At any rate, one day he said that his brother, Elmo, had agreed to spar with him. Al was balding, sported lots of rings, and dressed well, but as far as we could see he still moved lightly on his feet. Though he had run to fat over the years he circled professionally and exhaled with a hissing sound through his nose whenever he threw a punch. We thought his fat was probably deceptive. He looked a little like "Two Ton" Tony Galento, and Two Ton had knocked Joe Louis down, hadn't he? Elmo was slighter and shorter than Al, and his eyes looked frightened as someone helped him lace up his gloves. Al gave a little speech about how good it was of Elmo to help him out in his demonstration—Elmo not being a fighter and all—and how he would take it easy on him. We were to observe closely the finer points of Al's technique as he boxed the pants off his brother. Al pushed out a couple of lefts at Elmo's nose, and Elmo, out of fear or whatever, hauled off and busted Al hard with a right on his nose, which started bleeding freely. Neither Al nor Elmo could stop the bleeding, and so the exhibition was discontinued. They both said it was a lucky punch and no doubt it was, but we snickered anyway.

One afternoon Al took me aside and told me that he thought I might become a very good boxer because I had "fighter's hands." He had me clench my fists and he turned them over and over, rubbing and appraising them as if they were chunks of precious metal. I went home that day and talked my folks into letting me buy a pair of boxing gloves from Chris Jennings at Rosenbergs'. Jesse declined my challenge to spar, but he did fill a gunny sack with grass clippings and hang it from the eaves of the woodshed so that I could bob and weave and jab at it. I had decided to be a dazzling boxer like Billy Conn or Ray Robinson, not a heavy hitter like Joe Louis or Tony Zale. I danced around and hissed through my nose and grunted and punched the grass-filled sack.

That spring I lost interest in boxing because I found my first girlfriend. Betty Hutchinson lived on a farm way out on Dry Creek Road, and we spent most of our time outside school in dark Saturday afternoon matinees. Betty was what we called "stacked." She was about my age, since she was a year behind me at school, but she was really developed for a girl of twelve.

Betty seemed unaware of her figure, which made her more desirable. We spent Saturday afternoons necking in the darkness of the old Plaza Theatre, and I was consumed with her all week long. I would lie on my bed "mooning," as my mother called it, about Betty and listening to sentimental songs on the radio: "Sentimental Journey," "I Can't Begin to Tell You (how much you mean to me)," "Stardust." Then on Saturdays I would ride my bicycle out to Betty's farm, where she would mount her own bike, and we'd ride to town for the movie. After the show we'd ride back out to her farm, and then I would pedal home. Some Sundays my lips were so chapped and cracked from necking with Betty that it hurt to sing in the choir. Sometimes Betty arrived at school on spring days bursting out of a T-shirt. That made me so jealous that I packed my block sweater to school—no matter how warm it was—and insisted that Betty wear it. I couldn't make her wear my sweater to gym class, though, and a crowd of boys would gather when Betty played softball in a T-shirt and shorts.

The old Plaza Theatre was built sometime after World War I. The 1906 earthquake that levelled San Francisco had also damaged the whole business block on West Street. The Plaza Hotel was the first structure to be rebuilt, with supposedly earthquake-proof construction. One by one, other stores were restored, and as a final touch the Plaza Theatre was erected.

The Plaza Theatre was immensely popular. Movies changed several times a week. The Tuesday-through-Thursday double bill usually featured two B movies, since the theatre was not well attended on those nights. Friday and Saturday features were always action films—jungle movies, Westerns, war or pirate movies (with a serial and several cartoons and the *March of Time* thrown in at weekend matinees). Serious dramas, romantic comedies, and musicals usually played on Sundays and Monday nights when whole families were likely to attend.

The theatre itself was a gloomy cavern—dimly lit with wooden seats and dark carpets. The Plaza's walls were covered with murals depicting what appeared to be Greek warriors pursuing nymphs, and dimmable chandeliers were suspended from the theatre's ceiling. The orchestra was divided into three sections, separated by two aisles. Generally, families with their young children occupied the center section. We elementary school boys, with our girlfriends or dates, sat in the left section toward the rear where it was darkest. Unattached boys and girls usually sat farther up front in the same section. Often, a boy and girl from the unattached section got together and moved back to where the couples were. Drunks and strangers tended to occupy the right side of the orchestra exclusively.

This seating arrangement was not always self-imposed. Young usherettes in silk harem-like outfits and carrying flashlights, escorted customers to their seats, and they were as responsible for the theatre's segregation as anything else. These usherettes were never the brightest girls in town; most of them were poor and trying to make enough to buy school clothes. But in the way of small towns, wearing a harem outfit (unless you were Yvonne De Carlo) indicated that a girl had sunk so low she might even smoke cigarettes or wear tight sweaters and short skirts. The theatre manager protected them. One thing they were never allowed to do was to escort any-one to a seat in the balcony. The balcony was small and very dark and was the only section where smoking was allowed. Its only illumination came from the movie projector's smoke-filled beam overhead. This balcony was where the hot-blooded, reckless high school boys and girls congregated. Rumors abounded that, besides smoking and drinking, orgies sometimes took place up there—"daisy chains" we called them. We heard that the bal-cony's carpets had been removed so that cigarette butts could be extin-guished on the floor, and that some of the seats had been ripped from their moorings to accommodate the daisy chains.

Decent townsfolk regarded the Plaza Theatre balcony as the pit of Hell and often campaigned to have it razed. Others saw the balcony as a neces-sity to protect decent citizens from contamination. I could hardly wait until I would be old enough to move up there myself, with or without Betty. For Betty and I broke up that summer after I caught her necking with Bruce Holbrook under the Merryland pier.

Jesse and Mother were both very busy that spring. Mother with Red Cross and PTA, and Jesse with his new duties as Chancellor Commander of the Knights of Pythias—an honor he referred to as "being made the 'high-muckety-muck.'"

In addition they assumed responsibility for a now very large Tippy, since I became bored with his training. Tippy was clumsy, but friendly and eager to please—a dangerous combination in our small house. Mother cre-ated a "jail" for Tippy behind the living room davenport where he was often banished after breaking something. He could not turn around in the small space behind the sofa once he was in there, and Mother used to shake a yardstick at the tunnel-like entrance and say, "Bad boy, Tippy. Bad, bad boy. You must stay in your jail until I take this stick away. If you try to come out and knock the stick over, I will beat you with it." Tippy must have under-stood because he stayed crouched in the darkness behind the sofa, some-times for hours if Mother got busy and forgot about him. Often we remem-bered that Tippy was in jail only at dinnertime when he finally whined because he smelled food, or when someone remarked on how unusually peaceful the house seemed to be. Tippy would not go to jail for any of the rest of us. He would grin and pant at us as if we were the dimwits if we threatened him—but he was terrified of Mother's anger.

Jesse assumed responsibility for Tippy's evening walks. They mean-dered through the wood next door and circled round the block until Tippy "did his business." There were many other dogs in the neighborhood—

mostly unleashed—who were liable to come rushing out of the shadows to battle Tippy. Jesse had to fend them off as best he could with a stick he carried. Then, too, Tippy sometimes did his business on neighbors' lawns. When this happened, a screen door would slam open and the neighbor would rebuke Jesse sharply or swear at him. When this happened Jesse came home chagrined, and I would offer to go fight the neighbor (but not to take over walking the dog). Jesse then had to calm me down. "Don't go flying off the handle," he would say. Tippy loved me anyway. We romped and wrestled for hours in the backyard where he was usually secured on a long chain.

After school, when I wasn't thinking of Betty, I was practicing on my new trombone. It wasn't brand new but was purchased used from a music student who'd lost interest in music. The bell was dented, the slide did not run smoothly, and the whole instrument was slightly tarnished. But in spite of being a little battered, my trombone with a hitch in the slide played fine.

My parents must have wished they had never bought me the instrument at all. Not that I didn't take care of things they bought for me until I lost interest in them. I carefully worked neatsfoot oil into the scratches and chips on my boxing gloves, and I shined and oiled my trombone vigorously. But I was an awful trombonist.

I did not aspire to play the trombone in the first place. Old Charlie McCord, the music teacher, first recommended that I take up the tuba. The tuba! My aspirations were higher than that. None of the big bands that played at Palomar or Mirabel Park or Melody Bowl or even at school dances had a tuba. We eventually settled on the trombone, and until my parents bought an instrument from one of his students Mr. McCord lent me one to use at school. Ownership of an instrument and studying from Mr. McCord qualified me to play in the small elementary school band.

I was given music books to study and exercises to practice, but instead of using them I sat on my screened porch and endlessly practiced "Margie"—a popular song that year. Every afternoon I played "Margie" over and over, sometimes stopping in the middle of the song to repeat several problematical notes and then returning to the beginning. If my parents did not complain it was probably because they sensed that the trombone was another passing fancy. But I am sure they, and our neighbors too, hoped it would pass quickly. I fooled them this time. I played my trombone all through high school, though I never learned to read music and never advanced beyond third chair in a three-person trombone section.

But it was at the movies, when I wasn't necking, that I began to speculate on my future and to formulate a philosophy of life. Looking back, the writers of those old Westerns had a tremendous influence on me. My beliefs about good and evil, about honesty, about the corrupting influence of wealth and power, about the defenselessness of the working man were formed watching Westerns. The dialogue was terrible, but the plots were right out of John Steinbeck. The evil people were always the mayor, the city council, the banker, the land speculators, the large property owners and their greedy wives. The downtrodden that Gene Autry, Roy Rogers, Lash La Rue, Bob Steele, Johnny Mack Brown, and Wild Bill Elliott fought to protect were good honest folk: small farmers, shopkeepers, workers for the railroads, miners, homesteaders, schoolmarms and other working women who were considered "loose." The law was often in the pocket of the rich and powerful, and the hero was a brave and noble drifter—a knight errant.

Fifteen years later when I was playing gunfighters in Hollywood television Westerns, the plots had not changed much. The scripts were more sophisticated, but the central characters usually followed the pattern of the old Saturday-afternoon-matinee Westerns. By this time, though, I much preferred playing villains to playing heroes: the characters I acted had far more meat to them than the cardboard heroes did. My fellow hired guns included some of the finest actors of the American stage: Alfred Ryder, Everett Sloane, Jack Palance, Andrew Prine. But sitting in the Plaza Theatre in 1945, of all the futures I could have imagined for myself, acting in Western films would have been the farthest from my mind.

Movies were more important than just an afternoon or an evening at the Plaza Theatre. Sixteen-millimeter films were rented and used as fund raisers or at social gatherings when live entertainment was unavailable or too expensive. Though my interest in Boy Scouting had waned, our patrol met only a block away in a neighbor's garage, so I attended meetings. The neighbor's son had shifted some of the Owl Patrol's attention from earning merit badges to raising money for activities. Our patrol showed movies to the public (mostly our parents) and used the money to go to other movies. We rented the elementary school auditorium, sold popcorn at the entrance, and Jere Holbrook operated the projector. The neighbor boy and I told jokes from his mail-order joke books during reel changes, and a prize was presented to the champion ticket salesman.

Local service clubs showed movies too, if a speaker was unavailable. James Vogt, the high school chemistry and physics teacher, was always ready in a pinch to show the same movies to the 20-30 Club as he showed

136

to his students. Two of Mr. Vogt's favorites were "Diesel Engines" and "Forest Fire Prevention."

Many new service clubs and social groups were springing up in this first post-war year. A Business and Professional Women's Club was organized, the American Legion announced that they would sponsor a summer veterans' baseball team, the Sotoyome Literary Club resumed readings at their weekly teas. There were bridge parties galore, and the Healdsburg Golf Club tried to revitalize interest in a Healdsburg Country Club, an idea that died with the onset of the war. Mr. Gibbs was elected chairman of the club and won the inaugural tournament.

Jesse and Mother were seldom invited to join in these clubs or to be guests at their parties. They did not play bridge or other serious card games, though Dad did attempt to teach me cribbage, a game that he loved. Mother regularly beat the rest of us at rummy. Jesse performed one particular trick with a deck of cards for Margaret's benefit. He called the trick his water buffalo routine. When the rest of us were seated at the dining room table, Jesse stood in the kitchen doorway facing the dining room, and held a deck of cards behind his back. He made water-buffalo-mooing sounds and simultaneously plopped the cards on the kitchen floor behind him. This routine absolutely broke up Margaret. Most evenings, though, our family played board games like Parchesi or Chinese Checkers.

What we called the holy roller churches became more active after the war. The Reverend Brink's Christian Church grew to be the third largest congregation in town—after the Roman Catholic and the Federated churches. The Foursquare Gospel, the Assembly of God, and the Baptist churches all began to flourish. In 1945 the Christian Church organized all of these evangelical sects into a conservative coalition, held large revival meetings, and began to exert local political influence.

The Federated Church still contained Healdsburg's old Methodists and Presbyterians, and Smith Robinson led the most admired youth program and choir in town. It was made up of Boy Scouts and Girl Scouts, honor students, De Molay boys, and Rainbow girls—all the young people who would grow up to vote for Eisenhower. But the holy rollers were growing militant in their demands for censorship of movies and books, and they crusaded against smoking, drinking, and dancing.

The city council, the chamber of commerce and the Healdsburg *Tribune* all grew more Republican (or pro-business, as they would have said), and the gulf between Republicans and Democrats became deep and plain. The political divisions that were largely disregarded during the war when everyone "pulled together" were out in the open again. Republicans who had suffered Roosevelt's "New Deal" in order to recover from the Depression, now chafed under the continuing "socialism" of Truman's "managed economy" and stridently urged a "return to free enterprise." These divisions trickled down to the schools where monetary and social prestige became issues among the children. Invitations to parties and outings were stratified where only a year before there had been a measure of equality. Children of parents who had been air raid wardens together or who had hosted at canteens or made surgical bandages were now puzzled because they were not invited to classmates' birthday parties any more. Social status became important. Girls left the Girl Scouts to join the Junior Russian River Riders, and boys left off affordable scouting or sports to join the Junior Flying Club or to play golf.

The president of the chamber of commerce told the city council that the city must expand. He said it was a mistake to have been inactive during the war while other communities grew, and he urged that Healdsburg be developed to it's "full potentialities." The *Tribune* echoed the president's speech under the headline: "Merchants Favor Active Program of Development," and the city council, while admitting it had been short-sighted in not promoting industry, pleaded lack of sewage facilities as the reason.

Meanwhile, the federal government appointed a fact-finding board to consider oil workers' demands to examine oil companies' books, a possibility that horrified the *Tribune*. After categorically stating that oil companies "endeavored to pay fair wages, while giving a fair return to investors who had risked their life savings to invest in the companies," the editorials warned sternly against "creeping socialism." Picket lines were deplored because they kept "honest managers and owners from their property." Farm workers were being recruited in Mexico to replace departed POWs. A *Tribune* headline proclaimed that "California Farm Workers Are the Best Paid in the World."

On my birthday Sir Alexander Fleming won the Nobel Prize for discovering penicillin, the "wonder drug" that kept me from getting scarlet fever. The Greyhound bus schedule to San Francisco was printed as a public service. It showed three buses leaving Healdsburg daily. The buses left Healdsburg at 2:10, 7:25, or 10:25 A.M. and arriving in San Francisco at 2:25, 5:25, or 10:20 P.M.—about twelve hours later. The Golden Gate Bridge toll was cut to $.50 for cars and $.05 each for passengers. A state law was passed that required second-time drunk-driving offenders to post an $11,000 bond to get their licenses back. The bond would be held and used to defray medical expenses in case they injured anyone when driving drunk again.

The cash register stolen from the Villa Chanticleer on the night it burned down was found by a county road crew in a rural ditch. Bill Wolking, the Villa ex-manager, said there was $160 in the register when it was stolen along with Villa records and several slot machines. No clues to those items were found at the scene of the cash register's discovery.

Clipper Smith, trained again by Chris Jennings, finished second in the Petaluma spring marathon with a clocking of 2:52:49. Dance halls opened in May. Palomar featured Ernie Layton and his orchestra, while Lawrence Welk appeared at Santa Rosa's Melody Bowl.

In May, right after Shirley Temple's eighteenth birthday and about the same time the paper announced that Morris Ruby was returning from a brief pastoring stint in Alameda to "instruct boys and girls in physical education at the elementary school," I got into a fistfight with Grandin Worden in the schoolyard. As soon as we began to scuffle I forgot everything Jack Butler and Al Barbieri had taught me. Instead of throwing the crisp left jabs and hard right crosses I'd practiced on my gunny sack, I found myself wrestling with Grandin, rolling over and over, yanking on his clothes and hair.

Jesse had yard duty, and he separated us. Grandin was ushered first into a small supply room and I could hear the whacks of Jesse's paddle through the door. When my turn came, I just sat and waited—probably hoping that I would be let off the hook. But Dad appeared in the doorway and said, "Come on." So I went into the supply room and Dad said, "Bend over." I did, and he gave me three sharp, stinging smacks with his paddle. I thought he hit me much harder than he did Grandin. At least the whacks he gave Grandin sounded a lot less severe than the ones he gave me. I don't recall that I said anything about the fight, but I remember what Jesse said to me.

"Fighting is not allowed in the schoolyard. But if you can't avoid it, remember that the point of fighting is not to wind up on the bottom where you were."

Jesse was popular for the spring skits he staged in the grammar school auditorium. One popular skit that Jesse organized and at which he did a watermelon-thumping monologue was a minstrel show. My father pretended to check a prop watermelon for ripeness by thumping it. While doing this he lectured on how to interpret the pitch of the thumping sound. Another popular skit was one he produced right after Japan's surrender. In my father's comedy, white-robed scientists first tried to split an atom the

My sister and me, ca 1942

Jesse, Margaret, me, and a tiny Tippy

Mother, Margaret, Jesse, and a big Tippy

Alice Zacharias, me, Mother, Margaret, Aunt Theo and Jesse

Jesse in the garden

size of a pea with sledgehammers on an oversize anvil. The "Anvil Chorus" played during this scene. Then when the atom was split and the bomb was dropped on a presumed Hiroshima, children dressed as Japanese and wearing buck teeth made of colored paraffin flew all over the stage. Jesse certainly meant no harm by these skits. Their content, which now appear vulgar and racist, were considered to be very funny then and suitable for the whole family.

Memorial Day featured a big parade and memorial service. The high school band, the Boy Scout troop, and color guards from service clubs and fraternal orders gathered at the American Legion Hall and marched to Oak Mound Cemetery where Don Kirkpatrick, the Boy Scout bugler, played taps.

The Healdsburg City Council announced the next week that a "plaque of Healdsburg heroes" would be cast soon. For their part, the county board of supervisors proposed buying Merryland beach and turning it into a war memorial. The only catch was that to do this they would have to buy the rotting dance pavilion behind the beach from Syd Grove, president of the Russian River Riders, who was asking a fortune for it.

The patriotism of Memorial Day seemed to inspire the *Tribune* to new rhetorical heights. They opposed a loan to Great Britain, who wanted it to "fight communism," by saying that the United States had already become an "Uncle Shylock" to the world. The editorial writers went on to blast "liberals" who supported "one-arm bandits" at resorts (exempting, of course, Bill Wolking, who only employed them as a means of raising money for charity). It further said that real estate prices were too low compared to construction costs. The column, as usual, blamed the federal government and said "we are tired of being kicked around by the bureaucrats who fix up sugar-coated pills."

There was also a large political ad: "Must a Justice of the Peace be a lawyer? We who know Judge Ed Quinn say NO! His Four Terms of Service Prove It. None should fail to cast their ballot in the June fourth election."

Judge Quinn lost the election to an ex-navy officer, though he was kept on as a minor judge—issuing fines and county jail terms for misdemeanors. The police chief resigned about this same time and one of his officers replaced him as chief. It was fairly common for a local boy to apply for the Healdsburg Police Department after he graduated from high school. And if the boy was accepted and stuck around and kept his nose clean, it was not unlikely that he, too, would become chief some day. It helped if the boy had been a football player, a boxer, or a power-hitting baseball star. There weren't many opportunities for boys who weren't going on to college or who weren't sons of ranchers. They frequently joined one of the armed services to learn a trade. Others opted for law enforcement jobs with the local police or the county sheriff's department.

Both the high school and grammar school baseball teams won league championships, but I wasn't sorry to see the season end. I hadn't played much. The new coach who replaced Mr. Ruby did not think I was a very good right fielder. Eighth graders were all required to write an essay on "Americanism" before school closed, and I thought I had written a very patriotic one about emigrating from India and learning to love America. But Jere Holbrook won the gold medal and I didn't even get an honorable mention.

The new summer swimming instructor was hired. He had been a wartime tank commander and when his corps arrived in Paris he had been wounded by a sniper. As Boris told us later, he was riding in the tank's turret clutching a bottle of champagne in one hand and a bouquet of flowers in the other when he was machine-gunned. He rehabilitated himself through swimming, and the campaign organizers thought he would be a fine role model.

The swim campaign aside, the chamber of commerce had big plans for Merryland that summer. Bill Wolking hoped to hold a summer's end Harvest Fair. Chris Jennings would arrange for top amateur swimmers and divers to compete, and a torch-light parade would pass on barges under the bridge and past the beach where a grandstand would be situated. Such a big festival was planned that a chamber of commerce "band concert committee" was formed. This committee's goal was to relieve merchants from having to foot the bill for the popular free summer band concerts and allow them instead to put their money into the hopefully lucrative Harvest Festival. To this end the band concert committee asked "the average citizen" for donations to help "defray costs" of the band concerts. They argued that, since stores were closed during the concerts, the concerts could not be considered a commercial venture and therefore business shouldn't have to pay for them. An alert citizen wrote the *Tribune* inquiring if, since the Harvest Fair barges were to be "torch-lit" and hence the parade would be nocturnal (when businesses weren't open), the "average citizen" would be expected to be asked to "defray the costs" of that event also. The *Tribune* wasted no time in issuing a scathing reply that scolded the writer for his ignorance in matters of "modern merchandising." This *Tribune* rebuke took precedence over another editorial roasting "the new deal outfit," as the paper was fond of calling the federal government.

You might have thought city leaders would enjoy springtime instead of getting so worked up. Spring was always beautiful in Healdsburg. The weather warmed up in April, flowers and trees bloomed, and the country-side turned a deep green. There was the smell of blossoms in the air and wood smoke in the evenings. The weather became warm enough after dinner for games of kick-the-can and hide-and-seek in our street and the wooded lot. Spring was abalone season too, and men made weekend journeys to the coast to pry abalone off the rocks at low tide just as faithfully as they hunted deer in the hills in autumn. And like deer hunting, abalone-ing was as much an excuse to get away for camping, drinking, and story-telling as it was to put food on the dinner table.

Abaloneing wasn't much fun. Low tide usually arrived at about 4:00 A.M., and you had to wade out into the cold northern California surf to pry off the shellfish with homemade scrapers—usually forged out of tire irons and crowbars. It was a lot easier to endure this ordeal if you stayed up all night drinking whiskey and shooting the bull next to the campfire. Then you hardly even felt the icy surf at all. In fact, men usually met in a bar on a Friday evening and got pretty well oiled before an abalone trip began. Then they would all head back the next morning about 10:00 A.M. with sacks of abalone, stopping here and there at pre-arranged saloons, so that they trooped home sometime Saturday evening in pretty sorry condition. Men looked forward all year to the trip. Abalone had to be thoroughly tenderized to make them edible. Men thought it was their job to hunt abalone and the woman's job to tenderize their catch and to cook it. Jesse only went abaloneing once. The Knights of Pythias took a yearly trip, and Jesse tagged along in 1945. Jesse was not much of a drinker so he didn't suffer a hangover. He even tenderized the abalone for Mother. But I don't think the trip fell into his personal list of greatest thrills. None of us liked the abalone very much—we thought it tasted like rubber.

The high school and elementary school orchestras always played spring concerts. As third trombonist about all I did was sit on stage in a shirt and tie and play an occasional note or two.

The grammar school auditorium was acoustically very sound. It boasted a raised stage with a heavy velvet proscenium curtain. Since it doubled as a basketball court, the floors and walls were wooden and the small curtained windows were high up on the walls. Seats were stowed under the stage and arranged in rows for assemblies, concerts, or for graduation.

After the spring concert, janitors prepared the auditorium for graduation. Graduation speakers were chosen by a committee of teachers and by Mr. Gibbs who judged our class essay contest. The topic was, "My Future Occupation as...." I wrote about "My Future Occupation as a Merchant

Seaman." My essay lost, and that depressed me. More than being depressed, I doubted myself. I wondered if something was wrong with me for not wanting to be a businessman or a doctor or a teacher. I did not wonder why I was being asked to plan my future when I was twelve.

Mother ironed my shirt and trousers on graduation day. I did not own a suit, but Mother made me a blue sport coat with brass buttons. I took a bath, washed my hair, and when I returned to my porch my clothes were hanging neatly by my bureau. Mother even selected one of Jesse's ties for me to wear. There was a green folder lying on my bed that was not there before. I picked it up to look at it. The cover said "'Paddle Wheel Days in California' by Jess Manley." In the folder was an essay my father wrote when he was at Stanford. The first page noted that "illustrations and also typographical errors" were by the author. I sat to read Jesse's old essay, and this is how it began:

I have chosen this topic for at least two reasons. First, an interest in the subject as a colorful phase of California's early history. Second, almost anything that floats intrigues me. I believe this fascination for the water began in my infancy when I made a trip halfway round the world as a babe-in-arms. I recall very little of this adventure, but I have been told that I was a poor sailor, almost a dead one before reaching my home port of Boston. Since that time I have circumnavigated (I like that word) the globe and have found each landfall a thrilling experience. From Portland, Oregon, to Portland, Maine, by boat, two weeks drifting in a luxurious houseboat in the Vale of Kashmir, aground in the Suez Canal, accosted by a stranded and insolvent U.S. mariner on the docks of Marseilles—all this and more, are memories recalled with keen pleasure. No doubt you may come to the conclusion that this is to be the autobiography of an "old salt" who has spent his lusty days sailing the seven seas and has finally found a snug harbor in which to drop his anchor. That is hardly the case. These side trips have been but brief interludes in a life spent in the dusty confines of a schoolroom trying to enlighten youthful minds in the mysteries of the Pythagorean theorem and other such trivia. Maybe in my next reincarnation I will go down to the seas again. Perhaps as a majestic albatross, that wanderer of the southern seas. To sail on great outstretched, tireless wings the restless winds. Ah, what joy to dip my great webbed feet in the flying spume that plows from the crest of a storm tossed wave; to wheel and turn, to spiral up, up, up, screaming defiance in the teeth of the gale that blows but to do my bidding. Ah, who can tell.

His essay went on to describe the paddle wheel steamers that once plied northern California rivers, but I hardly read those parts. At dinner I thanked my dad. He said, "Keep your chin up."

We had a fine graduation. Mr. McCord led the band in a patriotic tune, and Squirt Moore, our unlikely class president, led the Pledge of Allegiance. Jere Holbrook, as student body president, presented the school with the class's gift—a gavel and stand. As class advisor, Jesse addressed the class and told us that there was no limitation to what we could be, but whatever we wound up being, to be as good at it as we could. Mr. Gibbs presented us with our diplomas, and we all sang a special farewell song written and composed by Lucille Peterson. My parents gave me a Schick injector razor as a graduation present.

Nine

JESSE AND MOTHER SEEMED HAPPIER than they'd been since I'd started to gauge their happiness. Dad spent a lot of time in his wood shop, mostly making new handles for implements. He always said that it was the handles that gave out first on American-made items, and so he carved replacements out of hard wood: axe handles, pick handles, even new handles for Mother's pots and pans. He would whistle and carve while Mother weeded in the garden. Mother's weeding outfit embarrassed me as much as the clothes she wore to my swimming lessons. She sported her coolie hat and a pair of faded knee-length shorts, but it was her top that caused me discomfiture. On hot days she wore her brassiere as a halter, a modest brassiere to be sure, but a brassiere nevertheless. I did not think that any other woman in Healdsburg gardened so immodestly, even in the privacy of her own backyard. It didn't bother Jesse. He whistled and carved and occasionally came out into the garden to show her his handiwork. I assured myself that if Betty Hutchinson were my wife, I would never allow her to garden with only a brassiere on.

There was a girl in my Junior Lifesaving class whose breasts rivaled Betty's. Every boy in the class tried to snag her for a partner in lifesaving drills because the most common method of helping a drowning person to shore was called the cross-chest carry. In a drill the "victims" would swim out until the water was over their heads. Then, when Boris the coach blew his whistle, the victims would thrash about and scream for help, and the victims' partners would dive in the river and swim out to rescue them. Some partners were not very good swimmers, and so some victims had to thrash around for a long time before they were rescued—and the way Boris taught the rescue it was tricky. When a partner arrived at a spot about five yards from where the victim was drowning, he or she dove underwater and swam to the victim's ankles. The partner then grabbed the victim's ankles, turned him or her around, placed the left hand (if one were right-handed) under the victim's bottom, and the victim was boosted to the surface on his or her back. At the same time the rescuer's right arm was thrown over and across the victim's chest as both rescuer and victim broke the surface. Holding the victim's chest firmly, the partner would sidestroke back to shore using one arm and a scissors kick. If a victim panicked and clutched a rescuer, threatening to drown them both, as often happens in real rescues, Boris instructed us to try to knock the victim unconscious by punching him or her on the chin. No one tried this in our classes, of course.

Though gentle by nature, Boris looked very forbidding. He was short, dark, and hairy. His war wound was a wide and ropy scar that ran out from under his swimming trunks and up to his breastbone. Boris tried to pair youngsters fairly for practices, but there were more boys than girls so the girl with the big chest often got rescued by several boys during the same exercise. Small rescuers would sometimes of necessity be paired with big victims, and there would be lots of floundering and sinking. An unequally matched pair often emerged coughing and flailing from beneath the surface. This pair occasionally collided with another pair, and soon four or five people would be flailing and coughing and sinking. Frequently Boris himself had to take to the water to straighten things out.

My assigned partner was a big, blond football tackle, who belonged to the Federated Church's youth group—that gang of do-gooders who had taken vows never to cheat at anything. He would not give me any help at all when I tried to save him, and the first few times he nearly dragged us both down to the bottom of the river. When, with great effort, I finally got him turned around, boosted to the surface, threw my arm over his chest, and began to stroke toward shore, he would go limp, letting his legs drag down behind him. As I kicked, my legs would become entangled in his and I would pull us both under.

Boris came to my rescue. "Under the circumstances, David," he whispered to me, "it would be all right with me if you used the 'hair carry' when rescuing your partner."

The hair carry was usually employed only when you knocked out your victim and he or she was a dead weight. I welcomed Boris's permission to use it on the do-gooder. When I boosted him, instead of throwing my arm over his chest I grabbed a fistful of his hair, and now that my feet were clear of his dangling legs I could swim easily. I received my Junior Livesaving certificate, and Mother finally stopped accompanying me to the beach.

Some 212 youths took part in the 1945 swim campaign. Chris Jennings, as Red Cross Water Safety Chairman, scheduled a water carnival and swimming races for the final day. Regulation lengths for races were going to be observed, and attendance by the whole town was encouraged. Mr. Gibbs was to be the official starter, armed with a real starter's pistol. Jesse would be a judge, but Boris was relegated to a spectator's role—this being strictly Chris Jennings's show.

On the day of the races a serious problem arose. Jimmie Jennings didn't have anyone to race against. Contestants had been divided into age groups as well as skill groups—the highest group being boys fourteen years and older. I was twelve and was registered among the advanced swimmers ten- to thirteen-years-old. But Jimmie was fifteen and no one showed up to challenge him. Chris tried to enlist me, adding magnanimously that he would give me a ten-yard head start. I knew I couldn't beat Jimmie, not even with a ten-yard head start. But how could I argue with Mr. Jennings? I looked beseechingly at Jesse, but he did not offer to intercede.

Chris said, "Look at it this way: it's a sure second-place ribbon."

I almost beat Jimmie. He won by three yards. The charade was repeated in the backstroke. For the day I won two red ribbons to go with the blue one I had won the year before. I kept the blue one pressed between the pages of a book and threw away the red ones. Later that summer I persuaded Jesse to take me to a baseball game; he seemed embarrassed when the ticket-taker accused him of trying to sneak me in as a twelve-year-old when I was obviously at least fourteen.

"Come on Mr. Manley," the ticket-taker had said, "I'm surprised at you, being a teacher and all, trying to sneak in your son for half-price."

Jesse paid the adult price for me without a word.

Well, I *had* grown very quickly. My parents adapted in different ways. Since I was now too big to spank, Mother took a new tack. When I did something wrong, she walked out the back door, past the garden and into the garage. She would sit and cry there, loudly enough so that we could hear her sobs from the house. Margaret and Jesse would pointedly ignore me. Their silence was so rebuking that I would finally trek out to the garage to find Mother sitting with her face in her hands.

I would say, "I'm sorry, Mom."

This apology only intensified her sobbing. Eventually she would reply, "It's my fault. I don't know what I've done wrong in raising you to make you behave this way."

"No, it's not your fault, Mom," I would say. "It's mine, and I won't do it" (whatever "it" was) "again."

After this admission and promise, Mother would rise and we would hug each other, her wet face against my chest. Then we would walk back to the house together. The incident would be over. Everyone pretended nothing had happened—until the next time I got into trouble.

I used to promise myself that the next time Mother fled to the garage I would just not follow her if I thought I was in the right. But when the inevitable next time came, I would wait and wait until the silence in the house was too loud to bear. Then I would heave myself up and walk out to the garage to make my peace with Mom, who seemed so pitiful and frail huddling there.

She must have been afraid for me. The special protections of India were gone. Gone were my "uncles," and gone were the genteel social events where I might meet missionaries' daughters with ribbons and starched dresses. I would not be involved in sports like boxing there. I would be hiking, perhaps, not playing basketball and baseball. I intended to play football in the fall too, and that frightened Mother.

My summer job at Meese's Pharmacy was a lot easier than prune picking. Mr. Meese, a tall, balding man, tried to interest me in the drugstore business. He had plenty of time to do that because he owned the smallest drugstore in town. Meese's Pharmacy was not like Tomasco's Drug Store, which was a noisy gathering place.

Tomasco's was next door to the Plaza Theatre and boasted a soda fountain with a counter and upholstered booths. We gathered there after school and Saturday matinees to drink a variety of Coca-Cola mixtures.

Old-timers played poker in a back room at Tomasco's all day and into the evening until the store closed. Sitting in booths, we could hear the click of chips and the clink of change. You could see the old players hunched over their cards through windows in the door to the back room as you walked down the hallway to the restroom. If you watched for more than a moment or two, hostile glances moved you on. No one admitted that the back room existed, but a lot of money changed hands there.

In college I met someone who was working his way through school by gambling. During vacations he and a partner worked their way from San Francisco to Eureka and back, hitting all the back rooms in small towns. He told me that the back room at Tomasco's was always "worth a bundle." The gambler did not graduate but I ran into him again in Hollywood. He had a regular role as a lawman on "The Outlaws" TV series, and I was playing a member of the Dalton gang.

150

Another aspect of Tomasco's drugstore was that the owners had a license to sell liquor. Most professional people drank on the sly in Healdsburg and were never caught publicly buying a bottle of liquor. A lot of them drank at the country club and held small parties in their homes. When they stocked up, they usually went to Santa Rosa. In an emergency, however, they could always pop down to Tomasco's for a bottle of aspirin and a magazine, then ask the owner to pop a fifth of scotch or bourbon into the bag. Adults bought liquor this way so the young people in Healdsburg wouldn't know that they drank.

Brown-Wolfe, the second largest drugstore, was the oldest pharmacy in Healdsburg and was all dark wood and subdued lighting. The gentry patronized Brown-Wolfe.

Meese's Pharmacy was located between Brown-Wolfe and Tomasco's. When I went to work there, Mr. Meese was trying to broaden his clientele. He had installed a magazine rack at the front of the store and, next to it, a large red metal chest containing ice and soft drinks. For a nickel you could drink a Coke or Cream Soda or Royal Crown Cola and peruse the magazines.

My job was to keep the shelves stocked and dusted. I also received shipments on the rear loading dock: opening them, pricing them, and arranging them on the shelves. I opened all the boxes of magazines and "censored" them for nudist magazines and movie magazines with sexy pictures in them. I hid these to take home with me—usually leaving one or two for Mr. Meese to find. I did this because Mr. Meese was himself the real censor and did not know that I had taken on that job. When he had taken out all the nudist and sexy magazines after my inspection, he shipped them back to the supplier, usually with a brusque note. *Esquire* was my favorite magazine because they featured a "Vargas Girl" in every issue. *Esquire* was too thick to hide, though, and I had to look at it quickly before Mr. Meese regularly rejected it.

As the summer went on Mr. Meese gave me more responsibilities. He let me mix simple prescriptions under his guidance. I used mortar and pestle to grind ingredients into powder and then poured the mixture into capsules. When he was busy mixing more complicated concoctions, he let me wait on the customers. That made me feel very adult, though I sometimes abused the privilege. In those days the purchase of condoms was more furtive than buying hard liquor. Condoms were not kept out in the open, but were hidden behind and below the counter, well out of sight, and the same age laws applied to contraceptives as to liquor. This law was based on the logic that if youths under twenty-one could not buy prophylactics they would simply not have sex. Condoms were a controversial item because married people, theoretically at least, had no need of contraceptives and would never admit to employing them. So the only reason for buying a box would be because one was having sex outside of marriage.

Since Meese's Pharmacy was never crowded, it was considered a good place to buy condoms. A buyer was not likely to be observed. But I could usually spot a condom customer. He would poke around aimlessly, looking at this and that until the other customers had left. Then, if I were at the cash register, he would approach me and ask, "Is Mr. Meese around?"

I usually replied truthfully, "Mr. Meese is making up prescriptions. May I help you?"

The customer would mumble something like, "Thanks, but no," or "It's not important," rather than make such a personal request of me, and leave the store.

But sometimes, in an emergency, a customer would place his order with me. Almost whispering, he would say, "A pack of Trojans."

Perversely I would ask, "What?"

The man would wince, then repeat his request a little louder.

When he did, I would say in my best helpful clerk's voice, "One pack of Trojans coming right up!"

Before I left my job at Meese's Pharmacy to go back to school, I filched a single rubber, a Ramses I think it was, for myself. A boy was considered especially worldly if he carried a rubber in his wallet. The rubber had to be placed so that after about a month of sitting in the wallet, the round impression of it showed through the thin leather when the wallet was opened. You had to be careful when you opened your wallet on a date, but around other boys the round impression gave notice that you were ready for action at all times.

******

Baseball was the most popular male participatory sport in Healdsburg. There were no women's teams, but there was a baseball team for which nearly every man or boy could play. Among them were a number of softball leagues with divisions within each league, a city hardball team, and an American Legion youth team, plus school teams. The baseball season began in March with high school games, and ran straight through until mid-September. Children who were old enough to catch and throw a ball played on just about every street and vacant lot in town until it was too dark to see the ball.

One of the first games to which my father took me was a popular novelty game called Donkey Baseball. Each player was given his own mount and a batter was allowed to stand at home plate to take his swing, but if he connected with the ball he had to mount his donkey and ride to first base. An infielder could field his position standing, but was required to mount his donkey and ride to a base for a putout. Outfielders stayed mounted and could gallop after balls, dismounting to retrieve a ball and return it to the infield.

These donkeys were veterans of many small-town Saturday afternoon games of Donkey Baseball. But they were nevertheless stubborn and irascible. Often they just stopped while en route to a base or while galloping toward an outfield hit, and then refused to be budged. When this occurred, a batter or fielder was allowed to dismount and tug at the reins or push the animal into motion, but once he got his donkey moving the player had to remount to complete his play. Often when a rider dismounted to urge his donkey into motion, the donkey simply galloped off—leaving the player with the ball racing frantically in pursuit so that he could complete the play. Sometimes a donkey, for no apparent reason, would gallop off with an uninvolved player on his back. This created chaos. The other donkeys became agitated and started running around aimlessly, bucking and spilling their riders all over the field until the whole ballpark was a madhouse of running donkeys and chasing ballplayers. Every time this happened, the umpire called time out until order was restored. Then the game proceeded until the next incident. It was all great fun, and Donkey Baseball usually took up a good part of a summer afternoon, what with all the stopping and starting. The best fun for a boy was watching adults make fools of themselves. The players took their humiliations in good grace, throwing up their hands in exasperation, laughing, and kicking at the dirt in disgust.

On the afternoon my father took me, one batter hit a ball to the outfield, mounted his donkey and dashed to first base—only to have the donkey ride over the bag and continue out along the right field line, picking up speed as he went. When the donkey approached the right field fence and could see that he had nowhere to go, he swung left along the perimeter of the outfield and galloped all the way around, following the fence to left field. Then, with his rider hanging on, he headed for home plate. The donkey galloped past the bleachers and around in front of the grandstand and then headed out to right field again, as if he were on an oval racetrack. We spectators stood and cheered the donkey on, while the other players laughed so hard that some fell off their own mounts. The donkey made three or four circuits of the ballpark before he finally stopped, exhausted, with his legs trembling and his tongue hanging out. Jesse loved Donkey Baseball. He knew about donkeys from his days on the Kansas farm, and he would grin and shake his head and say, "Those damn donkeys."

Then there were the Saturday evening band concerts in summer. Some 2,000 people showed up for the first one after the war in July to hear Armand Girard, "noted singer and radio artist," perform "The Desert Song," "Old Man River" and "Short'ning Bread." On the bill with Mr. Girard were Sonia and Yurok from "Old Russia" who performed a Russian dance. "The Gypsy" was sung by tenor Jimmy Kenney, a parole officer from San Quentin prison, and the band played a selection of marches and foxtrots. There was a special prize for the oldest couple present, and the concert concluded with a community sing of "The Star-Spangled Banner."

The Healdsburg *Tribune* was sold again that summer, but not before the old editors got in a few parting shots. They vehemently opposed proposals to raise the minimum wage, which had remained at $.40 an hour since 1938, to $.65 an hour. They wrote, "In some places, wages have soared as high as $2.50 an hour, but people are too proud or too lazy to work. They prefer to loaf or strike. We have gone a long way in California to create a class composed of those who are too proud to work or else too lazy, plus those who sit back idly and live for a time on unemployment benefits." The editorial concluded by accusing "outsiders" of agitating for higher wages at the local apple-packing plant.

That same week, a chamber of commerce proposal to install 325 downtown parking meters was met cooly by the majority of residents. A local man was arrested for buying liquor for an Indian at Tomasco's drugstore. The Indian, after receiving the liquor, returned to his shack, fell into a stupor while smoking a cigarette, and burned himself to death.

By this time Al Barbieri had moved his boys' club to the American Legion Hall. A regulation ring was set up when the club met, and Al always had a couple of fighters working in the ring, training them. It was understood that personal grudges between boys could be settled in this ring, and it was available to them whenever the club met. Though I had given up boxing for Betty, I was still a member of the club.

One evening I stepped into the ring with Grandin, the boy I'd fought with on the elementary school playground. We both put on headgear, and Al laced up our big, padded gloves. Grandin hit me with a couple of hard rights and I started to swing at him, turning on my right leg. All of a sudden, while twisting, my knee just burst with pain. It felt like some muscle that held my leg together from groin to ankle exploded and the muscle was unraveling. I could feel it pop and rip the whole length of my leg. I writhed and screamed on the floor of the ring.

Poor Grandin stood transfixed in his corner. Al leaped (as much as Al could leap) into the ring to help me up. My leg stiffened so I could only bend it while clenching my teeth, and then I could not straighten it again. When the pain abated, I limped outside, mounted my bike and clumsily peddled home.

In those days knowledge of the knee's mechanics was primitive and was unexplored among Healdsburg's doctors. We didn't even bother to call Doc Robinson. When I arrived home, Mother boiled some water and alternated applying hot and cold compresses. This did not help the stiffness, but the knee did not swell badly, and the compresses dulled the pain.

Mr. Meese excused me from work and suggested I prop up the leg and continue Mother's compress treatment. In a week I could walk normally, though the knee remained very tender and unstable. I wrapped an Ace bandage around it to keep it from buckling, and in two weeks I went back to work at the drugstore.

In early August, Dad wrote to Bill:

This is a busy household. I am working in the prune dryer, getting it ready for the prunes that will be coming in within a few more days. Ernestine is working as an apple packer, and although she is only a beginner, she is doing very well. She gets twelve cents a box and hopes to get up into the $12.00 a day class—by next year. After less than a week, she is doing better than some who have been packing for two seasons. Margaret takes care of the house and gets a noon meal for David and me. She also does the shopping. We feel that she does remarkably well for a ten-year-old. David is working at a drugstore for the summer. He is getting eighty-five cents an hour. I told him that when I was his age I worked for fourteen hours and still didn't have quite as much as he will get at the end of one hour. Remember those "good old days" in Kansas when we used to pull weeds for ten hours a day and get sixty cents for it? Oh boy. So you see, we are quite busy. It all helps in the general struggle to keep ahead of the high cost of living, so we don't complain. But it is rather a hardship on Ernie, as she feels she must keep the house up to the same standard as always. Drop us a line and let us know how things are getting along.

Except for grapes, which were always the last crop to be picked, the summer harvests were nearly over in late August. Mexican laborers, who were housed at the old prisoner-of-war camp began going home. The county board of supervisors voted to buy Merryland beach for $18,000 and make it a war memorial. Then they changed their minds and dropped the purchase. The supervisors were divided because, while they wanted a "fitting memorial," they didn't want to spend that much of taxpayers' money for it. Healdsburg's promised Harvest Festival featured barrel races instead of hydroplane races at Merryland. A smaller-than-planned parade passed through downtown. For their depiction of Marines raising the American flag on Iwo Jima, the American Legion won the best float trophy. The Russian River Riders, with flying pennants and waving Stetsons, trotted their horses down West Street. Midget race cars raced for three evenings at the ballpark. They roared around a makeshift track and rattled the old grandstand as they thundered by. Shifting gears, the little racers zipped around the same circuit the mad donkey had taken a month or so before.

Dad was now a foreman at the cooperative prune dehydrator. He counted trays and drove a forklift. After the harvest, Syd Grove, the Coop manager and Russian River Riders president, invited some employees and their families out to his ranch for a cookout. We drove out to the Grove ranch with another family, bouncing over the same dirt road I had traveled to pick prunes.

The cookout was held in a clearing on a bank of the Russian River. Here, where the river flowed slowly and deeply among orchards and vineyards, was where ancient Indian villages had been. The river's surface was a deep green, reflecting the leaves of overhanging trees. It was full of trout in season, and its banks were always home to crawfish.

The day contained examples of why I had mixed feelings about my father. I loved him but often wished he would be more adult, more serious. At Syd Grove's wiener roast and beer bust, most adults stood around in groups drinking beer, talking about the harvest, and leaving young folks to fend for themselves. Jesse stayed with the children. He helped get the fire going and supervised the selection and cutting of wiener-roasting sticks, which was a specialty of his. He walked among the trees choosing green, thin branches, about the thickness of a child's index finger, and slicing them off with his pen knife. Then he presented each child with his or her personal stick. One by one, girls first, he shaved the sticks smooth and tapered them to fine points for wiener roasting. He arranged children so that each one had a clear space to hang his or her wiener out over the fire and he helped the smaller children avoid dropping their sausages so close to the flames that they caught on fire. The secret to roasting a good wiener, Jesse always said, was to roast it slowly and well away from the fire, turning it over and over so that a fine sweat would break out, but the wiener's skin wouldn't burst. It took concentration, Jesse said, and this slow-roasting process got all of us very hungry and impatient, so Jesse entertained us.

He did a sort of duck walk around our circle, making funny faces and sounds and noises as if he were a cannibal at a missionary-boiling ceremony. During dinner Jesse pulled some of his famous little tricks on children. He would pull out a cigarette. Then he would tell a small boy or girl, "I'll bet you didn't know that I'm the only man on earth who can blow smoke out of his ears." The boy or girl would laugh, and Jesse would say, "It's true. Put your face up here very close to my ear and watch closely, because the smoke is sometimes hard to see." He would then light a match, fire up his cigarette, and take a deep puff. Then, after shaking the match out surreptitiously, he would touch the warm head to a boy or girl's bare leg, causing them to jump in alarm.

He also liked to tell the youth sitting next to him during dessert to look off somewhere. "Now what do you suppose that is?" Jesse would ask, pointing. The youth would look, and Jesse would quickly exchange the youth's full ice cream dish for his own empty one. Children had no fear of my father, and they would wrestle him for their own full dish of ice cream, shouting in mock anger. Dad would always plead innocence, then relent. When all of the children had eaten so much that they said they couldn't eat any more, Mother produced a bag of marshmallows she'd brought as a surprise, and Jesse, who had told them to save their sticks "just in case," positioned marshmallows just so on the stick tips, and another round of roasting began.

Jesse's public performances for children always embarrassed me. They seemed undignified. So I was glad when our family finally broke away from the picnic. Jesse actually had to sneak away from the children, who followed him everywhere.

He led us down to a boat dock, untied a small rowboat and we shoved off into the stream. Under the late summer sun, the river was dappled with sunlight. Jesse's wet oars, as he rowed, caught sunlight on their blades and dripped pendants of water, before cutting into the river again. It was the first time our family had been together in a small boat since I was a child.

I watched my mother as she sat upright in the rowboat's stern, a light, bright red sweater loosely fastened around her shoulders. Her dark hands clasped the gunnels of the boat, and she ignored the wisps of her hair that occasionally blew across her face. I had observed her earlier at the picnic.

A group of animated, excited women were gathered around Mrs. Grove. But Mother had stood a little apart—calm, aloof, more listening than talking. Now she was smiling slightly, and when my mother smiled she was transformed. She smiled and looked at Jesse's back as he rowed.

"I didn't know you could row a boat," I said to my father. Before now I only remembered him poling our punt on an Indian lake.

"Oh, yes," he said, "a one-legged pirate I met in the Dry Tortugas taught me how."

Margaret and I were sprawled in the bow of the rowboat, and Jesse winked at her. I could see past Jesse to my mother who gave Jesse a mildly reproachful look, as if Margaret might actually believe that Jesse had been a pirate.

Jesse had boated the oars now, and we drifted slowly back downstream. He turned to straddle the rowing bench and faced west, into the setting sun. Margaret clambered back to snuggle next to Jesse. As I looked at them together, and then at my mother in the boat's stern, I wondered again at how much alike my sister and father looked and how closely I resembled Mother. We both looked deeply tanned, while Jesse and Margaret seemed unaffected by last summer's sun.

"What would you name this boat if it were a *shikara*?" my mother asked Jesse.

"Well, let's see," Jesse said, "maybe we'd call it 'Jumping Jehosophat.' That has a nice ring to it."

Jesse eased the rowboat into the dock. I reached from the bow and held onto a wooden railing so that my mother and Margaret could climb out. Then I jumped up to the pier and waited for my dad. He stowed the oars neatly and removed the wooden benches. Then he turned the benches face down so they wouldn't weather so badly and packed them next to the oars. When he joined us on the dock he expertly tied the rowboat up to a small metal stanchion. I wondered where he had learned all these things.

Summer officially ended the next Saturday. We joined the 4,000 people who jammed the plaza that evening for the final band concert of the season. San Francisco columnist Herb Caen was the guest of honor, and Armand Girard sang selections from light opera. That same night, the Palomar Dance Hall closed, following what the *Tribune* described as "a near riot that occurred when groups of Mexican and white-skinned youths engaged in a free-for-all that sent one boy to the hospital."

Ten

THE FIRST SECONDARY SCHOOL in Healdsburg was the Agricultural and Mechanical University of California, which became the Sotoyome Institute, then the Alexander Academy, and finally the Healdsburg Institute. In 1882 the school was bought by the Seventh Day Adventist Church for $3,750 in gold coins and renamed the Healdsburg Academy. By the end of that year, the school was again renamed. It was christened Healdsburg College because the citizens of Healdsburg favored "college," rather than "academy." It boasted 152 students.

In 1883, five acres to the northwest of Healdsburg College were purchased to build a dormitory for the boys and girls. A four-story building with accommodations for seventy was built there and christened North Hall. Shop buildings rose in the orchard surrounding the dormitory. By 1884 shoemaking, tentmaking, and blacksmithing were taught in addition to core courses. Boys raised cows and horses; girls tended the kitchen and worked in the laundry and dining room. By the end of 1884, enrollment had jumped to 200 students. Healdsburg College held on until 1905. When it finally failed, its demise was blamed on "unwise borrowing for expanding industries, some not essential to the college." By the time of its failure, the college had twenty industries working to support the school.

When the Adventist school closed in 1906, the school district purchased the old University Street building and held high school classes there until 1917, though by 1915 the *Russian River Flag* said "the outside of the building brings back dreams of Dickens." This school building was finally moved to a street near the prune dehydrator where it was operated as a boarding house and bar until I was in the seventh grade.

In 1917 the Healdsburg College dormitory that was now a private sanitarium was purchased for $9,500. It was razed in 1918 to make way for construction of a new high school.

The high school still stood when I became a freshman in 1946. Its architecture was the same as most post-World War I schools but it seemed massive and daunting.

Set on a knoll and fronted with green lawns and flower beds, the high school filled the entire block. A broad cement walkway led from the sidewalk to a series of steps that led up to the school's big oak entrance. The school was two stories high with a large basement. It housed a large auditorium that occupied much of the first floor, and all of the classrooms had windows opening on lawns and trees. The orchard to the rear of the property had long ago been dug up and graded into level land, where a large gymnasium now stood flanking two football fields.

I tried out for the junior varsity football team, which started practice before school actually began. The high school fielded two teams, a varsity and a junior varsity team called the "Ramblers." Everyone who tried out made the Ramblers unless they were physically deformed or mentally unstable (and even these were not necessarily disqualifications). Each team suited up twenty-four boys, so the crowds were large for football games.

Practically every boy tried out for one of the teams. It was considered a sign of character and courage to play if you were physically able. Even the very studious became reserves. Most farm boys did, too, because fall was the one season when they could play, summer harvests having been completed. The few boys who could or would not play football played tennis, joined the marching band or, at the very least, volunteered to move the yardage sticks or to sell tickets and soft drinks. Almost everyone participated in football games in one way or another.

If a boy succeeded in high school sports, his future in Healdsburg was assured. It was not uncommon for a man in his forties to be identified not by the nature of his work, but by a magnificent broken field run he had made to win a game "back in 1923."

The Healdsburg *Tribune* published a special fall feature on the new high school football coach, Art McCaffrey, who was returning to coach his alma mater. "Coach Art," was introduced as "the greatest forward passer ever to wear the red and black" (the high school colors). The article went on to say that "his sixty-yard pass to Taylor York in an Armistice Day game against Ukiah is still a topic of conversation among football filberts." Art, who was redheaded, freckled, and still looked very young, predicted a successful season for his varsity. He noted that since Lytton Home boys now attended Healdsburg High and were eligible to play, three big Bay Area boys from Lytton would join last year's budding star Johnny Hassenzahl in the starting backfield.

I made the Rambler team, along with everyone else under fourteen who tried out. Our coach was the woodshop teacher, who coached us in the single-wing offense. Coach Art employed the Notre Dame box with its backfield shift that was created by Knute Rockne and used at the University of San Francisco where Art had starred. Both formations are alike, being fundamentally a power running offense to the right, or strong, side. In both formations, the tailback is the star, taking the snap from center, carrying the ball on 80% of the plays or passing it if he chooses. Since there was no free substitution rule, a player operated on both offense and defense. The tailback usually played safety on defense, returning kickoffs and punts.

The other backs were primarily blockers for the tailback, with the exception of the fullback who ran all his plays straight into the line. There was nothing fancy about the single-wing. Except for a rare, long, downfield pass to catch an opponent by surprise, it was predictable and plodding. I was installed by our coach as the second-string right halfback. I also played defensive left end, which meant that the other team's right halfback generally got to knock me down on their running plays. Our football formation was by no means antiquated, as the "T" formation with its concept of backfield trickery and forward passing was considered "new fangled" and awfully risky. Most other schools still used single- or double-wing formations. Even Coach Art's box formation, with its shift from "T" formation to modified single-wing, was considered pretty daring.

A freshly mowed and watered football field gives off a smell that still snaps my head up. During the summer the school custodian, Ralph Sandborn, spent long hours getting the football field and the gymnasium in shape. Ralph could always be found in a summer's twilight standing on the track that circled the field and watching the huge sprinklers rotate. He moved them after a precise amount of time so that the entire field was evenly watered.

Ralph gave the main school building the same careful attention. During summer vacation he waxed and buffed the green tiled floors until they reflected images. He washed the cream-colored corridor walls and ceilings thoroughly and oiled and polished the dark wood of the old balustrades and bannisters to the color of mahogany. The three floors of the school (including the basement) were separated by ramps, and since there were no stairwells the building had an open, airy feeling. The individual rooms were large and bright, except in winter. Blackboards were scrubbed, the wooden floors and desks polished.

Aside from Coach Art, the teacher who most influenced me was Mrs. Long, the English teacher, though we had our differences. The first book she assigned us to study was *Silas Marner*, a novel we all loathed. She followed *Silas Marner* with Shakespeare's *Julius Caesar*. Mrs. Long's idol in the play was Brutus, a man I found almost as colorless and humorless as Silas Marner.

Mrs. Long seemed very old. She was probably in her late fifties and held herself aloof from other faculty members as well as from students. She had unruly gray hair and seldom smiled. We played practical jokes on other teachers, but never on Mrs. Long.

The Spanish teacher talked of her summer trips to Spain and of suave Spanish men. Our algebra teacher was young and pretty. She was recently divorced from a well-known local Don Juan and everyone sympathized with her. My old elementary school social science teacher had been promoted to the high school, and my classmates and I joked that Wednesdays and Thursdays were still her only hangover-free days. While I was getting acclimated at the high school, Jesse was offered a better-paying teaching job in another town. He offhandedly mentioned it to us at dinner one evening as if the very thought of us moving was the silliest thing in the world.

Bruce Holbrook succeeded Jere as the elementary school student body president, and Betty Hutchinson was elected girls' yell leader. Jesse called them the "lovebirds."

"Juvenile delinquency" would not go away in spite of Al Barbieri's boys' club. Fifteen of the new downtown parking meters were vandalized, and delinquents were blamed for the damage. The *Tribune* said, "the hoodlums must be caught and punished and must be made to work off the cost of the meters. We must protect the rights of property owners." The *Tribune* blamed most criminal acts on "the people living in the auto courts," which meant the Okies (who weren't property owners). Suddenly, in spite of Smitty Robinson, blacks became suspects too. A *Tribune* headline claimed that black gunmen were terrorizing the county, holding up banks and pistol-whipping clerks. In their zeal to capture the outlaws, deputies and local police forces zeroed in on every black in the county. Healdsburg police arrested two local blacks (ages twenty-two and sixteen) for vagrancy, and Judge Quinn gave each thirty days in jail. Another local black, Osborne Winfrey, was ordered out of town by the judge. Winfrey had been a popular bootblack for several years at the Plaza Hotel, but after the pistol whippings, he was watched carefully and suspiciously. A local store owner finally accused Winfrey of shoplifting a can of crabmeat, and Judge Quinn set his bail at a whopping $250 when Winfrey had the temerity to plead "not guilty." Since he obviously couldn't post bail, Winfrey offered to change his plea to guilty and leave the county. It was so ordered by Judge Quinn.

I read about Winfrey's misfortune at school. The *Tribune* always arrived at the high school before my fifth-period study hall, and a group of us gathered at a table to read it. We looked for references to school activities but skimmed news items too. Since the story about Winfrey was on the front page, we couldn't miss it.

The other reason I read news stories and editorials was because my parents began subscribing to the San Francisco *Chronicle* when I was delivering it. I devoured the "green sheet" for all the sports news, and Jesse read the rest of it. Sometimes Jesse would snort with disgust over a story, and I would go and get the paper to read the story when he had finished.

Whenever I read a story about something that seemed unfair to me, I'd go home and wait to see what Jesse's reaction would be when he read the same paper right before dinner during the radio news. On the evening that the story broke about Osborne Winfrey being kicked out of town, Jesse did what he often did when something struck him as wrong and sad: he shook his head, dropped the paper into his lap, and stared off into space for a moment or two. Then, without a word, he resumed his reading. If I asked him what he thought when a situation like this arose, he would always reply "It doesn't seem fair." Mother was more vocal in her disapproval of inequities because she often dealt with the poor and disenfranchised at the Red Cross office. But their disapproval never extended beyond our house.

The Healdsburg police were angry because they were denied pay raises by the city council, even though they claimed they were being paid less than "fruit workers." At the same time the city council and the chamber of commerce were still trying to persuade the board of supervisors to "establish a magnificent memorial beach park along the river at the south edge of Healdsburg." Besides buying the beach, the rotting old building behind the beach would be "transformed into a restaurant, soda fountain, and bath house facilities." The final touch would be "seats built into the banks both above and below the highway bridge on the banks across from the beach, so that spectators may view water sports." Their argument concluded by stating that "Healdsburg leaders say this will be a boon to the Harvest Fair."

None of us believed that this plan would ever materialize. We especially doubted the bleachers built into the west bank part of the proposal. For the past two summers it became a contest between those of us who swam at Merryland to swim the river, clamber up the twenty-foot west bank, run up to the highway bridge, cross it as quickly as we could, and circle back down to the beach. The hardest part of this game was struggling up the west bank, for it was steep and composed of slippery clay and crumbling shale. It was common for a boy to get most of the way up, only to have his handhold give way and to slide back down into the river.

I reinjured my knee in the Ramblers' fourth game of the season—which also happened to be the team's fourth straight loss. (Actually it was our team's *fifth* loss, as we played an off-the-record touch game with a grammar school team coached by Morris Ruby and lost that game too, 6-0.) The week after I hurt my knee, the Ramblers were beaten by Santa Rosa 44-0.

The year 1946 was a congressional election year. Harry Truman was president, and workers were striking all over the country. Anti-labor sentiments were getting stronger, industry and business wanted to reform the Wagner Labor Relations Act, the Office of Price Administration was under fire, and an end to rent controls was sought by real estate interests. Safeway and Purity stores opened in Healdsburg and small, family-owned groceries went out of business. For awhile locals remained faithful to small grocers, but their resolve weakened and cheaper prices prevailed.

Though Earl Warren was a popular governor, he sponsored a health insurance bill that was criticized as "socialized medicine." In November, along with news that Herman Goering had cheated the hangman and that butcher shops would close on Mondays, the *Tribune* applauded the new Republican congress. The editors, saying Truman faced "certain defeat" in two years anyway, advised him to resign and let the GOP run the country properly. They concluded by saying it was time that government got in step with the people, who were turning "right"—away from "leftists."

On December 20th, Mr. and Mrs. Gibbs hosted the 50th annual faculty tea, at which Mother was "among those pouring." The holiday spirit may have ameliorated Mr. Gibbs's autumn-long bad temper—for he not only lost the race for state Kiwanis Club's lieutenant governorship, but the local golf championship as well.

On New Year's Day, Dad wrote to Uncle Bill:

Santa was very generous with us. Margaret insisted that the pooch be remembered, so Tippy got a beribboned weenie all his very own. Boots the cat was also remembered in the same way.

David is quite thrilled with the big game picture you sent him, for he fancies himself a hunter, although he hasn't shot a gun yet. Keeps talking about getting a .22 but I feel he is rather young. Howsoever I know I'll have to break down one of these days, although I haven't done any hunting for a long time. Still most kids go through a "shootin' iron" phase even if they don't follow through and become famous nimrods. I can easily recall tramping the hills as a kid, with my trusty single shot .22. It was lots of fun and I'd be a heel to deny it to Davy. Love from all the gang.

In mid-month "Shorty" Grimes, a popular bartender at the Sportsmen's Lodge, was arrested for selling liquor to minors. Shorty was apparently caught in the act of serving beers to two underage servicemen by board of equalization agents posing as customers. A slick assistant DA from Santa Rosa was brought in to prosecute Shorty in front of Judge Condit (who had defeated Judge Quinn) and a jury of locals. The Healdsburg attorney who defended Shorty told the jury that the whole thing was a setup. He reminded the jurors that Shorty had been tending bar for over twenty years, and that any experienced bartender could spot a board of equalization agent from a mile away because they always tried to dress like their heroes, FBI agents. Shorty's attorney said that with their snap-brim hats and trenchcoats on, they stuck out like sore thumbs. In his closing argument to the jury, Shorty's attorney said he didn't contend that Shorty was the "brightest person who ever came down the pike," but they all knew Shorty and knew he wasn't so dumb that he couldn't spot a board of equalization agent. To everyone's delight, Shorty was acquitted. It made a hero out of the local attorney and Shorty too. The victory was also counted as a blow against Santa Rosa city-slickers.

Santa Rosa seemed much farther away than fifteen miles. It was the big city and any victory over them was counted as a major achievement. None of Healdsburg's athletic teams had ever scored a victory over a Santa Rosa team. In the same month that Shorty was acquitted, the high school varsity basketball team lost their first game of the season to the Santa Rosa junior varsity even though Healdsburg was playing at home with a new electronic scoreboard purchased with money made from the alumni football game.

The basketball Ramblers, for whom I was playing, was made up of boys who could not easily coordinate dribbling and running at the same time. Our uniforms were not even uniform. A Rambler player sometimes wore basketball shorts that were used in 1932 paired with last year's model jersey.

But we played in a beautiful gym. It was one of the best high school gyms in northern California. The court featured a "floating" floor, and Ralph polished it as if it were glass. The acoustics were wonderful. The ball boomed off the floor in an empty gym, and when the bleachers were full the crowd noise was thunderous.

The Healdsburg 20-30 Club tried to raise $20,000 so the baseball park could be lit for night games. At the *Tribune*'s urging, this plan was expanded to create a whole new recreational district. This ambitious scheme was revealed in the same issue that a letter to the editor from a young ex-GI appeared. The veteran castigated the city council for refusing use of the old hospitality house to the Teenage Club because the club had "no sponsors." The ex-soldier had attended city-sponsored dances at the hospitality house during the war and wondered why the city wouldn't sponsor the Teenage Club dances. I read these articles in study hall. The entire back page of the paper was taken up by an ad that said, "It Is About Time The Butcher Bosses Listen" and condemned the Monday closing of meat departments. The ad was signed by the managers of the Safeway and Purity stores.

The varsity basketball team won three straight games. A new student from Lytton Home called "Tea-Head" was scoring frequently. A new chant "Tea-Head, Tea-Head," became fashionable, although local fans did not understand what "Tea-Head" stood for. Most of the boys and girls from Oklahoma had dropped out of school. Squirt Moore was one of the few to continue, but Squirt dropped out too before finishing his freshman year. Very few Lytton Home boys or girls finished high school either, but it was hardly ever a matter of choice for them. They were relocated by the state or returned home.

Ira Rosenberg, the founder of Rosenberg's Department Store, died in February. All retail businesses in Healdsburg and Santa Rosa closed for the entire afternoon the day he died. I had delivered papers very carefully to the Rosenberg mansion. I caught glimpses of almost every customer on my route at one time or another, but I never saw Mr. Rosenberg. It was as if no one lived in the huge mansion. But Rosenberg money was widely in evidence, and when he died the community worried whether a source of patronage had died also.

On the day that Mr. Rosenberg was entombed at Oak Mound Cemetery in the family mausoleum, another man was buried in Potters' Field. He was an unnamed sixty-three-year-old Irishman, freshly released from the county jail where he had served a term for drunkenness. Dead-ended in Healdsburg on his way to Eureka, he was arrested for "drunkenness" and "begging" the day after his county jail release. In despair he had hanged himself with his belt in Healdsburg's single-cell jail.

Jesse and his Cub Scouts were pictured on the front page of the *Tribune* on their third birthday. At a large Boy Scout program at the elementary school, fourteen-year-old "Kirk" Kirkpatrick became the youngest

Healdsburg boy ever to be awarded Eagle Scout rank. The minister of the Federated Church read the poem, "I Want to Be Like My Dad," at the ceremony, and during intermission the audience sang "Home on the Range." By now, my interest in scouting had seriously dwindled away.

Many indoor events took place during the winter of 1947 because it rained so hard and long that year. Mother even appeared in a PTA play for Founder's Day at the grammar school. The play was called "Tale of Three Letters" and featured seven other "mesdames." I cannot imagine Mother willingly consenting to be an actress; she must have *had* to appear because she was president of the association. Stage productions were very popular in Healdsburg. Several "entertainments" were planned for the winter, including a production of *Dear Ruth* at the high school. A teenage drama club was also being formed.

Even the Russian River Riders planned a "Revels of 1947" at the American Legion Hall. The "Riderettes," a "group of pretty Healdsburg girls" that included Betty Hutchinson, would provide the entertainment. A picture of the Riderettes in shorts and Western boots was featured in the *Tribune*. Next to the Riderette picture was a photo of the actor Dean Jagger and his Chinese bride. The photo was taken in New Mexico where they flew to be married because California had denied them a wedding license. "East-West marriages" were not legal in the state in 1947.

******

The biggest entertainment of the season took place in the high school gym. A boxing tournament was staged there when basketball season ended. So many boys submitted their names to enter the tournament that a series of elimination bouts had to be held. None of my friends made it past the semifinals. Even my idol Johnny Hassenzahl was beaten by a big farm boy in the 175-pound division. To top off the evening, my honest lifesaving partner who had just been elected vice-president of the teenage drama club, scored the only knockout of the evening when he demolished his opponent in the 145-150-pound division.

Frank Carvalho, the football team fullback, won the Joe Louis trophy. The award was presented to him in mid-ring by Al Barbieri. Frank's father, Manuel, was a hero in his own right. He had been awarded a Carnegie Hero Fund bronze medal for attempting to pull a pilot from a crashed and burning fighter plane in October, 1945. The plane crashed on a ranch where he was the foreman. Mr. Carvalho badly burned his hands trying to pull the

167

pilot, whose legs were trapped under the seat, out of the aircraft. Mr. Carvalho said he could have rescued the pilot if any of the other ranch hands would have helped him. But they were afraid the plane was going to blow up and so they stood at a safe distance watching. Mr. Carvalho could not manage the job by himself and finally had to give up the rescue effort. The pilot burned to death in his cockpit.

A blind xylophonist presented a show for one of our high school assemblies. His manager stopped me in the hall before the concert and asked conspiratorially, "Hey, kid, where's the head?" I replied straightforwardly that I didn't know for sure, but I thought our principal, "Bud" Christensen was in his office. The manager fixed me with a scornful stare and said, "No, no, I mean the mens' room." I was so happy to have added a cool expression to my vocabulary that I tried using it at home.

"Where's your sister," Mother asked me one evening. "In the head, I guess," I replied nonchalantly.

Mother surprised me by knowing the expression's origin, "This house is not a barracks, young man," she said.

The Plaza Theatre was temporarily shut down that winter by the fire marshals. They said the balcony was a firetrap and had to be fixed up. Extremely heavy rains continued and by February a total of fifteen and a half inches had been recorded. "Agents of Death"—depth charges, mines, bomb fuses, and mortar shells—were among the debris from World War II being washed ashore on county beaches. There were big timber strikes to the north in Mendocino County; police used tear gas to disperse the strikers and arrested many of them. All gambling was prohibited in the city except for the Catholic church's bingo games (and, of course, the poker games in the back room of Tomasco's drugstore). Mother was especially affronted that the Catholics were exempted from the gambling ban and even read us excerpts from a long letter she wrote on the subject to Grandfather Neudoerffer.

Under the headline "Youthful Check Forger Nabbed," the *Tribune* announced that our old keep-away nemesis, "Charles Hulburt, 16, was arrested for forgery. The check was for $51.50 and was used to take a trip with an accomplice to Glendale, Arizona, and back." Hulburt confessed, the paper said, and was certified to juvenile court. A week later the paper amended Charlie's real age to 18. In that same issue it was noted that Max Lingo, Ace's brother, was arrested in Healdsburg for being AWOL from Fort Lewis, Washington. Lingo had reportedly come back to visit his mother "who works at the Basalt plant." The paper also said that many children were being arrested for stealing auto parts from junkyards.

Baseball season began and I did even not make the junior varsity team. So I tried out for the tennis team and was assigned the last singles spot. Meanwhile, Jere Holbrook won the 75-yard dash and the broad jump at two track meets.

Major Taylor presided at the traditional Lytton Easter sunrise service. Easter services at St. Paul's were not mentioned in the *Tribune* listings because Mr. Kent seldom felt the need to announce church services in the paper. St. Paul's was always jammed on Easter Sunday with people we never saw on any other Sunday of the year. On Easter and Christmas, Mr. Kent always delivered a stern sermon about church attendance to the congregation. He was always forthright and colloquial. "Our pew," as my family referred to the pew that Jesse picked and where my folks and sister always sat, was a good place from which to view the colorful congregation on Easter. Mrs. Sheriffs, the second richest parishioner at St. Paul's (next to Mrs. Richardson, the wife of Lt. Richardson of the wartime Windsor Rifles), always wore her mink coat. In those days all of the ladies wore hats and gloves. Dad's Christmas hat comments were repeated at Easter.

Mother (Mrs. "James" Manley, the paper said), "appeared" on a Santa Rosa radio station in a PTA discussion. Mom then left us to our own devices for the first time in our lives: she flew to a week-long PTA congress in Long Beach. Margaret, who had decided she now wanted to be known as "Peggy," took over the cooking.

"Kraft Cheese Time," featuring free bar snacks between 4:00 P.M. and 6:00 P.M., was initiated at the 339 Club. Max Lingo, 19, was dishonorably discharged from the Army for being AWOL. The next Friday night he was picked up for disturbing the peace and punching a Healdsburg policeman in the eye. Max got a six-month sentence in the county jail from Judge Quinn, who also fined him $500.

In May the Sonoma County district attorney ordered all nudist magazines off drugstore shelves as part of a statewide drive against lewd literature. Chief of Police "Tiny" Stefani reported that he was unable to find any such magazines in Healdsburg. Particularly singled out for banishment was *Sunshine and Health*, a harmless publication that extolled the healthful virtues of nudism and featured pictures of real nudist families at camp. The photographs of these real nudists were about as titillating as pictures of naked aborigines in the *National Geographic* and far less titillating than the real live "dancers" provided for the smokers at the American Legion Hall.

The city council announced that although it had denied all previous building permits on the south end of town, it would now help develop two new businesses there. One development would result in a Chevron truck and transfer station, and the other would house a tractor and farm implement company. Since there was nowhere to grow at the east or west ends of town, Healdsburg was being stretched out at its north and south ends. Ground was broken just north of town for the first postwar subdivision, "Solar Terrace." A full page *Tribune* ad declared Solar Terrace was a "moderately priced subdivision" with "complete homes from $7,500 and up."

Spokespersons for Sonoma County taxpayers were vigorously protesting war memorial taxes. In opposing a twenty-five-cent war memorial tax, the wealthy Sebastiani family—of Sonoma's Sebastiani Winery—made a presentation to the board of supervisors. After their presentation, the board went on record in favor of "helping veterans as much as possible," while opposing expenditures for "anything the county doesn't badly need." This vote put a big roadblock in Healdsburg's plan for a Memorial Beach.

In February, Nick DeJohn, a "one-time Chicago gangster," was slain in San Francisco. DeJohn had been living in Santa Rosa without the knowledge of local police, who initially identified him as "a retired furniture man." Rumors had long circulated that the mob had secretly bought Villa Chanticleer to use as a resort and meeting place for mobsters. But spokespersons for the burned-out resort denied knowing DeJohn, who was found strangled and "stuffed into the trunk of his fancy automobile."

My nemesis Grandin Worden and I reached a truce since we both played on the tennis team coached by his father Al Worden, the biology teacher. Mr. Worden was the only coach that players called "Mister" instead of "Coach." He was very polite and courteous and did not curse or smoke. Tennis was still old-fashioned: players were expected to be civil with their opponents and wore white uniforms, not school colors, for matches. But at the highest levels, the game was changing. Jack Kramer and Pancho Gonzales were turning tennis into a sport that featured booming serves and volleys. Healdsburg High's best player was an American Indian of the Pomo tribe named Stan Smith.

My mother and my father had played tennis in India, and I had learned the rudiments of the game from them. Mother was considered a good player. She displayed surprising agility and possessed a nifty underhand serve. Jesse's twin brothers, Amasa and Emerson, were state champions at boarding school. One evening I talked Dad into playing me at the lighted golf course tennis courts. I thought I would polish him off quickly, but Jesse only moved slightly when I hit balls at him from everywhere on the court. He picked off my shots and lobbed them back accurately over my head into the far corners of the court so that I ran and ran until I was exhausted and finally called off the match in frustration. Jesse did not work up a sweat. Though he beat me I didn't consider his style to be real tennis.

Healdsburg High School graduated its fifty-fifth senior class on June 19th, the same day sugar rationing ended. Every store in town ran out of sugar by 3:00 P.M. The stink from ponds at Miller's potato dehydrating plant was becoming unbearable. Unlike the grower's cooperative prune dehydrator, Miller owned his plant privately. He processed potatoes in winter and apples (at the shed where Mother worked) in summer. Miller refused to clean up the ponds and neighbors were getting ugly.

Dr. Oakleaf spoke to the brand new Business and Professional Women's Club on the subject of mental health. He concluded his remarks by asserting that "living has become more complex, and extraneous influences bearing down on us in these high-pressure days have caused mental hazards." He asserted that 20% to 30% of all hospital patients were mentally ill.

At the beginning of summer, the county grand jury demanded enactment of a tough law to "throw slot machines out of the county." The board of supervisors agreed that slot machines were bad influences but approved their use, hoping to tax them. In this way, they reassured the public, they would be taxing the immoral people who used them without really approving of their use. At this same meeting, the supervisors ordered the city of Healdsburg to clean up Merryland beach.

The beach was in worse shape than ever. While waiting for the county to transform it into a memorial park, the city stopped maintaining it. The beach was littered with broken glass and cans and empty cartons; the three-year-old pier was shaky (it had to be removed and reassembled every year at the same time the gravel dam was demolished and rebuilt); traveling bands of gypsies occasionally stopped to bathe in the river; there was a hobo jungle underneath the railroad bridge. In late June, the *Tribune* warned that another polio epidemic might strike.

It was because of the polio scare that I started swimming around Fitch Mountain at Del Rio Woods. My friend Ira, or "I.I." as he was nicknamed, had been swimming around the mountain for two years after he had contracted polio from swimming at Merryland. The disease left I.I. with a stiff wrist and a slightly atrophied calf, but I.I. was still very big and strong and was a very good football and basketball player. In fact, he had found a summer girlfriend the year before from among the ten or so Bay Area girls who vacationed with their families in the Del Rio Woods "cabins." I.I. rode to the Del Rio beach with Wally Wood, whose father owned the Dodge dealership in town. Wally drove a black Dodge convertible. Soon all three of us were tooling around the mountain in Wally's slick convertible to swim.

Driving around Fitch Mountain, the narrow winding road dipped sharply, curved up and around in front of Bill Wolking's cliffside home, then climbed to a high bluff before descending to Camp Rose. Camp Rose had a public beach, as well as a store and summer cabins for rent, but the river was not dammed at Camp Rose and so ran shallow except for a spot where the river swept around in a looping curve. There were two trees at this curve that hung out over the water. One was heavy with foliage and had a rope attached to a lower limb so that boys and girls could swing out from the high bank and drop into the current. The other tree was a gnarled old oak. This tree's roots were exposed from the river's chafing at the bank. The trunk of the oak stuck out over the river at a steep angle and was devoid of limbs. At its top the amputated trunk formed a crude platform, and the tree was known all over the river as the "diving tree." The platform, which was a shattered fork where the trunk had broken off in a long-forgotten storm, was around twenty feet above the river's surface. Diving from this tree was a very competitive sport among some Healdsburg boys. It was dangerous because the river shifted subtly every winter so that diving holes beneath the tree had to be recalculated at the beginning of every summer. Often, an angle had to be figured precisely in order to hit a particular hole. The competition then was to see which boy could perform the most difficult dive from the tree given the conditions. Swan dives were very popular and also half-gainers. The tree's fork would become slick from the feet of many divers, and often after slipping, a boy would have to abort a dive in midair, twisting frantically to land in a hole.

Past Camp Rose, Fitch Mountain Road climbed steeply to a vista point where one could look down on the curling river for a mile or so in each direction. From there the road descended abruptly around a turn where a rutted dirt track ran off to the right, leading to Del Rio Woods. The dirt track led into a parking lot for the small Del Rio store and the Palomar Dance Hall. The parking lot was on a bluff that overlooked a wide sweep of river, and a series of wooden steps led down to the beach. Here the river was wide and deep—a long, gravel dam with a wooden spillway and pilings spanned the river at the western end of the beach. A wooden raft mounted on metal barrels was anchored two-thirds of the way across the river. Scrub oak and madrone covered the far banks, and sandy paths crisscrossed through the trees and brush. The other side of the river was perfect for games that ended in flat running dives off the banks. The dam itself was ten- or twelve-feet wide— large enough to spread out blankets and towels—and its sides were steeply angled. The pilings anchoring the spillway had slots in them where boards could be inserted to control the flow of water over the dam, and on the spillway's downside the water cascaded into deep miniature rapids of foaming water.

"Big Tom" Moran's daughter, Nancy, was the unquestioned princess of the beach. From the parking lot above the beach you could pick out Nancy, lying languidly among other girls on the raft. Nancy wore a yellow bathing suit to match her hair and to show off her deep tan. Up close, Nancy had odd green eyes with flecks of gold in them, smelled of the sun and coconut oil, and had a lithe easy grace. I left the beach at Del Rio for two weeks to take the Senior Lifesaving class at Merryland, and when I came back Nancy was gone. She had left for Hawaii with Big Tom.

The lifesaving course was easy because I didn't have a partner trying to drown me. My partner was Bobby Frost from the Frost Ranch, and he offered me a job as a hop picker. A hop-picking job was a good choice because prune and apple prices were down. Prune pickers were leaving to work in Napa County, where growers were paying eighty-five cents an hour. Money seemed to be in short supply everywhere. Local merchants refused to continue supporting the band concerts, and volunteers were trying to raise money to keep them going.

Sixty-seven people attended a city council meeting at which the smelly dehydrator ponds within the city limits were outlawed and Miller was told that he faced criminal action for not cleaning them up. Miller threatened to close the whole dehydrating plant rather than clean up his waste ponds and said he would move his operation downriver. Miller did shut down his plant without cleaning up the foul ponds, and a recall movement was mounted against the city council. The recall fizzled, but a group of "prominent citizens" recommended the city "be more cognizant of industries that bring payrolls to this city." In the end, it appeared that the city would have to pay for the cleanup, and Miller would move his potato operation. Healdsburg merchants "chipped in at the last minute to save the band concerts."

Once again Chris Jennings promised a Harvest Festival extravaganza on Labor Day. There would be wine barrel races and swimming and diving competitions featuring the "finest Bay Area athletes." Five local girls became candidates for Harvest Queen. The queen would be chosen for gumption, not beauty. The girl who sold the most contest tickets, ballgame tickets, and coronation tickets would be crowned.

Eleven

W E HATED TO LEAVE THE RIVER after a month of summer vacation to work on farms or in orchards. Harvest jobs started at dawn and didn't end until after dusk, and during the season you worked six days a week. Most of us dreamed of the day we'd be old enough for summer work in a sawmill or planing mill—but you had to be at least sixteen to work around machinery. I didn't even have any hope of that: I wouldn't be sixteen until the summer of my graduation from high school.

Hops were used in the brewing process to give beer, ale, or other malt beverages their special flavor. World War II bombing wiped out the hop industry in Germany, so California ranchers were reaping the benefits—sending millions of tons of hops to Europe. Many ranchers went so far as to plow up their other crops and plant hops.

Mr. Frost owned over 100 acres of Russian River bottomland on the West Side. His ranch was not nearly as big as Warren Richardson's huge Windsor hop ranch, but was one of the largest and most profitable in the county. At planting time in early spring, a hop ranch with its latticework of fifteen-foot-high poles and wires and strings looked naked. When the hops had climbed up the strings to the wire ceiling—but not out onto the overhead wires—it was time to harvest them. The harvesting always began right after the Fourth of July.

Hops had always been harvested the same way. Flatbed trucks with racks behind their cabs and two "crow's nests" built up on either side of the cab rolled along slowly in first gear between the rows of hops. Two field hands wielding machetes walked in front of the truck, slashing the hop plants free at their bases so that they hung loose from the wires. As the truck passed the severed vines, the men in the crow's nests cut the tops of the plants with their machetes and flung them backwards onto the truck's bed. Several workers on the truck bed then fastened the vines onto the racks until the racks were full. The cutters rested then while the truck made its way to a processing shed. The racks were lifted by a winch up to a stripping machine, where the hops were stripped so that only the buds remained. Then the buds passed down conveyor belts in the shed to be culled by other workers—usually girls or older women. At the end of the belt, the hop buds were sacked for drying in a kiln.

Chet Frost was the first rancher to invest in two new machines that combined the whole process into one operation. The future looked very profitable, and Chet Frost, a prudent and careful man by nature, had sunk just about everything he owned in 1947 into modernizing his equipment.

Chet's new hop-picking machines are difficult to describe because they were awkward-looking. They most closely resembled the amphibious vehicles that were used to transport troops during the war. They were long and deep-bellied, and with soft, large tires. The bay of the machine, where troops would have normally crouched, housed a wide, rotating steel conveyor belt that stripped the hops, and with great clanking and groaning emerged to crawl across the top and down into the machine again. The machine still featured two crow's nests and two workers trudged in front of it hacking at the vines, but now the machete-wielders on the crow's nests tossed the severed vines down onto the machine's back. Two more workers seated at the sides tied the vines to metal pegs on the conveyor belt. The conveyor belt rotated, and the vines were stripped inside of the machine. Only the hop buds were sucked up into a chute at the back of the machine and blown down into a bag. A bag-handler standing on a small platform at the machine's tail managed this operation. He would tie a full sack and drop it off, choke off the chute's flow while he positioned a new bag, open the chute and repeat the process. The whole machine was beetlelike in appearance. It had a large metallic shell, the slender piping of the crows nests resembled antennae, the residue was eliminated like larvae, the bags of buds were dropped like burlap turds.

I worked as a machete man in one of the crow's nests. We bundled up as if we were in a blizzard instead of in the heat of summer because the vines stung like nettles when they touched bare skin and because of the dust in the fields. We wore heavy, long-sleeved shirts, buttoned and with the collars turned up. Our gloves were safety-pinned to our shirt cuffs to protect our wrists. We masked our faces with large bandannas, wore surplus aviator goggles and an assortment of caps. I drilled a hole through the wooden handle of my machete so that I could tie it to my right wrist. The machine would not stop for you if you dropped your machete, and it was a precarious climb down and up from the crow's nest. The machine was a self-contained processing shed but could not move by itself. Bobby Frost pulled it with a big tractor. We worked long, hot, dusty hours, and there was no opportunity to slack off because Bobby never slowed the tractor.

******

We were never too tired from the long, hard days in the fields to forego Friday night band concerts, weekend movies, or skating at Palomar, which had been transformed from a dance hall to a roller rink because of a skating craze. I was strictly a sidewalk roller skater and not any good at roller rink skating—nor was I any good at asking girls to skate with me. I stood on the sidelines with I.I. and Wally and maybe Bobby Frost and watched. Every evening was programmed like a dance. The announcer called out a certain type of event, the couples gathered on the rink, and the recorded organ music would start. Partners dipped and crossed and swirled around and around the floor. After paying to enter the rink, patrons were fitted for skates in the foyer. What was once the coat room for dances now had racks of skates, numbered and arranged by size. A soft drink bar with a big mirror behind it covered one end of the rink. There were benches along each long wall of the rectangular room and at the far end, next to where the bandstand had been, was a large stone fireplace.

The "cool" Bay Area boys wore white T-shirts and unwashed, shiny Levis with the cuffs turned under at the ankle so that they were stiff and heavily creased behind the knees. The most daring of these boys also unbuttoned the top three buttons of their pants and rolled the waistband under so that a "V" was formed that went right down to the crotch. This was accentuated by the fact that they wore their Levis as far down on their hips as decency would permit. Though some of us aped city styles and wore our Levis fairly low-slung, we didn't unbutton them. I had enough trouble persuading Mother not to wash mine and ruin their sheen. Not all of the city boys dressed this way. Some wore khaki pants and Hawaiian shirts—probably to prove they had been there.

One Saturday night some Okie boys terrorized the roller rink. I was standing on my skates near the bar, and Jack Butler was sitting on a bench along the wall. They burst in—five of them—knocking people out of the way. They chased the boys with the unbuttoned Levis and beat them badly when they caught them, overturning pinball machines and benches when the boys tried to hide under them. The city boys did not fight back. Those who were lucky enough to be wearing khaki pants cowered in a group near the fireplace. I couldn't see the whole melee because I was trapped against the bar with about three rows of frightened boys and girls in front of me. Suddenly the rows parted and I stood looking at Buck Butler again. It had been a long time since Buck had punched me out at the movies, but he must have remembered me because he said, "Ain't you had enough, kid?" and hit me so hard that my skates rolled out from underneath me and I crashed into the floor on my back. I got up and removed my skates, intending to use them as weapons, but the Okies had finished wrecking the rink and were leaving. I followed them to the front door where one of them turned around and drawled, "I'd turn 'round and go right back in there if I was you, boy." After they roared off into the night, I asked Jack why he hadn't done anything to stop them since he was the only one who might have made a difference. He shrugged and said that they were "kin." I never saw Jack again after the roller rink brawl; he moved up north soon after his kin were all arrested.

When they were arrested, the *Tribune* reported it this way: "Once more the urgent need for a deputy sheriff for Fitch Mountain has been emphasized. Last Saturday night a group of bullies banged their way into the Palomar skating rink and for an hour or so created a virtual reign of terror. The helpless owner of the place frantically telephoned both Healdsburg and Santa Rosa for help, but none was given. Youngsters skating at the rink were kicked and beaten by the group, fixtures in the place were smashed; all-in-all it was a disgraceful small riot. It was not for hours that the group was apprehended by Healdsburg police—long after they had grown tired of wrecking Palomar and left for 'fun' elsewhere. Fortunately, no one was seriously hurt, but for that no credit is due the sheriff's office." That was the editorial. The front page story read: "Five Men Charged in Big Brawl; Night of Terror in Calistoga and Fitch Mountain. Roscoe Stanley (21), Billy Joe "Ace" Lingo (16), Jim Bell (16), Bill "Buck" Butler (21), and Claude Butler (20) were arrested for assault, disturbing the peace, and wrecking property. After the group had terrorized the Palomar skating rink around Fitch Mountain, they left for Calistoga and seriously injured two people there."

Nancy Moran came back from Hawaii shortly after the riot at Palomar. In her absence I bought a new swimming outfit—matching yellow trunks and shirt with a green palm tree on the shirt pocket and the thigh of the trunks. I jettisoned the old green trunks that Mom had made me—the ones with the lifesaving patch that were faded and worn.

Nancy and I started going out together toward the end of summer. I.I. was dating Nancy's best friend. We would meet the girls at the Plaza Theatre on a weekend evening and after seeing the movie we would walk them home around the mountain. I fell hard for Nancy Moran. On the day she left we stayed late at the beach, huddling together in a blanket while the wind that always began to blow in the late afternoon swept downriver.

During the summer a man named Manuel Modena broke the prune picking record by picking 100 boxes of sixty pounds each in nine and a half hours. Taxpayers once again refused to pay for new sewers, and the county sanitation engineer said that Sonoma County had the distinction of leading the state in inadequate sewage systems. The Harvest Fair lost $696, and Gloria Nicoletti, who was crowned Festival Queen, chose $600 cash instead of a Hawaiian vacation. The hops were harvested in time for me to partici- pate in early football practice. I was not listed in the paper among the coach's "hopefuls."

Grandfather Neudoerffer visited us just before school opened. Every fifth year he was sent "on furlough" to the United States and Canada for a combined vacation, conferences with his superiors, and money-raising for his mission. Grandfather did not always take his furloughs if he felt there were more important things to be done in India. We were excited, but Grandfather arrived agitated and angry. When his ship docked in San Francisco, he was met by members of the mission board who hustled him off for a welcoming dinner at Fisherman's Wharf. Then as now, especially in the tourist season, one could not simply walk into a popular wharf restau- rant. Lines sometimes extended down the street for half a block. According to Grandfather, the Lutherans took their place at the end of the line and chatted about his voyage—Grandfather, in his black suit with clerical col- lar, enjoying a pre-meal cigar. Fisherman's Wharf is in a predominantly Italian Catholic neighborhood, and very quickly a waiter appeared at Grandfather's elbow. "Father, you don't have to wait. Please come right in," he said apologetically.

You might as well have called Grandfather "Beelzebub" as "Father." He declined angrily, not neglecting to tell the maitre d' sternly that he repre- sented Martin Luther, not the Pope. Then he insisted on waiting his turn and eating in the restaurant even though it must have been terribly uncomfort- able for everyone concerned. I took him, or perhaps he took me, on long walks about Healdsburg. I liked showing him off—and showing him the playing fields of Healdsburg and the river. As I think of my grandfather now, it occurs to me that he probably never played a game in his life. I don't even remember him watching the English or the East Indians at play. And he could not have been terribly impressed with our river; even in its occasional floods it could not hold a candle to the Godavari. He was surprised at how tall I was and said he thought I would grow sturdy enough to withstand the rigors of India if I should decide to become a missionary. I did not tell him that my ambition was to be a third mate on a tramp steamer.

Only later did I realize that Grandfather took this particular furlough so that India's independence would be celebrated without him. He arrived on August 3, 1947, and on August 15th, India became self-governing. This greatly saddened Grandfather. Though the colonial system had done him no particular favors, he thought East Indians too politically naive and religiously fragmented to govern themselves. Mother told me that he could not bear to read the papers during this time, and so she read the news to him.

Before he left Healdsburg, Grandfather spoke at the Federated Church Missionary Society. The *Tribune* said that "Dr. Neudoerffer's topic was religion and politics of India and was based on his forty years' experience in that country."

For several months following Indian independence, my parents were also in demand as speakers. Jesse addressed the new Rotary Club on "politics and religion in present-day India." The paper quoted him as saying "politics run rampant with public graft almost taken for granted." The British rule was beneficial to the country, Jesse said, but he hesitated to predict a future for India in the face of its present religious unrest. The article continued, saying that Dad had spent five years as a teacher in India and traveled extensively. This was the first time I heard of Jesse expressing opinions about Indian politics or religion.

I never saw my Grandfather again. When he made his final visit in 1952 I was away at college. When he visited us in 1947, however, Grandfather brought other news that directly affected our family. Papers were filed in Sonoma County Superior Court on August 8, 1947, that would change all of our lives dramatically.

A solid rain began to fall in early September. The main topic of conversation in town was the low market price for prunes. State Senator Barry Abshire, who lived in our county, told the Kiwanis Club that unless prune prices escalated, many veterans who had bought small farms would be wiped out. Judge Quinn collected an all-time high amount of $1,580 in fines during August. Some eighty-four arrests had been made, fifty-one of them for public intoxication.

When school opened I was elected president of the sophomore class. I tore ligaments in my right knee during Rambler football practice that same week. This time Doc Robinson taped up my leg, and Mr. Meese lent me a pair of crutches. I left home for school a little earlier in the mornings, hobbling on a shortcut through the elementary school playground.

Sophomore English literature featured Dickens' *A Tale of Two Cities*. Since the novel takes place during the French Revolution, our English teacher that year was Miss Destruel, the French teacher. I faced geometry and the dreaded Pythagorean theorem from pretty Tillie Iverson who had been married to the local Don Juan, and ancient history from Bob ("Bunny") Fletcher (who could not pronounce Nebuchadnezzar). We had a new band teacher as well—Mr. Finne—a small, fine-boned man with a clubfoot.

I still absorbed the *Tribune* in study hall. The hot news locally was that the restaurant and tavern owners agreed to follow President Truman's request for meatless Tuesdays, chickenless Thursdays, and breadless bills of fare. Only one slice of bread (not two) would be served with every meal, and no bread or butter at all would be served unless "demanded." In the same issue's editorial it was suggested that since the president had called for less use of grain so that it could be shipped to "war-torn Europe," Californians should drink wine and brandy and cut out beer because it would help local vintners. (I wondered what Chet Frost and Warren Richardson thought about that.) The editorial concluded by hoping that the *Tribune* would not be criticized for "advocating the use of alcoholic beverages."

Mother passed out ballots concerning universal military training at the last meeting over which she presided at PTA president. She thought it would be fairer for the poor because college students would not be exempted. She also announced that the PTA would sponsor a children's Halloween parade. Margaret asked Dad to make her a parade costume, and in great secrecy Jesse fashioned it in his shop. On the morning of the parade, Jesse's creation was unveiled, and Margaret broke into tears at the sight of it. None of us understood why. It was a wonderful and original costume. Jesse had crafted a huge orange pumpkin out of wire and papier-mâché that would cover Margaret's entire body except for her feet. The pumpkin had a girl's eyes, with long eyelashes and a great grinning mouth. Jesse had painted it gaily and authentically. Mother had even made green, leafy slippers to complete the outfit. When my parents finally persuaded Margaret to stop crying and tell them what was wrong, she sobbed to them that boys wouldn't think she was pretty. In fact, since they wouldn't even be able to see her under that big orange ball, they would think she was a fat girl who had to wear a pumpkin costume because she couldn't fit into anything else, Margaret said. I was dumbfounded that my little sister would be thinking about boys at all since she was only eleven. Mother saved the day by making up a story about a princess who hid herself in a pumpkin to fool a handsome prince. Margaret finally donned the pumpkin suit and won the prize for best costume. After the parade, the pumpkin costume stayed in our attic for years, and Margaret never could be persuaded to throw it out.

Just about then, my parents bought their first car. It was a used black Dodge that they bought from Wally Wood's father a week before he sold his dealership. I think Jesse must have been promised some sort of closing-out deal by Mr. Wood because purchasing a car had not been mentioned around the house. Jesse just drove it home one afternoon. It was a very shiny black, but if you looked closely you could see wavy lines in the new paint job, and we realized too late that it had been rolled over at least once in a serious accident. The car ran crooked too—a sign that the frame was bent badly. Jesse had been taken, but at first we didn't mind. Mother could shop without having to walk to town, and she and Dad could ride into the countryside to hike on Sunday afternoons. They had missed hiking. It was only later, when the car was always in the shop, that we started to cuss it.

Before Thanksgiving there was an uproar over a movie that a Santa Rosa exhibitor wanted to show at the Plaza Theatre. The movie had been shown before for "educational purposes" and didn't create much of a stir, but this time the guardians of morality were moved to action. The *Tribune* headlined: "District Attorney Will Ban the Hygienic Films Production *Mom and Dad* from Sonoma County." The exhibitor protested that the film was previewed for a group of clergymen, mothers, PTA members, and city officials of Santa Rosa who voted fifty-four to one in favor of the film's release. But the district attorney said he would stop it anyway because "portions of the picture are lewd and obscene."

Predictably the DA was overruled, and now everyone had to see the movie. The ticket line stretched down the street past Meese's drugstore when they showed *Mom and Dad* again that fall. Children under eighteen weren't even allowed into the theater unless accompanied by their parents, but I.I. and I talked an usherette into sneaking us in through a fire exit. The movie was advertised as being so shocking that doctors and nurses would be on hand. Sure enough, the exhibitor had stationed women in nurses outfits along the aisles, and they all carried little first aid kits in case anyone fainted. The film started out provocatively enough: A slick-haired, fast-talking boy asked a nice girl for a date, and they ended up parked in his convertible in a desolate spot. The boy primed the girl with liquor and began kissing her, then suddenly you could only see the couple's heads, but you knew his hands must be doing something awful because she started protesting, "No, don't, no, don't." But he had her too hot and bothered by then, and they both disappeared out of sight behind the front seat. This passionate scene took up all the first five minutes of the film. Then, suddenly, the screen lit up with words that said something like: "Moms and Dads, do you know what can happen to your children if they indulge in sexual intercourse?" A doctor then came on the screen and for about an hour he showed pictures of gonorrhea and syphilis victims—lots of magnified diseased sexual organs—and lectured on the evils of premarital sex. Nobody fainted, but I came close to throwing up and so did a lot of other people. I learned something about movie promotion that night. *Mom and Dad* ruined any sexual desire a boy might have had, and I was grateful I carried a rubber in my wallet since the doctor said that prophylactics were the only way to keep from getting diseased like the people in the movie.

The HHS varsity football team with its "four speedy runners" was unbeaten. The Ramblers had lost all of their games, although Jere Holbrook was making "good gains."

The *Tribune* was sold again to two brothers from Duluth, Minnesota, who, according to the *Tribune's* own assessment, "don't have much newspaper experience." The departing owner, who had only published the paper for a year, appealed in his last issue for the election of a Santa Rosa real estate man for state senator because the man was a Republican: "We believe in the conservative and sound platform of the Republican party," the departing publisher said.

In November the real estate man won in a landslide, and the Greyhounds won the football championship. The team was compared by locals to the 1925 team on which Smith Robinson starred. Stan Smith led the tennis team to a championship too. As soon as my knee healed, I went skiing with a large group on Cobb Mountain. The snow had just dusted the mountain and no one really knew how to ski. I borrowed a pair of skis and made it about ten feet down a gentle slope before my knee turned and gave way again. Johnny Hassenzahl drove me down off the mountain.

I became despondent over the instability of my knees. Art McCaffrey was quoted as saying I was one of the players he counted on to play varsity basketball, but I didn't make the team. His vote of confidence was enough to keep me playing, though. I.I. and I wound up as Ramblers and we played a lot in that situation.

One evening in early December I was on my porch writing to Nancy Moran. I sat on my bed next to my little table with the one small drawer where I kept Nancy's letters, and which only had room on its top for a lamp. There was no room for a desk, so Jesse sawed and sanded a writing board for me—much like his own drawing board, but lighter—and I wrote hunched over with the board on my knees. My family seldom disturbed me when I was out on my porch, so when Mother came out and closed the door behind her I knew that something was up. Mother looked to be on the verge of tears, but in true Neudoerffer fashion she came right to the point. She began by saying that because a law was changed, she had to tell me something that both she and Jesse had hoped to spare me. Jesse was not my real father. She had been raped in Canada. I was a result of that assault. She had wanted to put me up for adoption, but Jesse, to whom she was engaged at the time, insisted that they keep me and raise me as their own son. Mother said I really had Jesse to thank, not her. Because of the changed law we all needed to appear at the county courthouse so that I could be formally adopted. Mother was weeping. I embraced her and told her it was all right, that I understood. She got up and left the room, squeezing my shoulder as she went.

Jesse never said anything. He behaved as if nothing at all had happened. Perhaps we were more solicitous of each other—our voices a little softer, our exchanged glances gentler. I know I watched Jesse closely, appraising him anew, seeing him in a different light. This was our secret, Mother had said. Even Margaret need not know; we would carry on as usual. And that is what we all tried to do.

On December 18th, Mother, Jesse and I drove to Santa Rosa in the black Dodge. The county courthouse stood in the center of downtown, so that traffic going north or south circled it on one-way streets. There was no waiting room in the office, and Mother entered the judge's chambers alone. Jesse and I stood together in the hallway (one of those marble hallways where whispers echo), Jesse held his hat in his hands and I shuffled my feet. Jesse stood with his head bowed, and his feet apart and planted. The bright overhead lights accentuated his bald head and reflected off his glasses. I did not look at him directly but cast sidewise nervous glances at him, trying to think of something reassuring to say. But no words came out of me.

Finally the door opened and we were summoned into the judge's chambers. He asked if I consented to the adoption and I said, "Yes." The judge then asked me if I would rather be known as David Neudoerffer or David Manley and I said, "Manley."

184

The judge signed the adoption papers and we left for home. Mother and Jesse, in the Dodge's front seat, occasionally remarked on the wintery landscape during the fifteen-mile drive, and I sat silent in the back seat.

I saw my father differently after that day. He became older, gentler, braver. He seemed at once more brave for saving me from an orphanage, more vulnerable for having suffered his fiancée's rape, more noble for not having abandoned her, and a subtle preference for Margaret that I had always sensed was now explainable.

Mother seemed more vulnerable too. The thought of the violence of the act and the scars it must have left horrified me, and I grew very protective of Mom. The adoption process hadn't shaken her a bit, though. Mother always endured.

She was also covering up. In 1980, after her death, I found the adoption records. In the document, my father is clearly listed as one "Robert Campbell, whereabouts unknown." So there never was a rapist at all. Then one of Jesse's old college chums sent me a copy of Mom and Dad's wedding picture. They are standing in front of Grandfather's mission, and I am positioned between them. On the back of the picture Jesse had written: "Meet the family! Ernestine, R.N. (registered nurse) and the boy. David is twenty-two months old and some boy. His Daddy was killed in an auto accident in Toronto, Canada, and I am going to try to fill the vacancy. Quite proud of my family." So Jesse, wittingly or unwittingly, was a part of the deception. I understand that a missionary's daughter could not tell an adolescent son that she had had a lover before she was married. That was not an option for Mother. I loved my mother and father more, not less, after the adoption proceedings, but I did not feel I could speak to them frankly about my feelings. Mother seemed bruised and beyond my comforting; Jesse seemed unable to smile at me. On the exterior nothing changed, but the deeper feelings of love that ultimately drew us closer together took time.

******

In its New Year's Eve edition, the *Tribune* welcomed the new Healdsburg Rotary Club and applauded the Rotary motto: "He who profits most, serves best."

On January 11, 1948, I turned fourteen, and on January 30th Mohandas Ghandi was assassinated. On the Sunday after Ghandi's assassination, while George Izzett and I were shrugging into our cassocks and surplices in the sacristy, Mr. Kent asked me what my grandfather had thought of the

Mahatma. I replied that I didn't know for sure, but that I thought Grandfather disapproved of his unstatesmanlike attire and bearing and of all the trouble he caused the British with his strikes and fasts and inciting of mobs. Mr. Kent said nothing to me then, but several weeks later he presented me with a just-released book titled *The Light Has Gone Out, But Ghandi Lives*. He had inscribed it: "To my young friend David from Frank B. Kent." I stuffed it away in my book collection and did not read it for years.

Our family was more taken with Nehru than Ghandi. Nehru seemed so English. I did not try to reconcile my recently acquired sympathies for the underdog sodbusters in Westerns with my defense of a well-ordered, benevolent empire. *A Tale of Two Cities* absorbed me in English class, but not because I sympathized with the French Revolution. I identified with Sydney Carton who rode to the rescue of a damsel in distress.

Locally, a small merchant was singlehandedly fighting a battle with the Healdsburg City Council. W.H. Mallon, who was known to teenagers as "Mr. Mallon" and to my father as "Water" Mallon, owned what the *Tribune* called a "confectionery bus," from which he sold candy, soft drinks, popcorn, and peanuts. Mr. Mallon parked his bus in a lot he owned on University Avenue equidistant between the elementary school and the high school near the ballpark centerfield fence. It was a handy spot for youths to gather during school lunch hour or after games at the park. Mr. Mallon himself was a friendly, ruddy-faced man who discouraged fighting near his bus, and so it was a popular gathering spot for children, parents, even teachers. That winter, Mr. Mallon decided he would like to erect a small grocery store on his lot to better serve his clientele. To this end, he presented a petition to the council, signed by many locals; but even though many residents and teenagers appeared at a council meeting to support him, Mr. Mallon was denied a permit for his store. The council ruled that the lot was not zoned for business and that in allowing Mr. Mallon to build, as an exception to the zoning ordinance, they would be setting a dangerous precedent. Many of us wrote letters arguing that Mr. Mallon's confectionery bus was one of the few decent gathering places for teenagers and that it served as a meeting place for youngsters and adults alike. The council was also warned in letters from parents that their actions would be remembered in the March city council election. A second request to build by Mr. Mallon was quickly denied on the same evening the council voted to approve the construction of a new apartment complex just behind his lot. It was evident to all who had fought for Mr.

Mallon's store that the "big wheels" of the town did not want a small store patronized by often noisy young people near their new apartments. City fathers and downtown merchants were always encouraging youngsters to stop loitering in front of Tomasco's drugstore in the downtown business district and to find somewhere else to gather. The fact that they spoke publicly this way and then closed down the only other gathering place for youth was not lost on us. I asked Jesse if this wasn't a good example of hypocrisy, but all he would say was that it was "a damn shame."

Perhaps in an attempt to assuage youngsters and at the same time to lecture them, the new *Tribune* owners editorialized in favor of bringing a big league baseball team to the ballpark for spring training. The Minnesota brothers wrote that "this would keep the boys and girls of this city off streets and interest them in a sport that is beneficial to both mind and body." As an afterthought, they added that "this would bring the name of Healdsburg into the national sports world."

Mother declined to act in that year's PTA Founders' Day skits. But she accepted an appointment to a committee organized to find a "sports director" for the city of Healdsburg. The salary for the new sports director was to be $1,200 to $1,800 annually, and an attorney, a businessman, a city councilman, and Mother comprised the search committee. Cub Scout Pack 21 celebrated their fourth birthday and Dad, as scoutmaster, handed out the usual awards. It was announced at the birthday party that the American Legion would take over sponsorship of the pack from the elementary school PTA, which had sponsored the Cubs for the past two years. After I read the paper, I knew that Dad had continued on so long as scoutmaster for Mother's sake.

W.H. Mallon announced that he would challenge Art Smart, owner of Nelligan and Son Feed Store, for his seat on the city council. Art Smart's reelection slogan was: "Elect Art Smart for clean honest government." Ad space on the outfield fence of the "newly renovated" ballpark went on sale for $2 a running foot in eight- and ten-foot sections.

The Healdsburg High School varsity and "B" basketball teams won championships, and we Ramblers were undefeated. Lynn "Pappy" Waldorf, famed football coach of the University of California Bears spoke to the Healdsburg Kiwanis Club at noon and to the Greyhounds (the high school athletic club) in the evening. I was not a member of the Greyhounds because I had not played on a varsity team, but Johnny Hassenzahl, president of the club, reported that Pappy showed a film of the "Big Game" and spoke on leadership.

Lytton Home's Major Taylor was once the chaplain at San Quentin prison. Partly because the high school varsity won the basketball championship, partly because his son, Bob, was captain of the team and partly because he thought it would be a good game, Major Taylor arranged for the varsity to play the prison team. The game was a sort of post-season reward and educational trip and a test of how good our team really was. I say "our" because Coach Art included several Rambler players on the varsity for the last few home games, and so we were included in the San Quentin trip. We left in one of the yellow school buses right after classes on a Friday.

San Quentin state prison commands a promontory in San Francisco Bay sixty miles south of Healdsburg and one mile east of San Rafael. The prison walls are the color of the coastal rocks into which its foundation is anchored. From a hill, before the bus descended into San Rafael, we caught a glimpse of what looked like an ancient fortress. Ralph, our custodian/bus driver/sometime junior varsity coach turned the bus east from downtown, and when we came to the landing from where the ferry boats crossed the bay, Ralph turned right along a narrow road. The bus rounded a turn and San Quentin loomed in front of us. It was quiet in the bus when Ralph switched off the engine. You could not even see the top of the thick walls from the bus windows. We emerged into a damp, foggy evening. Art produced passes at an entry booth, and our team—about fifteen of us—was ushered up to the immense prison gate.

While we waited for admittance to the prison, a police car with two shackled men in the back seat pulled up. One of the officers opened the rear door and unlocked the prisoners' feet from where they were chained to the floorboard. When the two men were finally helped out of the car, they stamped to get their circulation back. The policemen guided them our way and they shuffled forward, trussed in leg irons and waist chains.

A deputy warden arrived and ushered us through a second set of high, barred gates that led into a large brick court with flowers and a fountain in the center of it. The courtyard was silent and empty, and tall inner walls entirely enclosed us. Our guide pointed out various prison wings and described the sort of prisoners who inhabited them. Then he walked us to the honor wing. Though uninhabited then, there were six tiers in the cell block, and the cells at floor level were open. Our guide explained to us, as we craned our necks, that the top row of cells, running along one wall of the square, was death row. From the top tier, condemned prisoners could look down on honor prisoners as they freely mingled on the main floor. An elevator was positioned at the far end of death row, he told us, for an inmate's last trip down to the gas chamber.

We were led through a steel door into the chamber itself. Painted a pale green, it smelled of disinfectant. I noticed it was spotlessly clean and wondered who kept it that way. Behind the chamber our guide indicated the elevator exit and the cell where a condemned man was given his last meal—"anything he wants"—and spent his last night. There was about four feet separating the elevator door and the cell and they interlocked so as to form a passageway from cage to cage. The escort told us that a condemned man's last hours were often spent in company with the prison chaplain. "Major Taylor can tell you all about that, can't you Major?" he said, rather than asked. The major nodded. Everything seemed to be marked out for the condemned man as the moment of his execution drew near. There was a narrow, lined walkway from cell to gas chamber. Our guide paused to show us the vat in which an executioner dropped cyanide pellets. The pellets, our escort said, when mixed with acid, produced a chemical reaction that filled the chamber with lethal gas. The chamber itself contained two square metal seats with armrests. It struck me that the gas chamber resembled the bridge of a ship and that the chairs, except for the black straps that hung from them, were like the captain's and the helmsman's chairs. They were bolted to the steel decking, and the chamber's one large window curved in front of the chamber like a bridge's wind shield. In front of the chamber, following the window's curve, was a circular railing, and behind this railing, spectators gathered to witness an execution. Our guide pointed out that witnesses were required in California prison executions and that, although dignitaries and newspaper and radio reporters had priority, any citizen could write to the warden and request to be a witness. There were lots of applicants when someone was executed for a particularly heinous crime, the deputy warden said. As a final treat for our team, we were all allowed, going two at a time, to sit in the chairs while our guide explained what a painless death the use of gas provided. "Not like the electric chair that fries you," he emphasized. He had us imagine taking deep breaths of the odorless gas and holding them in, so as not to cough. I remember when Caryl Chessman was finally executed some years later. I could visualize the whole process very clearly and was startled to realize that I had quite possibly sat in the same chair.

Our team was then escorted through the main yard into the prison dining hall. It was big enough to feed a multitude, and catwalks crisscrossed overhead. When we entered, trusties were busy clearing out tables, and a crew was mopping up the enormous tile floor. Clearly, this was to be our playing surface.

We were herded into a kitchen where we changed into our red and black uniforms. Then the guards collected our gym bags for safekeeping. While the portable bleachers were brought in to surround the space we would use as a court and the baskets were lowered into place, a guard told us that the San Quentin Lions had a good team. The team, he said, included a former Harlem Globetrotter and an ex-backup center from the University of California at Berkeley. Finally Coach Art gathered us around. He told us to watch out for their "rough stuff." Art needn't have worried. The referees whistled San Quentin players for the slightest infractions and gave us the breaks on calls. The bleachers, which were filled with honor prisoners, cheered loudly for us and booed their own team heartily. San Quentin won 64-60, but everyone seemed to think it was the best game a high school team had ever given the prison varsity. There was a lot of handshaking in spite of the guards' admonitions to avoid contact with prisoners, and the bleachers gave our team a standing ovation. We substitutes stood through the second half, but that was as much from the cold and dampness of the huge mess hall as it was from the game's excitement. Ralph drove us out of the prison, through the night lights of San Rafael, and back up dark Highway 101.

In what the *Tribune* called a "daring burglary," safecrackers robbed Rosenberg's department store and got away with $300. According to the paper two men between the ages of thirty and thirty-five planned the job from a room at the Plaza Hotel. They walked out of their hotel room window onto the roof of the store, sawed their way through the ceiling, cracked the safe and stole the money, and checked out of the hotel at 2:00 A.M. If the safecrackers would have waited another minute to make their escape, they would have walked out at 3:00 A.M., as the first Daylight Saving Time went into effect that same night at 2:01 A.M.

Twelve

THE HIGH SCHOOL BOARD OF TRUSTEES announced they would place a ballot measure before the voters to raise school taxes from $.75 cents to $1.50. They mentioned in the announcement that Healdsburg was the last city in the area to ask for such a raise. The *Tribune* editorial writers did not like the measure, but urged voters to "swallow this bitter pill quickly" for the students' sake. The PTA held a meeting to elect district officers in the high school music room, and the main speaker's topic was "The Influence of the Motion Picture and Radio upon the Character of Children and Youth."

I was not yet an insubordinate student, but I watched as some of my classmates exploited teachers' idiosyncrasies. Those teachers who were easily rattled or who were quick to anger were their favorite targets.

Though Mr. Fletcher, our ancient history teacher, had served gallantly as a naval lieutenant during the war, he was a favorite target of students' pranks. Mr. Fletcher spoke in a strange, throttled, barking voice that seemed to come from somewhere at the back of his throat, and when angry his face turned a deep shade of red and puffed up so that his eyes all but disappeared. He had married a young former student, who affectionately called him "Bunny," or so it was rumored. The implications of this nickname were obvious, and it was common for Mr. Fletcher to be greeted as he arrived in his classroom by crude drawings of rabbits on his blackboard. Or students in a group would approach his desk during a test to ask for clarification of a point and leave behind them a bunny pinned to the classroom wall behind his back. When Mr. Fletcher discovered the drawing, he would furiously tear it off, crumple it up, and hurl it into the wastebasket while loudly saying something like, "Class, you have gone hog wild." This would double up everyone and escalate Mr. Fletcher's rage to the unintelligible. Worse, Mr. Fletcher knew little about ancient history, and his lectures revealed that fact. He mispronounced names and places if they had more than three syllables. The crowning blow came one day when a student removed the hinge pins from the heavy classroom door, and as Mr. Fletcher briskly opened it, the door fell on him. His un-teacher-like oaths and curses from underneath the door and his threats of revenge when he was extricated set everyone to howling. Several years later, on a summer break from college, I worked side by side with Bob Fletcher on a planing mill green chain. He was a different man in an olive drab under-shirt and an old navy cap, and he worked as hard as anyone on the chain. But ancient history did not work out for him at all.

The new music teacher had the opposite problem. A traditional musician, he believed an orchestra should play serious music and like music seriously. Our orchestra members, except for the first chairs, had taken up their instru-ments because they liked music in a casual sort of way and because they thought it would be fun. None of us had aspirations to become terrific musi-cians. Mr. Finne's practice selections were generally intricate and dull, not lively or modern. He sat before us on a high stool because of his clubfoot and clicked his music stand delicately with his baton to begin a piece of music. Mr. Finne could not even march before our band in parades—as Mr. Linger would later do in spangled uniform and shako—when we performed. But several of us would always be grateful to Mr. Finne, though we did not know it then. Four or five of us had formed an interest in jazz and Mr. Finne encour-aged us, pointing out that great jazz musicians usually possessed a thorough understanding of classical music. In March, he arranged a trip for us to attend "Jazz at the Philharmonic" at San Francisco's Civic Auditorium. We pur-chased our tickets, and Mr. Finne went along as our chaperone.

We drove to the concert in two cars—one of them being Schuyler Richardson's family Cadillac in which Mr. Finne rode. There were more people at the Civic Auditorium than any of us had ever seen in one place. Jazz aficionados of all races and mixtures of races came to the concert in minks and tuxedos, checkered padded sportcoats, evening gowns, and over-alls. I had never been in such eclectic company.

I cannot accurately describe the concert or its lasting effect on me. The music was nothing like the polite, melodic jazz that was played on the radio or that was available on '78 records. There seemed to be no structure to the concert at all.

A new world of improvisation opened up for me. Lyric flights by Charlie Parker and Johnny Hodges. The deep soulful tenor of Coleman

Hawkins contrasted with the honking, driving frenzy of Flip Phillips to whom the audience roared, "Go. Go." The cool trumpet style of little Howard McGhee, who played with his left hand in his sportcoat pocket. Contrasted with McGhee was the flamboyant Dizzy, with his upturned trumpet bell, shooting out nonstop riffs, his cheeks bellowing in and out. I did not know of a trombone's possibilities until I heard Bill Harris. Bud Powell never changed expression as he played—the ultimate in "cool." J.C. Heard would go off on long thunderous drum solos that culminated in soft whishing on the high hat with brushes as the soloists rejoined the melody one by one. Ray Brown, in one bass solo, thrummed so fiercely that, sweating freely, he tumbled backward into J.C. Heard's bass drum. The whole auditorium rose up in agreement. "Yes. Yes," they roared. After intermission, Ella Fitzgerald sang jazz standards and a little scat. The concert concluded with Ella singing "How High the Moon." We were so excited that we babbled all the way home. But Schuyler said that Mr. Finne sat quietly next to a window in the Cadillac's back seat, staring out as the dark miles home rolled by.

Though I began to love music, I was a dud at dances. Formal dances were always "program dances." Boys and girls received programs when they entered the dance, and after a couple had settled on which dances they would dance together, the boys went round to the other girls filling out their program cards. The object of a program dance was to keep couples from dancing every dance together and to allow unattached boys and girls a chance to get in on the action. There were always girls who were overweight or skinny or who had bad cases of acne who seldom were asked to dance but who stolidly attended all of the dances anyway. And there were farm boys totally without any social graces who stood in clumps looking lost, and other boys like me who held themselves aloof and pretended to be cool. Jesse called boys like me "dopes." He occasionally asked me, after a dance, who I had danced with and almost invariably I said, "No one." Jesse would say, "You dope." Mother, on the other hand, knew who the outcast girls were and suggested it might be gentlemanly if I asked several of them to dance with me. I always avoided Mother after dances.

There were lots and lots of dances. Dances were the accepted method of keeping kids out of trouble. At one such casual spring dance, I got drunk for the first time. I.I. and I were occupying our usual positions in the stag line when he casually told me that his parents were out of town for the weekend. He suggested we might leave one of the rear exits cracked open, run down to his house a couple of blocks away, have several quick drinks of his father's bourbon whiskey, and then sneak back into the dance. I didn't hesitate to join I.I. My reaction to straight bourbon was a gagging fit, but we finally got several swigs down and hurried back to the dance before a chaperone checked the exit. As I stood again in the stag line, the strangest thing happened: a warmth spread through me and my head buzzed and I felt a surge of confidence. It was magic. I danced every dance the rest of the evening.

Later that spring Bobby Frost appropriated a bottle of his father's home-made brandy, and we drank it on the beach at Merryland one night. This time I threw up until I thought my stomach would turn inside out. My face burned like fire. It had been raining, and I caked my face with cold muddy water to cool it off. When I got home and went in to kiss my mother goodnight—it was the rule, for she never went to sleep until I got home—she was horrified by my face. I told her I had fallen face down in a mud puddle.

Track season opened with Jere Holbrook and Wally Wood starring in sprints and Bobby Frost in middle distance events. I was relegated to the Rambler baseball team, and I joined DeMolay because they had a summer softball team. The Federated Church youth group had a monopoly on all the important DeMolay offices. I was elected "marshall." The marshal got to guard the door, which was a lot like getting to play rightfield for the Hartnell Street gang. My DeMolay stint didn't last long. I.I. helped me join the Junior Oddfellows, a much more diverse group of boys who met in the Knights of Pythias hall. We peeked into the Knights' closets, and, sure enough, they were full of robes and chain mail and armor and swords. It seemed to me that grown men who dressed up in suits of armor and acted like King Arthur's knights were the real dopes. In fact, when Dad became the high-muckey-muck of the Knights, he was the farthest thing from my image of a knight that I could imagine.

The Rosenberg's safecrackers were identified from their handwriting in the Plaza Hotel registration book and apprehended in San Francisco. They turned out to be Seperon Balenzuela, 29, alias Joe Garcia, and Frank Richards, 64, a former Sing Sing convict. Joe Lombardi of the Santa Rosa Bank of America pleaded with Italian-American residents of Healdsburg to send letters to friends and relatives in Italy, urging defeat of Communists in state elections.

The *Tribune* published a local election extra with the headline, "City Progressives Win." Slim Price was reelected mayor, and a new police chief took over when, for no apparent reason, Tiny Stefani resigned on election day. Art Smart defeated Henry Mallon, and the school tax was voted down.

Its defeat left Mom and Dad depressed and angry. Ranchers and business-men cast the largest nay vote, in spite of the fact that Chet Frost was president of the school board and Mr. Gibbs was now the district governor of the Kiwanis Club.

The California Commonwealth Club voted to "attack first with the atomic bomb if we have reliable information the enemy intends to attack us." A study showed that DDT was killing bees and other "good insects," and urged scientists to develop "more powerful stuff, but also more selective." The Air Force unveiled its new jet fighter plane, the "Shooting Star," and President Truman ordered a government takeover of the railroads.

The high school varsity baseball team edged unbeaten Geyserville and their future Pacific Coast League pitcher by a score of 3-2. This tied them for the league championship. Our own pitcher won the game in the bottom of the 13th inning. He hit a solo home run off the centerfield fence over 400 feet away. The Geyserville pitcher had struck out 12 batters and our pitcher fanned 21.

Jesse umpired grammar school softball games that spring. He volunteered because Morris Ruby was coaching the team. Jesse's flair for umpiring made him very popular. Townsfolk came to grammar school baseball games just to watch Jesse. He called balls and strikes with a flourish, and loudly. He would sweep up his right arm, two fingers stabbing the air, as he called out, "Stee—Rike—Uh—Tuh!" just as a professional umpire would have called a second strike on a batter. Dad thought games ought to be fun. Not all visiting coaches or teams felt this way, however. Many elementary school coaches took winning and losing very seriously.

One day, on my way home from high school, I happened on a game Jesse was umpiring. I sat down on the home team bench to watch the end of the game. Dad was crouched behind the catcher with a face mask on to protect his glasses. Except for taking off his jacket, he was in his teaching clothes. Healdsburg was playing Sebastopol and their coach, like Mr. Ruby, was a part-time preacher. He was a big man with a reputation for being hot-tempered. On this afternoon he was being abusive because his team was losing. Dad, for all his theatrics, was a scrupulously fair umpire. He would not have given the home team a break any more than he would have given me a break in his math class. But the Sebastopol coach repeatedly argued Dad's calls—interrupting the game and towering over Jesse, he shook his finger in Dad's face. Finally, the coach exploded at one of Dad's calls. He rushed Jesse and pushed him toward the backstop screaming and cussing. I ran to pry him off my father. I pulled him off and turned him round so that I stood face to face with him and I said something like, "Leave my father alone, or I'll bust you in the mouth." Jesse quickly tugged me away. "This is none of your business," he said. "Head for home." So I angrily turned away and as I left I could hear my father shout, "All right, settle down. Let's play ball."

When Jesse came home he found me on my bed with my hands clasped behind my head staring at the ceiling. He came in with his sport coat slung over his shoulder and sat down on the edge of the bed. We didn't speak for a moment or two, and then I asked, "Who won?"

"Healdsburg did," he finally replied, "but no thanks to you." I retreated into sullen silence, and he went on: "Since his team was losing, the thing that coach wanted more than anything in the world was to be able to protest the game. If he could have baited me into a fight or even an argument, he could have protested and his protest would most likely have been upheld because I had lost my temper. Now that wouldn't have been right, would it?" I didn't answer, so Dad answered for me. "Of course it wouldn't. The best team wouldn't have won the game, and those players would have had a right to be awfully sore at me. Or you," he added as an afterthought.

"There are times when you may have to eat a little humble pie in order for things to work out the right way," he concluded. I understood what he was saying, but I didn't like it at all.

Toward the end of May, a Summer Events Association was formed to plan, among other things, the Saturday night band concerts. To no one's surprise, Mother's summer recreation committee hired Morris Ruby to direct the program at $200 a month for three months. I was anxious for summer vacation to begin because, according to Nancy's letters, her family would spend the whole summer at their cabin.

The Boy Scout/DeMolay/Federated Church ticket was defeated in the high school elections. An athlete, Keith Walker, won the student body presidency over Kirk Kirkpatrick. Jimmie Jennings, who was now called "Jim," lost the vice-presidency. His new name was accepted more quickly than might be expected because Chris started calling Jimmie "Jim" in all his press releases for the *Tribune*.

The week before school closed, my old lifesaving partner rescued a Petaluma boy from the treacherous surf at Dillon's Beach while on a DeMolay picnic. According to the paper, the boy was struggling 100 yards offshore, and my ex-partner used his Red Cross lifesaving technique to pull the boy in through the undertow to safety.

A popular writer came up with a scheme to dam San Francisco Bay and make it into a fresh water lake. The writer believed that the state was running

196

out of water and so it couldn't grow. He cautioned readers to remember that Italy was about the same size as California and that Communists were trying to take over the Italian government using water problems to stir people up. The writer concluded that San Francisco Bay should be dammed somewhere out beyond the Golden Gate Bridge to allow California to grow without a Communist takeover.

Dad brought this scheme to Mom's attention because she was on the summer recreation committee, but Mother was not in a humorous mood. She was as angry as I had ever seen her. A family of ex-Oklahomans who lived several blocks from us were evicted from their rented home into the street. The father was disabled and his large family consisted of his wife, four sons, and a daughter—Sylverene. The owner of the house had kept one small room without a bathroom for himself. Police, when they evicted the family, said the owner collected bags of his own waste and stored them in a corner. The owner was able to relocate, but his tenants were living in the street. Police were trying to provide a tent outside the city limits for them because the city council wanted them moved. Their presence in the street was blocking traffic, annoying neighbors, and embarrassing the council.

Mother was outraged that the owner escaped responsibility while the family suffered. She collected a supply of food and clothing and insisted Sylverene stop at our house every afternoon to carry a hot dinner to her family. Mother did not believe this could happen in America. Until that Okie family's eviction, concerns over the homeless had hardly touched our family. Occasionally a hobo came to our house and asked for food in exchange for yard work. Jesse always found a job that needed doing, and Mom always provided a meal with dessert and coffee—or iced tea if it were summer. The man usually departed with a pack or two of Camels, which Mom and Dad smoked.

The day after school closed for the summer I headed for Del Rio Beach and my routine seldom varied. At ten in the morning I walked to the corner and sat on the curb in my trunks and moccasins waiting for a ride around the mountain. After a week of hitchhiking, I didn't stick out my thumb any more because drivers knew where I was going. I just sat on the curb in the sun until somebody stopped. Often the local shoe store owner, Mr. Schwab, stopped. He would pull up in his Model A Ford sedan and invariably say to me, "Hop in, Speed." He nicknamed me "Speed" because I had started mimicking the pigeon-toed slouch of some black athletes. When I stepped out of his car at Camp Rose, where he lived, the shoe-store owner always said, "You're on your own now, Speed."

But often a new friend, Gil, picked me up in his green 1938 Plymouth. Once at Del Rio we walked down the wooden steps and out across the dam to spread out our towels near our girlfriends. Our circle included Emil, the new student body vice-president, another basketball player named Charlie Morse, I.I, Gil, and myself. We played a game in which we stood on the wooden spillway in ankle-deep water smacking a tennis ball against the onrushing falls. The ball shot back at us off the face of the falls, and we tried to scoop it up and hit it back before the ball skipped past us into the rapids below the spillway. The rapids were deep and full of strong currents. We played another game with a heavy stone: we cradled it in our arms and tried to walk across the river bottom beneath the rapids to the other side.

We played endless games of tag. It was not unusual to evade a tag, dive off the dam or raft, swim fifty yards or so to the beach, run barefoot down the beach to the dam, sprint the length of the dam to the falls, leap from piling to piling next to the spillway, and dive into the rapids. Swimming under water you emerged on the far side of the river, scrambled up the bank, ran through the woods and brush back upriver for several hundred yards, and sprinted into a long, flat dive off the bank back into the river. You always attempted to dive into a well-scouted hole between tangles of fallen trees and driftwood—bringing your pursuer up short on the bank. Beaverlike, you swam underwater through the tangled tree limbs to emerge some distance away.

The girls were totally indifferent. They lazed on the wet raft sunning themselves, occasionally reaching a hand over the raft's edge to splash themselves with cool water. On rare occasions they joined in our games of tag, but usually they paid no attention to us. About four o'clock, a cold wind blew down the river canyon, rippling the water's surface and flapping our rock-weighted towel corners. As I hitchhiked home for dinner in the sunset, the wind grew colder. I never was late for dinner. Mother's six o'clock deadline was sacrosanct. I usually arrived in the nick of time, and if Dad were on the front porch to see me shuffling pigeon-toed down the block, he would ask sarcastically, "Is that the athlete's slouch?" Mother accepted my dating an Irish-Catholic girl pretty well because she thought that a Moran would never really take a small-town boy seriously.

I played softball for the Junior Oddfellows on most summer evenings. We had a very good pitcher. John was so dominant that he sometimes wound up three or four times, windmilling his right arm in a big arc round and round and faster and faster, before hurling the ball at the plate. A lot of fans came to softball games, and though our city girlfriends seldom showed up, they celebrated our victories with us. If one of the girl's parents drove them to the Plaza Theatre on an evening we played a game, we picked them up after the show and drove them back to their cabins in Gil's car. And after Gil's car was wrecked, we walked them home.

Meanwhile, the family from Oklahoma was still living on the street. The school tax measure had been rescheduled for another vote—absentee ballots were mailed out—and it passed narrowly despite ranchers' vehement opposition. All Pomo Indians were awarded $150 each for usurpation of their tribal lands by the federal government. The prune growers association set an hourly summer labor rate at eighty-five cents. Grocery clerks struck, demanding a forty-hour work week. Mr. Meese was elected head of the city planning commission. The crowd at a band concert topped 2,000 and more seating was urged, though no one wanted to pay for it. It continually frustrated merchants and the city council that they could not figure a way to charge for the concerts.

On August 16th, Babe Ruth died. On August 20th, the 339 Club beat Concrete Pipe Company for the Class A softball championship, and the Junior Oddfellows won the B division by a score of 25-0 over DeMolay. After the game, following our usual routine, we picked up our girls at the Plaza Theatre and started around the mountain in Gil's small Plymouth sedan. Gil had played for the losing team, and perhaps to demonstrate his frustration he gunned the Plymouth on the mountain road's straightaways. Then, pretending to be out of control, he whipped the car back and forth as he negotiated the turns. Going too fast we hit the two deep dips in the road approaching Bill Wolking's home. As the car bounced up from the first dip, my head hit the roof, breaking the overhead light. The car hit once again, then became airborne heading into the second dip. I pushed Nancy onto the floor and shielded her with my body as we hit once more, bounced, and slammed into a telephone pole. The front left fender took the brunt of the collision and the little car swung wildly out into the center of the roadway, almost overturning. My upraised left elbow drove through the plate glass window before the car rocked to a stop, steaming. We separated ourselves from the wrecked car as people came out of their summer cabins to survey the damage. After we had checked each other to make sure no one was seriously hurt, we went around to the front of Gil's car to survey the damage. Someone, I.I., I think, first noticed the pool of blood on the highway in the headlights' beam and said, "Someone's hurt." It took us a little time to figure out that it was I because I was wearing a heavy sweater and it was absorbing the blood from my wound. But shortly, my left sleeve and my left trouser leg were soaked, and my left shoe was filling up with blood. I told everyone that it was a scratch, and they believed me. Had it not been for the timely arrival of Eagle Scout Kirk Kirkpatrick—who with my ex-lifesaving partner, just happened to be driving around the mountain when they saw their friend Gil's car—Doc Robinson estimated that I would have bled to death in five more minutes.

Kirk took charge. "Take off that sweater," he said to me and I obeyed. "Emil, flag down a car," he ordered, and Emil obeyed. "Charles, I'm going to twist this sweater into a tourniquet. Find me a strong stick to twine in the sweater so we can twist the tourniquet and stop the bleeding." While Kirk wrung the blood out of my sweater, Charlie ran to find a strong stick. The wound, once exposed, gaped. It was four inches long on the inside of my upper arm where the big artery is, and it went down all the way to the bone. When the tourniquet was tightened and the blood stopped flowing so freely, the gash was revealed to be a couple of inches wide and was a ghastly white.

Nancy fainted. By the time Kirk was convinced that the tourniquet would hold, Emil had flagged down a passing car, and he was holding the rear door open for me. "Ira, get in there with him and keep that tourniquet wound tightly," Kirk ordered, and Ira obeyed, though his face turned chalky and he began to sweat. Quickly, Kirk crossed to the driver's side of the waiting car and issued terse instructions on how to quickly reach the hospital. Then, with a smart slap on the car's top, he said, "Hurry." The couple in the car were probably going home to their cabin after an evening at the movies, but they followed Kirk's orders. Their car was big and powerful and we made good time. Although I.I. did his best to keep my tourniquet tight, I bled freely on the leather upholstery and plush carpeting.

As soon as we reached the hospital, I was rushed to the emergency room. Doc Robinson was telephoned, but he was away on a house call in Windsor, his wife said. The head nurse tried to reach my parents, but they weren't at home either. I remembered they were visiting teacher friends, and she reached them there. Mother did not believe the nurse who told her, "Your son has been badly hurt in an automobile accident. He's in the emergency room here at the hospital."

Mother thought it was me using one of my disguised dramatic voices, as I had done before. According to the head nurse, she said, "This is not a funny joke." Mom very nearly hung up before being persuaded that the call was genuine; then she and Dad arrived within minutes. Nancy arrived with them. Before long, Doc Robinson arrived too. Doc was not one to be rattled. He removed his hat and coat and asked, "Well, you big lug. What have you gone and done this time?" He administered some sodium pentathol and the next thing I knew, I was groggily aware that the Doc was finishing stitching me up.

Doc bandaged me and explained the severity of my wound and what he had done to fix it. He said frankly he was astonished no nerves had been severed and advised rest until my appointment with him in a week.

I walked out into the hospital lobby—still wearing my blood-soaked clothes—and was surprised to see that a number of people had gathered. I.I.'s dad was there, and all of our girlfriends. One man said he'd heard that my arm had been severed. I later discovered that rumors about my accident had spread quickly. Within an hour it was reported that I had broken my arm in anywhere from fifteen to one hundred places, that the nerves in my arm had been severed so that it would always hang limp by my side, and even that my arm had been cut off. The common thread of the rumors was that I would never have the use my arm again.

Gil, Kirk, and my lifesaving partner were allowed on my porch later that night by Mother. I told Gil it wasn't his fault. I thanked Kirk and my ex-partner. Kirk said anyone would have done the same thing. I accepted that. I figured that Kirk had been in the right place at the right time, just as my ex-partner had been at Dillon's Beach.

Doc Robinson told me Kirk had saved my life and that a miracle saved my arm. The plate glass window of Gil's car sliced cleanly and severed the radial artery and two veins. A colored diagram of the inner arm clearly showed how the pencil-thick artery that pumped blood from the heart was wrapped around with nerves. The doctor could not explain how the artery was sliced without nicking a nerve. He had used over one hundred stitches to close the wound. Though the underside of my arm would be numb from elbow to wrist for a year or so, the numbness would eventually go away. Doc Robinson recommended I forget about a summer job, but said I could swim if I took it easy. I could play football in the fall, too.

So while everyone else worked I had Nancy to myself at the beach. In addition, Nancy told her family that I pushed her to the floor just before we hit the telephone pole and now they treated me royally. Nancy and I became bronzed from the sun.

******

I had told I.I. about my adoption, and sometimes I worried that he would spill the beans. Once he asked me if my real father might have been an Indian since I was so dark. I didn't think so, I said, because I was born in Canada, not India. But it bothered me. I couldn't ask Mom what nationality the man who raped her was. I knew if I.I. told his girlfriend about his suspicions, it would all be over between Nancy and me. Before the Morans left for home, Big Tom invited me down to the ranch for a weekend. My friends and their girlfriends could join Nancy and me and we could have the run of the place, Mr. Moran said.

Mother did not take my feelings for Nancy Moran seriously. She called our relationship "infatuation." But in other respects she acknowledged I was growing up. For the first time I was allowed to choose my school clothes. Charlie and I.I. and I took the Greyhound bus to San Francisco on a shopping trip. We each came back with a MacGregor windbreaker and Pendleton shirt, a pair of scotch grain shoes, and a $20 cashmere sweater. That same year I bought a double-breasted glen plaid suit and a maroon porkpie hat in imitation of jazz musicians I had seen pictured in *Downbeat* magazine.

I also started smoking cigarettes. We had taken our girls to the county fair and I had won a miniature beer mug at a basketball-shooting booth. I kept the mug in the small drawer of my nightstand along with a pack of cigarettes. I smoked at night out on my porch, stubbing out my smokes in the little mug. One afternoon I came home to find a large ashtray on my stand. Since I couldn't pretend I hadn't seen the ashtray, I asked Mother why she had put it there. Mother gave me a great surprise by saying, "If you're going to smoke, I don't want you putting the ashes in your drawer. This is an old house and I don't want you to burn it down." She told me this calmly as she dried her soapy hands on her apron, but she asked Dad to speak to me, which he reluctantly did. We sat together on the back stoop, looking out over the vegetable garden.

"You know, if you're serious about being an athlete, David, you shouldn't smoke. It plays havoc with your wind."

"Well, I'm not seriously smoking, Dad. You know, I'm just fooling around with cigarettes a little," I said lamely.

"Don't you think you're too young to even be playing around with smokes?" he asked. "Maybe you ought to wait until you're sixteen or so to experiment, or maybe until you graduate from high school."

I thought I remembered Jesse talking about his own smoking habit, and it seemed to me that he said he started when he was very young in Kansas. "When did you start smoking?" I asked.

Jesse was ever honest. "Well, I was fourteen myself. But that doesn't make it any better for you."

202

I thought that I had somehow won the argument and so I left the ash-tray on my nightstand. My friends were amazed at how cool my parents were, and Mom and Dad's popularity skyrocketed.

When registration for the draft began on August 30th, many local boys tried to beat it by joining the new Healdsburg National Guard unit. The guard was building a $100,000 armory at the golf course's north end where Fitch Mountain Road completed its loop down off the mountain.

Hilmer Finne returned from attending a Fred Waring workshop in Pennsylvania. Lefty Ristau of the Sebastopol hardball team outpitched Clarence Ruonavaara of the Healdsburg Prune Packers for the City League Championship. Clarence was the new high school baseball coach. He was a local boy who had served in the U.S. Navy during the war as a lieutenant. More important, he pitched for the University of California at Berkeley after he graduated from Healdsburg High and often wore his blue Cal block sweater with about twenty gold stripes on each arm. He was lanky and had a shock of dark hair that flopped down over one eye when he pitched with his three-quarter sidearm delivery. He was more serious than Coach Art, especially about baseball. Coach Clarence said things like, "Give it a ride, big guy," and "That's the ticket," when some-one got a base hit.

The Miller Fruit Company's dehydrator was destroyed by fire just after Mother completed her summer apple-packing stint there. The *Tribune* reported that a son of the Okie family who were still camping in the street was accused by Healdsburg police of immoral acts with an eleven-year-old boy. The police also announced that they would begin to crack down on trucks speeding through town. The *Tribune* was upset because three rob-beries of local stores had not been reported to the paper. The new police chief was blamed. The final band concert was held on the first Sunday afternoon in September.

High school opened on September 21st and I made the varsity football team as an end. I was also elected the junior class yell leader. The job was meant as a joke. My old girlfriend, Betty Hutchinson, was elected sopho-more class yell leader.

Our football team opened the season by beating Willits 41-0. It was soon evident that I was not going to play much because the first-string left end was going to be a star. The first-stringer was the center on the basket-ball team and made a tall target for the tailback's passes. Coach Art liked me because I seldom dropped a ball, but I had lost any speed I might once have possessed because of my damaged knees.

John Wayne and Henry Fonda appeared in *Fort Apache* at the Plaza Theatre. After the Western, a trailer was shown promoting "Midnight Burlesque," a live girlie show that was going to be presented the following weekend. The trailer was tawdry and the girls were so ugly that everyone at the Saturday afternoon matinee laughed at them. Predictably, the *Tribune* chastised the theatre owners for showing the trailer. The editor thought that presenting "Midnight Burlesque" was all right because "one could see it in San Francisco" and, after all, it was for "adults only." But they disapproved of showing the trailer following a regular movie because "youngsters were exposed to something entirely beyond their years." Nevertheless the paper carried a large advertisement for the show: "Big Time Burlesque as You Like It," featuring "Arlene: Burlesque's most beautiful thrill dancer, plus Lotus Wing, Hillary Dawn, Peggy Bond, and two 'great comedians.'" The ad said the title of the live show was "Hollywood Revels," and that it featured a "cast of sexty."

In the same *Tribune* issue, Senator Eastland of Mississippi said America ought to drop the atomic bomb on Russia if they wouldn't lift the Berlin blockade. Clipper Smith, the marathoner, bought the Sanitary Dairy and announced he would bottle the dairy's milk in "wax-coated cartons" for store sale. He added that he would be available for youth coaching duties.

Our football team bussed up the coast on a three-day trip to play Ferndale, a small farming town just south of Eureka. I'd never been further north than Willits—sixty-five miles away—on Highway 101. In fact, I always felt when I passed Squaw Rock (a Pomo landmark whose name the tourist industry had anglicized) between Cloverdale and Hopland, that I was heading for the outer limits of civilization. Cities to the south of Healdsburg were considered to be arbiters of fashion and sophistication, and towns to the north were considered backward. We thought the farther away from San Francisco you traveled, the more primitive the natives and settlements became.

Highway 101 in those days was a tortuous logging road between Willits and Eureka. Several lumber trucks were lost every week on its twists and turns and steep downhill grades. A truck would not be missed until it failed to reach its destination, and then the whole stretch of highway with its forested canyons would have to be searched, because the canyons swallowed up big rigs. Brake failure and dense fog usually accounted for these calamities. Huge redwood forests flanked the highway for miles and miles, and were so gigantic that even in bright sunshine our bus traveled as if on a winding, shadowed trail, its old engine laboring.

After climbing steadily through the redwoods for thirty or so miles, we reached what seemed to me then a vast, flat meadowland of farms. Ferndale lay here—off to the west of the highway toward the ocean. We pulled into the small, old high school yard where the Ferndale players met us. They took us home with them, by twos, to spend the night before the game with their families. The quarterback and I were paired up, and if we expected our host to show us the sights we were disappointed. He lived on a farm and Saturday was no different from any other day on the farm. The only way he was able to play football was by doing his chores before mid-morning. That meant getting up at 3:00 A.M. tomorrow, he said. When my teammate and I were awakened for breakfast in the morning, the whole family had been out for several hours working up an appetite.

The breakfast we were served in Ferndale was not like any breakfast we had ever eaten: a platter of fried eggs and another of home-fried potatoes, a whole loaf of toasted bread, sausage patties and slices of ham, juice, milk, and lots of coffee. The quarterback and I gorged ourselves, and when we left for the game we were stuffed.

We played on a lumpy, sloping cow pasture with chalked stripes on it. I was knocked silly the first time Coach Art put me in the game, and I never fully recovered. It was not usual for me to play unless we were way ahead or way behind, and I should have suspected something was wrong when the first-string end took himself out and Coach Art called me from off the bench. Coach Art never took his star out of the lineup because the star didn't like it, so the only time he came out of a game was when he took himself out to get a breather. I came into the game just as Ferndale prepared to punt. Jere Holbrook gathered in the ball and I ran downfield looking for someone to block. I picked out my target and threw a body block, stretching out my body and leaving my feet to catch him just above the knees. To my surprise, I bounced right off the Ferndale player's thighs. My whole right side went numb, and my head was whipped back so hard it felt disconnected. I felt as if I'd tried to block the iron statue of the World War I soldier that stood in the plaza. Luckily for me, the star end returned to the game at the end of the quarter. The game ended in a 6-6 tie, and they would have beaten us if they hadn't fumbled once or twice in critical situations.

Irving Shulman's novel, *The Amboy Dukes*, was published that fall. The Amboy Dukes of Shulman's book were a New York City street gang who fought and drank and screwed lots of girls and flouted authority; they called it, "getting their kicks." Their cockiness and rebelliousness appealed to a few of us, and we started to run around together. We traveled in Bobby

Frost's pickup, since Gil's car was still not operable, and "Sky" Richardson only occasionally joined us in his family's Cadillac. Bobby controlled the transportation and always had a little money, so he was our ceremonial leader. But it was Gil who was the real brains of our outfit. Gil was a slender, bowlegged boy with a broken nose that gave him a slightly pugnacious look. Gil questioned teachers on their statistics, their political beliefs, and on their moral assumptions. Even Mrs. Long was not immune to Gil's cross-examinations, though he admired her. Mrs. Long said, for example, that Shakespeare believed in God because he wrote in *Hamlet* that: "There is a divinity which shapes our ends, rough-hew them how we will." Gil pointed out that the character of Horatio made this statement, not Shakespeare. Gil also said that Hamlet's line, "'tis fair thought to lie between maids' legs" should not be deleted from Mrs. Long's discussion of the play because the line showed a facet of Hamlet's character that ought not to be neglected. Gil was often dispatched to the principal's office for insubordination and became celebrated for it. Emil, Charlie Morse, and I made up the rest of our group. In Healdsburg there were two small identical twins, the Giacomelli brothers, who later became jockeys. Because we stuck together so closely and dressed alike we became known as the Frostomelli gang.

The other high school gang was the Grantomellis, whose leaders were the Grant brothers—Powell and Billy. Billy I had known since the seventh grade, when Alexander Valley became a part of the elementary school district. Powell was transferred to Healdsburg from Hollywood when his mother found him too difficult to handle. The two gangs got their kicks in different ways. The Grantomelli gang were belligerents. We Frostomellis liked to be smooth and cool. The Grant gang went looking for "beefs," as fights were called. The Grant brothers' names became as well known as the James's or the Dalton's throughout Sonoma County. The dangerous members of the Grantomelli gang were "Foxtooth" and "Deutsch." Foxtooth and Deutsch enjoyed fighting and searched out boys with equal reputations in other cities to have a showdown with—much as oldtime gunfighters were said to have done. If Foxtooth and Deutsch couldn't find anyone they considered tough enough to fight with, they sometimes fought each other, and that seemed to satisfy them. Several years later, when Gil was attending the University of California at Berkeley, Foxtooth and Deutsch dropped in at Gil's fraternity house for a visit. While Gil and his fraternity brothers were at their classes, Foxtooth and Deutsch demolished the inside of the fraternity house. Gil returned to find them sitting on the stairs, bloody and disheveled. He asked them what had happened, thinking that they had perhaps surprised some would-be thieves. But Foxtooth and Deutsch said they merely became bored and so had fought each other to pass the time.

Other boys occasionally joined the Grantomellis on their nights out: "Tille," "Bubby," and others. There was "Tiger Pat" who would remove his shirt when drunk and shuffle and jab like a prizefighter; "Cash" Watson got his nickname because he was always broke; "Papa Jim" who Powell thought looked like a young Ernest Hemingway; and "Satchel Jack" because he usually refused to drink beer like everyone else and instead carried a fifth of gin and a bottle of grenadine to chase it in a small satchel on outings.

Our gangs finally merged because Gil and Powell became friends. I was relieved when our gangs merged (to become the Frantomellis) because I occasionally caught Foxtooth or Deutsch looking in my direction, as if I might be a suitable antagonist. Powell could hold Foxtooth and Deutsch in check. And, for some reason, they both respected Gil too. Though merged, the two gangs kept their separate identities: the Frostomellis and the Grantomellis.

Like the Amboy Dukes, the rest of us had nicknames. Because I was dark and had long arms, I was nicknamed "Monk."

Our house became a principal gathering place for my friends. This was not due to my popularity, but to Mom and Dad's. My friends sensed that Mother and Jesse were genuinely interested in them despite their backgrounds or their interests. Dad kidded them and Mother often invited them to lunch or to dinner as if they were part of our family.

Our home was graced that fall by the presence of Alice Zacharias, a special guest from India. Alice was a young Hindu nurse trained by my aunt Theo who now administered a mission hospital in Guntur. Alice came to America for further nurse's training. After visiting with our family to acclimate herself, she would go on to the East Coast. Her everyday garment was a flowing sari, and she further adorned herself with many dangling bangles, anklets, and necklaces. She even wore a large nose ring. Alice sported a red caste mark on her forehead and spoke the singsong English of Indians who have been taught at British institutions. She was not only a great curiosity, she was the most exotic human being my friends had ever seen. Alice was a beautiful person too. She had a dazzling smile, a calm demeanor, and was as interested in my friends as they were in her. She took a personal interest in each of them. It was amazing to see these mostly rough-edged boys stop by to walk in the backyard garden with Alice. Several of them corresponded with her for a while, and none of them forgot her.

Mother was by now feeling more at home in America. This didn't mean that she wholly approved of American democracy. British rule in India, of which she and Grandfather so heartily approved, was founded on a paternal benevolence toward the natives. She found America less than benevolent to its own poor native sons and daughters. Maybe this was why she took to my friends—most of them came from the lower economic scale, except for Gil and Sky Richardson and Bobby Frost. She probably sensed that their bravado came from trying to prove they were as good as anyone else. As Jesse had done for Okie children, Mother dispensed kindness and encouragement, not reproach or judgment, as cures for anger and impatience.

Mr. Gibbs was appointed chairman of the local Red Cross chapter, and he persuaded the board to hire Mother as a full-time executive secretary. I don't think Mr. Gibbs or the board anticipated how much influence Mother came to exert through her small office. She championed the outcasts: the poor, the immigrants, the drunks, and the abused women of Healdsburg—as well as transients and "vagrants." Vagrancy laws were still very much in effect, and if a person were found with insufficient change in his or her pockets ("no visible means of support"), he or she could be jailed, though they were more often simply escorted to the city limits and told to keep moving. Slowly Mother changed this practice. She would scrape up cash somehow—Mr. Meese became a prime source— with which to provide gas money, or meal money at the Iceberg Cafe, or grocery money at Gromo's grocery. She began to collect clothing and soon had a room full of castoff garments. Years later when I returned to Healdsburg like a homing pigeon for a day or two, Chris Feeney—our town drunk—would weep into a cadged glass of muscatel for love of my mother. Even Cocky Lodge often stopped by the Red Cross office—leaning his "wheel" carefully against the building—to talk with Mother. He was always "Earl" to her, and even though she could not understand his garbled speech she would put aside what she was doing to listen to him. Mother also became district president of PTA and traveled occasionally to Sacramento and Los Angeles. But our home life seemed unchanged. Jesse, Margaret, and I still returned at noon for a hot lunch, and dinners were still at 6:00 P.M. sharp.

Thirteen

M Y FOOTBALL SEASON was again cut short by my right knee's frailty. We beat the team that was to have been our toughest opponent and prepared to travel to Ukiah for a non-league game. Perhaps in celebration over the Calistoga victory, or perhaps in anticipation of an unimportant game, our star end went out drinking and fighting with the Grantomellis and was suspended from playing in the Ukiah game by Coach Art. The end must have been in a terrific fight, because word of it got around the school, and Art had no other option than to suspend him, though the coach probably breathed a sigh of relief that it was a non-league game.

So I found myself sitting in the prized seat next to Coach Art and directly behind Ralph on the way to Ukiah. The coach ran over plays with me and tried to calm me down. Ukiah was a much larger school than Healdsburg and had a big, strong team, so we were not expected to win. But Coach Art had inserted some fancy passing plays especially for the first-string end, and their proper execution now depended on me. We took the field in our black and gold road uniforms, and it was no comfort to me to notice that a larger-than-usual Healdsburg contingent had made the trip to watch the game.

My knee probably rescued me from the ignominy of a horrible performance, for I tore ligaments in it on the third play from scrimmage. I had twisted to make a block, my knee buckled, and I hobbled to the sidelines in great pain. The third-string end entered the game. I somehow finished out that football season, but the only other game I played in was against Tomales, the league doormat. When we were ahead of them by something like 45-0, our star end let Art put me into the game. I caught a long pass and found myself with only one Tomales defender between me and the end zone. I could not make a cut to get by him and he tackled me easily. And so another chance at glory eluded me.

In the fall of 1948 I was taking political science from Miss Dorothea Shanahan, my old grammar school teacher who had been promoted to the HHS faculty. As I have mentioned, Miss Shanahan was most effective on Wednesdays and Thursdays. I don't think she was a naturally ill-tempered woman, for on Wednesdays and Thursdays she displayed a wry, sarcastic sense of humor. But something caused her to be jumpy and curt on Mondays and Tuesdays, and on Fridays she always seemed preoccupied and short-tempered.

Though we only suspected Miss Shanahan was a drinker, we knew she smoked cigarettes. She was the only female teacher who smoked. Neither Mrs. Long nor Miss Destruel would have defiled their bodies with the devil weed. The men on the faculty congregated between classes in the boiler room to smoke their cigarettes. My friends and I often banged on the big metal boiler room door when teachers were in there. We shouted things like "Fire!" or "Police!" or "Open up. This is a raid!" or "Smoking on school grounds will cost you five demerits," before scattering. One of the smokers usually poked his head out of the door and glared about angrily. The boiler room was a part of the gymnasium and faced the tennis courts across a wide driveway.

Along the street, next to the tennis courts, students parked their cars, and it was in these cars that they smoked. Smoking within a block of the school was prohibited, and if a student was caught, it would cost him or her five demerits. James Vogt, the chemistry and physics teacher, had the job of policing the line of cars parked on the street. Mr. Vogt used many ruses to surprise students smoking in their cars. Sometimes he hid in the bushes near the tennis courts and then sprang out, notepad in hand, to write down students' names. But the students posted scouts who yelled, "Look out for the Little Colonel," forcing Mr. Vogt to break into a run while holding his glasses in place. When he arrived at the cars, nothing would be observable but smoke pouring out of rolled-down automobile windows—not a punishable offense.

Miss Shanahan hated Communists, which was fashionable and politically correct, of course. So we would surreptitiously fashion small paper airplanes in class, draw red stars on them, and set them sailing through the air in armadas from time to time. Miss Shanahan would angrily stride around the room swatting at them as if they were flies. Stomping them to death on the floor, she would order the culprits—if she could pick them out—to dispose of them in the wastebasket "where they belong."

None of us faulted Miss Shanahan for being against communism. Everybody was mad at the Russians for setting up the Berlin blockade, especially after we had bailed them out during the war (I knew all about that from reading "True Comics"). I, for one, was mad enough to fight them, especially since we had the bomb and they didn't. I thought President Truman should have ignored the blockade and sent a division of tanks through the Berlin corridor to clear it out. But I didn't have any faith in Harry Truman. I considered him uneducated and crude—not at all statesmanlike. I thought that presidents, like monarchs, should be above cursing. So when newspapers convinced me Thomas Dewey was a crime-fighter as New York's district attorney and would be equally tough on Communists, I organized the Dewey-for-President campaign at the high school. Campaign headquarters for both parties was Miss Shanahan's room, and I obtained Dewey/Warren posters, buttons, and bumper stickers from Santa Rosa.

I could not interest my friends in the election. Most of the Frantomellis dismissed both candidates as rich crooks and refused to participate.

The humiliating thing was not that Truman won, but that he carried Healdsburg High School too. The entire county including the city of Healdsburg went for Dewey, but high school students voted overwhelmingly for Truman.

The Armistice Day parade in 1948 was the biggest in Healdsburg's history. "Spectacular," the paper called it. "World Unity" was the theme of the parade, and people set up camp chairs and packing boxes to view it from sidewalks and rooftops. The parade started in mid-morning at the Legion Hall, marched past the Plaza and turned down Matheson toward the cemetery. The biggest float was entered by the Veterans of Foreign Wars, and it featured a seated "gray-whiskered Uncle Sam holding on his lap numerous children dressed in bright costumes of many lands. At the other end of the float was a white-gowned figure of peace with children of Communist countries kneeling at his feet. Around the base of the float were the words: 'Destroy Communism Through Education and Truth for World Unity.'" The *Tribune* noted that the Russian River Riders were "smartly attired" and that the Healdsburg High School band won no prizes for excellence.

Occupying front page space with the Armistice Day news was a headline that read: "Drinking by a 'Few' Teenagers Aired at Public Meeting." The public meeting was called in reaction to trouble at a teenage dance at the golf course clubhouse. Though no names were mentioned, I knew several Grantomellis had been involved. One parent demanded that a policeman be assigned to all future teenage dances, and several others urged police to jail young offenders and notify their parents. The editors called for police presence as "the honor system doesn't work." Two unnamed establishments were accused of selling liquor to minors.

I did not play in the alumni football game that year, which was won by the high school 19-12. At halftime an "unbreakable watch" was dropped by the Finley Frisch jewelry company from an airplane. Several ribbon streamers were attached to the watch so that "spectators could follow its downward flight." Mr. Frisch himself retrieved the watch at midfield and presented it to the referee who announced to the crowd that it was still ticking.

"Gobbler, the Thanksgiving Turkey," who had been exhibited in the window of the Healdsburg Music Store, was won by a man named Earl Rex. Earl had most accurately guessed the number of kernels of corn "Gobbler" ate in a forty-eight-hour period. Over 3,000 people guessed, but Earl won Gobbler with his estimate of 2,396 kernels.

Shortly before Christmas, I.I., Gil, Charlie, Emil, and I went to Lafayette as guests of the Morans. We took a bus to Oakland on a Friday and walked to the Catholic high school that Nancy attended. She drove us out to the Moran estate. All of the adult Morans had gone other places for the weekend, leaving their home to us—which impressed us as being terribly sophisticated. The Moran ranch was set even farther back into the hills than Sky Richardson's ranch was, and it was bigger by far than Bobby Frost's hop ranch. Although it was called a "ranch," it was really more of an estate of rolling hills and clumps of oaks with nothing else growing on it. The house, set on a prominent knoll, was a long, rambling ranch house that featured a sunken living room with a beamed ceiling and flagstone fireplace. The formal dining room and kitchen occupied the east end of the house, and a long hallway to the west led to an assortment of bedrooms and baths. The Moran's garage was almost the size of the house itself to accommodate their many automobiles. A swimming pool, tennis courts, and a stable adjoined the house. By the time we arrived, it was evening and too late for anything but a quick tour before we visitors were assigned private bedrooms. Saturday we rode horses—or tried to ride horses. Except for Gil and Emil it was the first time any of us had been on a horse. My friends and I looked down on horseback riding, considering it a pastime fit only for farm boys and drugstore cowboys like the Russian River Riders. It certainly was not something that big-city athletes would do. The girls rode circles around us on tiny English saddles. My horse finally bolted. It reared suddenly, turned abruptly, and headed back to the barn at a gallop. It was Nancy who galloped alongside me, spoke to the horse by name, and reduced its gait to a trot. I tried to thank her, but for an inexperienced rider, a trot is no time to try talking. My words came out in short explosions of sound as I banged up and down on the saddle. That was not the last time that a horse ran away with me, but it was certainly the most humiliating time. Nancy spoke soothingly to the horse and to me, but when I dismounted my carefully combed Wildroot-Cream-Oiled hair was hanging in my eyes and I could not walk without staggering. I only partially regained my composure on the tennis courts.

The Morans employed a cook and maid who lived separately on the estate. The cook prepared a sumptuous dinner for us that evening and then we all retired to the sunken living room. Nancy turned the lights down and someone built a fire. Someone else began to play records on the phonograph—a long, low console of bleached wood—and we murmured and necked and danced. Gil and Emil, who had been the best riders, were the best dancers too. Though not athletes, they possessed the skills that most impressed the girls. How could that be? Charlie and I.I. and I had studiously avoided the pastimes that we considered "typical." Typical activities were not cool. So, while Gil and Emil—whom we thought we had rescued from the uncool world—twirled their partners in the Moran living room, the rest of us shuffled around and around uncomfortably with our dates.

The next morning we took the bus home. On Monday we arrived at school with chapped lips, which we complained about to everyone who would listen.

The front page of the Christmas Shopping Edition of the Healdsburg *Tribune* was dominated by pictures of the big fire at the old Merryland building. While being remodeled into a "Rollarena," the "memory-laden" building burned to the ground in a spectacular blaze witnessed by hundreds who stood watching on the beach and passenger bridge. The paper noted that Merryland Auto Court was saved. Just before Christmas, the Pacific Telephone and Telegraph company proposed rate increases. Individual residence rates would be upped from $3.50 to $3.75 per month and four-party line service (which our family had) from $2.50 to $2.75. Rates to San Francisco, however, would remain at $.50, the company announced.

Kirk Kirkpatrick went to San Francisco for a meeting of Junior Statesmen, and the "Varieties of '48" were presented at the high school. A boys' quartet composed of Gil, Kirk, my ex-lifesaving partner, and my choir partner sang barbershop favorites, and Lucille Peterson sang a solo.

Basketball season began and I made the varsity as a reserve guard. In December, we lost narrowly to a couple of San Francisco teams. After playing against the two smooth city teams, the Willits "Loggers" came to town and played the second half in their bare feet. We won that game and one other before Christmas vacation.

On December 20th, most everyone tuned in KSRO radio in Santa Rosa to hear a "live" Dennis Day sing fifteen minutes of holiday songs, including "Johnny Appleseed" and "Clancy Lowered the Boom." Mom particularly liked Dennis Day on the Jack Benny show and thought him a nice, polite boy. The popular "Varieties of '48" was repeated, and church choirs (but not St. Paul's) caroled about town. The American Legion hosted a Christmas party for "800 youngsters" where Smith Robinson led community singing. The *Tribune* rated the year's top stories as (1) Truman's victory, (2) the Berlin airlift, and (3) the high cost of living. Stories receiving honorable mention were Ghandi's assassination, Babe Ruth's death, the founding of Israel, and Princess Elizabeth's baby, Charles.

At Christmas, I received from a Santa Rosa sporting goods store a pair of "kangaroo skin" baseball cleats that I coveted. I thought the soft, lightweight, exotic shoes would increase my speed. After exchanging presents, our whole family went to see *Gone With the Wind* at the Plaza Theatre. Mother admired the movie's costumes and settings, but thought Rhett Butler unscrupulous and Scarlett decadent. I figured Rhett for a coward and Ashley for a sissy. Scarlett was awfully flat-chested, I thought, and her prissy sister wasn't any bargain either.

Just before New Year's, the *Tribune* advertised that *The Outlaw* with Jane Russell, Jack Buetel, and Walter Huston would be shown for two days only. My friends and I knew about the movie's scandalous scenes; the picture of Jane Russell in a peasant blouse was hot stuff. We just hoped *The Outlaw* wouldn't be as disappointing as *Duel in the Sun* had been. *Duel in the Sun* was just a lot of sweating and panting and French-kissing between Gregory Peck and Jennifer Jones. We hoped *The Outlaw* would show Jane Russell and Jack Buetel "going all the way," as the ads hinted the movie would.

But *The Outlaw* was just as disappointing as *Duel in the Sun*. When I was making Westerns in Hollywood, I picked up my script at the studio where the film or TV show was going to be shot. I used to hurry out to Universal, or Paramount, or Four Star, or Columbia and skim the script in my car, looking for some meaty dialogue—some scene with real emotions. But the few Westerns that tried to break out of the accepted formula were embarrassingly bad like *The Outlaw* or *Duel in the Sun,* or expensive failures like *Heaven's Gate*. Though my parts were usually more interesting because I played villains, not heroes, Western stories still had predictable

214

scripts. No writer has successfully written modern emotions for Western characters. And yet even I have retained at least part of the Western's myth of romantic love: the myth that the only woman you could truly love was the unattainable one.

After Christmas, my family bought a better car. Ralph, the custodian/bus driver/junior varsity coach, purchased a new automobile and Jesse, who knew Ralph because they drove school busses together, bought Ralph's old car. My family kept Ralph's old Plymouth until after Jesse's death, and Mother swore by Plymouths the rest of her life. She justified her loyalty by saying most taxicabs were Plymouths.

I was excited over the Plymouth's purchase. On my fifteenth birthday I would be eligible for a learner's permit, and I was eagerly looking forward to driving. Jesse was not enthusiastic about it. A well-known local boy had recently wrecked his parents' car with a load of his friends on board, and the memory of my injury while riding with Gil did little to persuade Jesse to trust me with the family's only mode of transportation.

Early in January, Herman Nock's hay and salt warehouse burned to the ground as 300 spectators watched. The fire was blamed on "tramps" that the *Tribune* said "often took refuge in the hay stored there." "Television in Healdsburg Assured" was a headline the following week. The accompanying story said that Al Barbieri of "Barbieri's Home Furnishings" had attended a television demonstration at the Occidental Hotel in Santa Rosa. A hockey game was shown, and Al was quoted as saying that "the puck was at all times visible."

Our varsity basketball team lost to Balboa High of San Francisco. Keith Walker, whom the paper had nicknamed "The Blond Bomber," scored 15 points. The *Tribune* said the game was played at home in the "Prune Palace." We believed it was because of dumb nicknames like "The Blond Bomber" and "The Prune Palace" that Healdsburg got the reputation of being a hick town.

Another teenage club dance was held at the golf course clubhouse and there was no trouble. The evening's peace was generally ascribed to the fact that a police officer was on duty to "help park cars." My sister was elected president of the Ta-Wan-Ka group of Camp Fire Girls. The girls received bolero jackets at a special hut meeting, and Margaret announced plans to include sewing and folk dancing in the group's activities.

My aunt Theo arrived on leave from India. Aunt Theo always brought real Indian curry powder with her, and pappadums and green mango chutney. She arrived with presents too, like *sari* material and glass bangalores.

Aunt Theo said Grandfather was slowly adjusting to Indian independence, and that Alice Zacharias was an honor student. While she was with us, she spoke to several groups. The *Tribune* carried a small item that read: "Theodora Neudoerffer, from India, gave a picture of her work for the Business and Professional Women's Club last Tuesday." I went to see *Man-Eater of Kumaon* after my aunt left. The movie starred Wendell Corey as a government hunter trailing a man-eating tiger in India. The job looked terrific. Wendell Corey spent his time reading and drinking and ordering servants around when he wasn't off hunting man-eaters.

After an undefeated league season, the varsity basketball team was upset by Calistoga, 29-24. Everyone attributed our defeat to the fact that the Blond Bomber had been held to eight points.

The Prune Palace always hosted several novelty basketball games during the winter. The Kiwanis Club sponsored a "blackout" game that required both teams to wear fluorescent jerseys. The ball, hoop, and foul lines were also luminous. Sometimes a player hid the ball under his jersey and ran to the opposing net unobserved while two teammates were positioning themselves under the net. One of the teammates would remove his jersey and hold the other teammate on his shoulders so that one gigantic player appeared to be standing under the basket. When the player with the hidden ball arrived downcourt, the ball seemingly appeared out of nowhere, leaped by itself high above the giant's jersey, and dropped through the net. At blackout basketball games, opportunistic young boys sat close to good-looking girls and tried to "cop feels" during the blackout.

The Colored Ghosts, a sort of traveling minor league Harlem Globetrotters, used to come to town too. The local 20-30 Club always sponsored these games, and the club's members always volunteered to be humiliated by the Ghosts. The *Tribune* always reported that the local players had been "good sports" about being humiliated, though it wasn't true. The 20-30 Club players always played very hard and seriously because their girlfriends and wives were in the stands watching them. This made their confusion funnier. They got angry, and when they did that a Colored Ghost calmed them down, handed them the ball, and escorted them downcourt for a free shot as you would a child. This made the 20-30 Club players even angrier and clumsier than they were before and the crowd would roar. The *Tribune* never reported the scores of these games.

Donkey Basketball—complete with rubber donkey shoes—was a wintertime staple at the gym as well. In these games, the Kiwanis Club always played the Rotary Club. But the biggest winter attraction at the gym was the annual high school boxing show, and I decided to make a boxing comeback for it.

The afternoon boxing class was scheduled just before basketball practice. A large room in the gym had been cleared out for the class, and with a big ring in the center of the room there was not much area left over. The boxing coach taught agriculture classes and liked hardworking rural boys. He recruited them for the boxing class. A grin would cross the coach's face when a big recruit dropped one of the school's "big wheels." While two boxers fought, the rest of the class crowded around the ring, standing tightly bunched together. Everyone perspired because the room was close and packed with bodies. The high school coach was not as instructive as was Al Barbieri at the boys' club. He let boys "just go at it." And he had favorites: if one of his favorites was losing, the coach sometimes climbed into the ring himself to demonstrate why he was losing. He would push aside the losing boy and say something like, "Here, see, you are dropping your left hand when you throw your right hand, and he's hitting you with his right over your guard. You've got to do it this way." Then the coach would proceed to jab and follow up with two or three hard rights to the winning boy's headgear. This would make the winning boy just dizzy enough so that his opponent could often finish the job. By "finish the job" I do not mean by knockout, of course, or even by a knockdown. Those were rare. But given the fact that we fought the usual three one-minute rounds with a minute in between each round, the coach's favorite often prevailed.

For some reason I boxed left-handed. Perhaps I thought that leading with my right hand would give my jab more steam, but the coach observed this weakness right away. He called over a boy named Dick Gardella and told him to put on headgear and the standard fifteen-ounce gloves. Dick did not look like the farm boy he was. He was shorter than I, had the reputation of being an intellectual, and normally wore a pair of thick glasses. He did look more powerful when he took off his shirt, though.

When Dick squared off against me I could hardly believe my good luck. He stood up straight, squinting hard at me, and held his gloves near his waist and wide apart. I circled to the right and Dick shuffled heavily in my wake. His face presented a wide-open target, and he didn't seem to be focusing on me. Since he couldn't get me in his sights, I began jabbing him hard as I circled, feeling him out. I should have been warned by the fact that he just kept shuffling after me and squinting at me as I popped his face with my right-hand jab.

By the opening of the second round, I felt confident. I resumed my circling and jabbing, when without warning, Dick lashed out with his first punch—a left—that hit me on the forehead and set me back on my heels. He followed with a huge right that caught me on the jaw and sent me sprawling. Everything whirled and now I could not focus or get my bearings and I flopped about on the canvas like a fish out of water. The coach counted to ten over me. Dick was gracious in victory, suggesting that his knockout was a fluke. No one could remember anyone ever being knocked out with fifteen-ounce gloves—which resembled pillows—so the rest of the class seemed to think my knockout was a fluke too. I decided not to push my luck any further and quit the boxing class that very same day.

It rained heavily during the winter of '49. Gil and I used to drive around the mountain in his newly repaired car and carve notches in the wooden steps that led down to the now flooded beach at Del Rio. We sat in his car in the rain and watched the brown river sweep small trees and debris downriver while waxing philosophical about our futures. When we did not go flood watching, we sat in a small cottage behind Gil's house and listened to jazz on an Oakland radio station—"where the elite meet to beat feet," the disc jockey said.

I regained my third trombone chair in the band after abandoning boxing class and journeyed with forty-five other students to Hopland for a concert at the little high school there. In Hopland, Tiger Pat, who was our drummer, launched into an impromptu, improvised, extended drum solo during our performance of Duke Ellington's "Caravan" overture. Mr. Finne got very red in the face and clicked his baton frantically on his music stand, but to no avail. There was very little he could have done anyway since he had no replacement on drums for Tiger Pat. Poor Mr. Finne had not wanted to add "Caravan" to the orchestra's repertoire. He included it as a sop to the jazz fans in the band who were quite numerous. Four of them had formed a small jazz combo called the "Bebop Boys." The Bebop Boys sometimes played at informal school dances, and other musicians could sit in on their sessions just as we'd heard the real pros did.

Gil was perhaps the least effective member of the combo. Being more cerebral than the other musicians, he was attracted to the new atonal bebop with which Miles Davis and other trumpeters were experimenting. Bebop, though, did not make good dancing music, and boys and girls would mill around restlessly during Gil's solos. In fact, not many Healdsburgians took to jazz. The Healdsburg Music Store refused to carry jazz records because the owner thought they were suggestive and not real music anyway. So when we wanted to buy a new recording, we had to hitchhike to a music store in Santa Rosa.

Mother and Dad did not object to my playing jazz records on my porch, but they disapproved of our Frantomelli escapades. These escapades were confined to Friday and Saturday nights because most of us weren't allowed to go out during the week. We drank beer and smoked and crashed dances, but we never did much damage.

We called our meeting spot the "La Granty Brew Pits"—after the La Brea Tar Pits. Faith Grant had taken her boys to see the black bogs in Los Angeles once, and it amused Powell and Billy to name our drinking spot after them. The Brew Pits were actually the abandoned remains of a gravel dredging operation, much smaller than Basalt's, that Bill and Powell's father, Del, had halfheartedly operated on the banks of Dry Creek.

The pits were located about a mile west of Healdsburg, under the Dry Creek bridge. Since they lay outside the city limits, and since Del still owned the property, they were technically outside local law enforcement limits. There wasn't much to the pits: a large, concrete slab about the size of a tennis court, an abandoned tin shed, and further down the bank some rusted dredging equipment. In nice weather the sandy soil among the rusting old hulks was a good and private place to make out with a girl. Girls, however, seldom visited the pits. The Brew Pits were strictly for Frantomelli use. Since the Grantomellis were poorer than the Frostomellis, they often resorted to creative means when procuring beer to drink at the pits. For example, Powell discovered that the railroad station had stacks of empty beer bottles in cases on the platform. He would buy one beer, dust off the empty bottles in the cases, pour a little fresh beer over them, and have Foxtooth and Deutsch turn in the cases at rural grocery stores for the deposits on the bottles. That trick worked pretty well.

I generally bought the Frostomelli beer supply with my altered DeMolay card. Bobby Frost and I usually went to the store after everyone chipped in their money. We parked down the street from Flossi's grocery at the north edge of town. I'd make sure no police were watching the place before I went inside. Mr. Flossi, a very old man, had a niece a little older than I who helped him in his store. The family lived in back of the store, and a bell was situated so it tinkled whenever someone entered. Mr. Flossi came from the back of the house, and we negotiated as if I had never been in the store before.

"Give me a case of Grace Brothers beer, please."

"You no twenty-one."

"Of course I am, Mr. Flossi. You've served me before. Here's my ID."

"This ID no good. You no twenty-one."

"Sure it is. It's a DeMolay ID, and DeMolays never lie. Look, here's my birth date. I'm twenty-one."

Mr. Flossi would then summon his niece. "Look here (showing her my ID). He no twenty-one. Right?"

"You're right, Uncle Gino, he's not twenty-one. His ID is a fake. Don't sell him any beer."

"This is absurd. If you don't want to sell me any beer I'll take my business elsewhere," I would start to leave.

"Wait a minute, wait a minute. OK, I sell it to you this time. But no more. I still no think you twenty-one."

I would pay up, collect our case of beer, and depart quickly. Sometimes I could hear, as I left, Mr. Flossi's niece berating him for selling me the beer.

When nobody had any money, we just cruised around town looking for an opportunity—and sometimes we got lucky. One time we discovered a beer distributor's truck parked in his driveway with a whole load of beer on it. The distributor's house was on the outskirts of town where there were no street lights so we parked down the block, took off our shoes and formed a beer case brigade. We passed cases quickly until we had Billy Grant's car and Bobby's pickup full. We cached close to thirty cases far out on Dry Creek Road in brush near the creek. Then we went home fast so nobody would suspect us. The next morning the distributor discovered the theft. The police questioned Powell and Bobby but couldn't prove anything. The cache didn't last long because too many boys knew about it.

Usually our two groups met at the pits about 8:00 P.M. on a Friday or Saturday evening. We parked our cars and pickups around the concrete slab, leaving room to build a fire. As the weather improved, we took the seats out of the cars and trucks, placed them around the fire, and sat around drinking and planning what we were going to do.

We drank a local brew, Grace Brothers beer, out of red cans with a little fuzzy green figure on them representing "Happy Hops." Happy Hops looked like a miniature "Jolly Green Giant." Eventually we had a huge pile of G.B. beer cans at the pits. We arranged them in a big pyramid on the concrete slab next to the creek, and the pyramid became the Brew Pits' sign. You could see it from the country road and the bridge as you drove by. Then Powell Grant discovered a carved wooden head buried on their ranch and, figuring it was an old Pomo Indian totem, we put it on top of the pyramid.

At around 9:00 P.M. our groups went separate ways. The Grantomellis often left in their cars to look for a beef in another city. We Frostomellis generally found a dance somewhere. Most often we drove to one of the dance halls on the outskirts of Santa Rosa, and sometimes in desperation, we even went to the Fulton or Windsor grange to hear what we called "shit-kicking" music. The Windsor Grange dances always featured the Johnson family, whose members each played an instrument. The father played fiddle, an older brother played saxophone, the mother played cornet, and a son who was my classmate played drums. The bass drum had a light in it that blinked on and off to reveal a pastoral scene painted on the drumhead. The Johnson family played a lot of waltzes and polkas. They were terrible.

Gil and Charlie and Emil and I traveled in Bobby's pickup. Most weekend nights we eventually wound up at the Russian River Cafe at the south end of town, near the passenger bridge. The jukebox was filled with old jazz records and we stopped in for hamburgers before going home. The owner brought down his own old recordings: Bix Beiderbecke, Billie Holliday, Charlie Ventura, Vido Musso. We listened and argued who was the best. The Russian River Cafe closed after the new all-night diner at the truck stop opened.

It was inevitable that we finally got into trouble, and it happened because Bobby needed a new front seat for his pickup. Bobby's front seat was worn out from everyone's sitting on it and dancing on it at the pits so that the springs poked out of the fabric. There was a small junkyard behind a gas station on West Street, and one Saturday night we decided to try to find a replacement there for Bobby's front seat. The station was closed and dark. We drew straws to see who would attempt to find a seat, and I lost. I sneaked through a drizzle down a slough behind the junkyard and poked through cars and stacked tires and junk until I found a fairly new seat I thought would fit the pickup. I hoisted the seat on my shoulder and went down the bank into the slough and waded to where the rest of the gang waited.

Flushed with success, we decided Bobby could use new hubcaps too. But this time the gas station owner—who must have been sleeping in the back of the station—woke up and came out after us, pulling up his pants and yelling. Bobby, Gil, Charlie, and Emil got back to the pickup and took off, but I was cornered by the owner. I stuck to the shadows while he told me to "stay right where you are. I'm going to call the cops." Then, when he went to the phone, I ran for home. I just got into bed when my companions woke Mom and Dad by knocking on the door. They told me they went back to the junkyard looking for me and the police caught them. Now we all had to go to the police station with our parents to appear before Judge Quinn. I managed to convince Mom and Dad that we really didn't think we were stealing anything but junk. The stuff looked like it was waiting to be scrapped, not sold. Judge Quinn, when we appeared before him the next afternoon, let us off with a lecture and three months' probation. We didn't take the probation the way it was intended. Like the Amboy Dukes we now had "records," and we reported monthly to an old desk-bound policeman. We usually reported to the police station on a Saturday afternoon with a tarpaulin covering the beer we'd just bought at Flossi's market.

The Federated Church Youth Group polled 263 Healdsburg high school students about their church attendance. Some 114 said they went "now and then," 94 reported they went "regularly," and 55 said they "never went." Among reasons given for attendance or nonattendance, 52 said they were often "too busy," 44 said they "never got started going," 20 said they were "not interested," 13 said their "friends didn't go," 10 said they "didn't understand church," 5 said they "didn't believe in God," 4 said their "friends would criticize them if they went," and 2 said "church was only for old people."

Our varsity basketball team won the school's fourth title in as many years by tying for the league championship. Baseball practice followed, and I was listed among prospective outfielders by the *Tribune*. The boxing show at the high school drew a capacity crowd, and the new Healdsburg Camera Shop announced "Oscar the Mechanical Man" from Berkeley would entertain visitors on the day the shop opened. The announcement said that Oscar the Mechanical Man could "stay in one position for a full ten minutes."

In March Nancy Moran asked me if I would escort her to her school's prom at the Oakland's Claremont Hotel in April. I agreed, but I was very nervous. The only suit I owned was my double-breasted glen plaid that I wore to jazz concerts. The only ties I possessed were bright knit ties with matching suspenders. My dress shoes were brown suede, and I still did not dance very well. The first thing I decided to do was get a haircut. The one barber in town that we patronized cut our hair the way we wanted it: short on top—almost a crew cut—but very long on the sides, and we swept the sides back into a duck's tail. We then ran a comb edge straight down the back of our heads, making a deep cleft there.

I persuaded the barber, Mr. Cherry, to cut off the sides to match the top so everything would be evened up and I wouldn't look like a *pachuco* at Nancy's dance. I'd radically altered my hairstyle since I had been to the Moran estate. If she saw me with my D.A., as we called the cut, I knew she would faint and Big Tom would throw me out of the house. It wasn't easy persuading Mr. Cherry to trim the sides of my head because he took great pride in his duck's ass cuts. But he did manage the job. I picked out a brown belt and a dark, muted tie at Rosenberg's to go with my brown glen plaid suit. Mom and Dad said they would drive me down, spend Saturday night with old friends from India who now lived nearby, and pick me up on Sunday morning. Jesse and Mother were as excited about the weekend as I was; it would be their first long trip in the new Plymouth, and they were planning a hike up Mt. Diablo.

Jesse would not have to give me driving lessons for a couple of days, either. I pestered him for lessons every weekend and made him very nervous by speeding and cutting corners when I could see there was no one coming from the other direction. Jesse would yell, "Watch out! Watch your speed!" and then become embarrassed because he'd gotten flustered. He would never instruct me in town but took me far out near the Frost ranch where there were long straight stretches of road with little traffic. Even then he got awfully jumpy. I had mastered the rudiments of driving, but had never driven in traffic or tried to park a car.

When Saturday arrived we went to San Rafael and took the ferry from a landing near San Quentin across the bay to Richmond. We drove through the spring-green East Bay hills, and when we pulled into the Moran's circular driveway our Plymouth, of which we were so proud, looked old and small beside Mr. Moran's stable of cars. The Moran family welcomed me warmly and made sure I had a comfortable room. Big Tom was in an expansive mood and asked Nancy and me which car we wanted to use for our date. I thought Nancy would do the driving, so I kept quiet. But Nancy didn't hesitate. "May we take the Cadillac, Daddy?" she asked.

"I don't see why not," Big Tom said grinning. He added more solemnly, "We all know what a fine young man David is." With that he clapped me on my back and slapped the Cadillac keys in my palm.

Dinner was in the formal dining room. All of the clan were there except for the oldest daughter, who'd recently gotten married and was building a home just over the first ridge. Most of the dinner conversation centered around everyone's plans for the evening. Tom Jr. was off to the theater in San Francisco, though he was without the promised tickets for himself and his date. Mr. Moran handed Tom a few bills and suggested he "grease a few palms." Neil, the youngest son, was vague about his plans. I gathered the family worried about Neil, for he was admonished several times to "be careful, whatever you do." Nancy and I dressed for the dance after dinner.

VARSITY

The football Greyhounds.
I am in the middle of the
second row from the top.
Jere Holbrook is on my left.
Coach Art is on bottom right.

Keith Walker
FORWARD

David
Manley
GUARD

N.B.L.
SECT. II
CO-CHAMPS

Charles
Morse
GUARD

Varsity basketball

Ira Anthony
GUARD

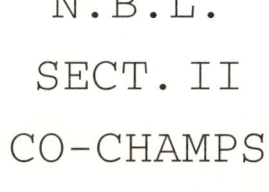

John
Tillis
FORWARD

Note my shadow plaid Pendleton shirt,
unwashed Levis, shiny Price shoes

My first theatrical photo at eighteen

When she finally made her entrance in her formal gown, everyone whistled. She was really something in a green dress to match her eyes and gold accessories. I'd bought an orchid corsage that Mother had gently cradled in her lap during our trip. Everyone applauded the corsage, though the orchid didn't match the dress very well.

The whole family hollered at us from the back door to have a good time. We walked to the garage and when Nancy stood by the Caddy's passenger door, I knew that I was going to have to drive. I got behind the wheel and confided to her that I'd never driven a Cadillac. She told me how to start it and shift it. Though I didn't have any major problems, I was very nervous driving through neon-lit Oakland.

It wasn't Nancy's fault that the dance was a disaster. She did her best to keep my spirits up, but I could tell that I looked like a hillbilly to the slick, sophisticated boys in their tuxedos and dinner jackets.

They stared at me curiously, whispering, and chuckling among themselves. I couldn't dance well, and when other boys cut in—which was often—I was left to stand alone on the sidelines feeling even more conspicuous. The chandeliered ballroom was immense and ornamented with glittering decorations that far outshone the crepe paper that was common at Healdsburg dances. And the band at Nancy's prom must have consisted of at least fifty musicians, while at Healdsburg High we generally employed the same ten-piece band for every dance.

The band at the Claremont played syrupy arrangements of popular songs; the reed section tooted and peeped without any muscle or drive. Whenever Nancy introduced me to another couple, they shook my hand and then ignored me while exchanging inside jokes and gossip about other wealthy friends. "Where are you from again?" they would ask me.

The next morning Mom and Dad arrived while we were finishing breakfast. They sat alone in the sunken living room, Mom holding her purse and Dad leaning forward uncomfortably with his old hat in his hands. They sat there looking around the room, while we all talked gaily at the breakfast table. I felt somewhat redeemed after the dance fiasco because Mr. Moran mentioned my heroism during the car wreck.

I glanced at my parents sitting in the living room. They looked very shabby and small to me amid all this splendor. For an instant I was ashamed of them. Then, just as quickly, I was ashamed of myself.

As we drove away, waving at the Morans, a carload of boys drove up and piled out of their convertible. They wore tennis outfits and I guessed they had come to play tennis with Nancy. I was reading *The Great Gatsby* and had a fleeting thought that the East Bay crowd were as shallow as Fitzgerald's East Egg characters. I sat silent on our way home—looking out the window as Mom and Dad talked of their visit and their shared memories of India. I wondered how they could talk of the time they were invited to dine with the maharajah of Jaipur and yet still seem so out of place in the Morans' living room.

Fourteen

I HAD BECOME A PRETTY GOOD BASEBALL PLAYER. With the Blond Bomber pitching, the varsity won its first couple of games.

The first "serve yourself" gas station was being built a half-mile north of Healdsburg, and a city sewer bond was finally passed by a margin of 5-1. A smoker being planned at the Legion Hall was billed as "an evening of fun at a men's event." It would benefit band concerts and other summer events. Emil's girlfriend's father bought the Brown-Wolfe drugstore and the family was moving to Healdsburg because they wanted out of San Francisco. None of us could understand that.

A local boy won an appointment to the Merchant Marine Cadet School in Mississippi. The last two years of his school would be at King's Point, New York, where he would be commissioned. The boy qualified for the academy because of his high scores in a nationwide competition and I went to talk to him. I wanted to find out what I ought to study my senior year if I wanted to try to qualify for the maritime academy. The thought of becoming a merchant marine officer appealed to me. I visualized myself as a tough, unshaven third mate on a tramp steamer. We would visit regularly at infamous ports like Marseilles and Casablanca. I would walk down the gangplank of our rust-streaked ship in a dense fog and sit in a smoky cafe— waiting for a girl who looked like Rita Hayworth to walk through the door.

The boy who had won the appointment brought me back to reality. I needed to know the rudiments of spherical trigonometry, so I'd have to ask for special instruction in fourth-year mathematics. I'd never heard of spherical trigonometry, and Jesse claimed ignorance of it. In any case I knew I would have to study hard because I was just barely passing third-year math.

An unusually early spring followed the heavy rains of winter. One of Mother's great pleasures was wildflowers. She loved Sunday afternoon drives to view the purple lupines that carpeted entire hillsides in Alexander Valley. She packed a picnic lunch on Saturday night so no time would be wasted on Sunday. After church we would drive out into the country and hike a little before settling on a spot to spread a rug in a field full of flowers. It was easy to find unfenced fields then—fields with gentle slopes and with a creek nearby.

Tippy would be unleashed so he could run to his heart's content. After lunch, Jesse would tilt his felt hat over his face and snooze. Mother read or took out her knitting, and Margaret and I chased Tippy and threw sticks for him to fetch. Margaret was now almost thirteen, though she was four years behind me in school. A delicate, very pretty, blonde-haired, blue-eyed girl, she was so shy that we seldom talked much except on those outings. She had dropped "Peggy" and now wanted to be called "Marge."

I was promoted to the regular left fielder's spot on the varsity and we beat Ukiah twice on one Saturday. The *Tribune* noted that "except for Dave Manley's three-run triple, the Healdsburg batsmen ingloriously divided eight base hits."

The new chiropractor in town joined the Knights of Pythias and somehow convinced Mother that he could cure my knees without surgery. It wasn't true. My knees did not pop out of joint when I injured them, the ligaments kept tearing. But I began to take weekly chiropractic treatments. They consisted of manipulation, during which I thought my legs were being broken. This was followed by treatments with hot pads, and other pads that pulled and tugged at my knees through some sort of electrical current. The chiropractic office was on the second floor, and when I left I could barely negotiate the steps, my knees were so wobbly. The chiropractor said this meant they were improving.

The high school did not have a training room. The best Coach Art could do was get me out of an afternoon class so that I could put medicated salve on my knees and bake them under a heat lamp. This never seemed to do much good, but I used the heat lamp treatment often because Coach Art always signed a slip for me to get out of an afternoon science class whenever I said I wanted to use the lamp. One afternoon I skipped my weekly chiropractic appointment—for which the baseball coach excused me from practice—and went swimming instead. Gil and Bobby and I went out to Dry Creek near the brew pits, figuring no one would spot us there. The creek was full from the rains and it was a warm afternoon. We dove off the clay banks and lay around in the sun. Somehow, Coach Clarence found out about it, and he suspended me for a game. Art might have overlooked a minor infraction like swimming, but Coach Clarence was serious. He had been a naval lieutenant, and duty was duty. The team traveled without me to Cloverdale and was beaten. And when Cloverdale traveled to our ballpark the next week I was not in the starting lineup. But The *Tribune* said, "in desperation, Coach Ruonavaara called on pinch hitter Dave Manley in the bottom of the seventh inning, who obligingly blasted out a three-run hit."

For the first time since he became the permanent lay reader at St. Paul's, Mr. Kent was asked to conduct the Easter Sunrise Service at Lytton Home. American Legionnaires lined up a "galaxy of stars" for their upcoming smoker. "Breakfast in Hollywood," a national radio program, selected Smith Robinson as its "good neighbor of the day" and planned to present him with a "good neighbor's orchid" on the show. In figures disclosed by the state, Sonoma County topped California counties in wine production by processing 8,064,000 gallons, 25% of the state's output. A representative from the California Physicians Service spoke to the Kiwanis Club on "Socialized Medicine." He said that thanks to Blue Cross, other insurance companies, the California Physicians Service, and county hospitals, the general public had adequate hospital and medical services without going into complete socialized medicine.

The county taxpayers' association griped loudly about aid to the aged. They also pointed out that aid to the needy went up in February of 1949 to $71.20 per month compared to $55.06 in February of 1948. Mother considered aid to the needy a job for churches, civic groups, and the Red Cross. She had an unshakable faith in the goodness of people, although the Anderson case had rattled her faith. Mother believed that ignorance, rather than greed, caused people to be miserly, and that education could overcome most of society's problems. Jesse never argued with her, but occasionally wondered aloud how people would feel about government assistance if another depression came.

In the meantime, our varsity baseball team won six more games in a row before losing to Eureka. The Eureka team bussed down the coast and slept overnight in our gymnasium. Smitty Robinson was not flown south to appear on "Breakfast in Hollywood" as our community had eagerly expected. Instead, the producers sent him an orchid and the program host read a letter from his "fans." The high school newspaper, The *Red 'n' Black*, printed a composite profile of the ideal freshman, sophomore, junior, and senior boy and girl. Though Jere won most of the body parts, I was the junior nose. The girl's composite did not include things like breasts, legs, or derriere, but did include "personality." My friends and I thought the girl's composite was worthless. Lonnie's Coffee Shop opened at the south end of town next to the new Chevron truck stop. The Russian River Cafe went out of business soon after.

Mother was thanked for her extra work during the spring Red Cross campaign that collected $3,870. But Mother was feeling let down. Her favorite actress had failed her. In a fit of passion, the beautiful Ingrid Bergman had left her family and fled to the arms of the gnomelike Roberto Rosselini. Ingrid's infidelity devastated Mother, who like most people confused movie stars with the characters they played.

Our varsity baseball team played the tiny town of Tomales Bay, where the diamond sloped so sharply toward the ocean that from left field I could see only the batter's head. Once, running far downhill to catch a long fly ball, I ran completely out of sight and clambered back upslope with the ball in my upraised glove. The umpire called the hitter out, but I could just as easily have chased the ball all the way down to the beach and returned holding it aloft without anyone questioning whether I had caught it or not. The *Tribune* reported of that game that "Fly-chaser Dave Manley came through with a run-scoring single in the sixth to score the winning run." It was all to no avail, however, as Geyserville beat us in our final game, 2-1, to win the league championship. The tennis team with Stan Smith playing first singles did win the championship that spring.

Dad occasionally wandered over to the ballpark when we played an afternoon home game. He would sit by himself in the sunny left field bleachers and bask in the warmth of a spring afternoon for a couple of innings. Of the sports I played, excepting maybe tennis, Jesse liked baseball the best. He told me once that he'd played third base himself when he was young, until a ball had taken a bad hop on him and shattered his glasses, cutting him over the eye. Baseball was the only sport he helped me with uncomplainingly. We went out into the alley and, using the garage door as a backstop, I pitched to him from the fringe of the wooded lot. We played catch in the late afternoon before dinner when the sunlight sifted through the grove. Dad caught my fastballs with an old outfielder's glove because we hadn't a catcher's mitt. When he came to my games unannounced he never stayed long. I would look in from left field and he would be there with his jacket off and his hat tilted back on his head.

We had regular fans who attended every game and even some practices. They came to high school, softball, city league, and Junior Legion hardball games. Most of them were old-timers who'd been around since the ballpark was built, and most of them had played baseball there when they were young.

I didn't start out to run for student body president because it was a foregone conclusion that Jere Holbrook would run unopposed. There wasn't a boy in school who could challenge Jere's popularity. However, Jere was struck down by spinal meningitis just after Easter, and no one knew whether Jere would fully recover. So I ran. The biggest factor working against my election was my Frantomelli membership. Jere supported my opponent, a transfer student, and through his flying club contacts arranged for campaign leaflets to be dropped from a plane onto the football field during lunch hour. Most of the leaflets blew off the schoolgrounds, but Deutsch and Foxtooth restrained students from picking up those few that were on target. My opponent then attempted to make a speech from the gymnasium roof, but someone sabotaged the microphone cables. I got blamed for these strong-arm tactics, and it didn't help that I wouldn't condemn my friends.

Charlie ran for vice-president with me. We had placed big banners reading "VOTE FOR MONK AND CHUCK" in all the hallways, but even Charlie deserted me and threw in with my opponent. When I lost the election, I knew I had lost to Jere again, not to the transfer student.

When school reopened in the fall, Jere was elected senior class president—the highest student office left unfilled. All told I lost six elective offices to Jere over the years, not including the Greyhound Club presidency, which I lost to him later that year.

As the senior class valedictorian, Gil spoke on "Modern Man's Dilemma." The Blond Bomber won the "coveted" Kiwanis plaque. He also wrote, "Good luck from the Blond Bomber" in my *Sotoyoman*. The first-string left end inscribed under his football picture, "Get out there and hold down left end." Coach Art wrote, "I hope those knees hold out for one more year." It did not look like I would ever ship out as a third mate. Before school closed Miss Vranna disclaimed any knowledge of spherical trigonometry and, in fact, discouraged me from taking a fourth year of mathematics. I did not have an aptitude for it, she said.

******

The summer of 1949 began in tragedy. Just after graduation, Johnny Hassenzahl broke his neck diving out of the ancient Camp Rose tree. Johnny had graduated the year before and married his high school sweetheart, but like many boys he wanted to prove that neither graduation nor marriage nor a steady job had dimmed his athletic prowess. The dam at

Merryland, which deepened the river around Fitch Mountain, was not in place when Johnny dove.

A crowd was watching him because he was known for his elegant swan dives; Johnny seemed to hang in midair with arms outspread like wings before hurtling toward the water like a dive bomber. I wasn't there but I was told that the water was so shallow Johnny's waist didn't even break the river's surface. His head drove into the mud, and his legs—straightened out for the dive—stuck up out of the river, twitching. Someone ran to a phone while Jim Jennings and others pulled him from the river. By nightfall everyone knew that Johnny was paralyzed from his neck down. The *Tribune* carried a picture of Johnny in his football uniform and urged that the old diving tree be cut down. A benefit baseball game under the new ballpark lights was planned.

In June the annual Red Cross swim campaign was canceled because there were no beach facilities, even though the city council had promised the previous March to build a bath house. The police cracked down on the Grantomellis. They picked up Foxtooth and booked him for driving without a license, failure to produce proper identification, and giving a fictitious name. Judge Quinn fined him $10, which was more than Foxtooth had. He was given a choice of going to the county jail or joining the Marine Corps, so off he went to boot camp. The chamber of commerce began promoting "tourist and resort" trade and the idea of turning Merryland beach into a lake resurfaced. Mr. Gibbs told the *Tribune* that the elementary school might have to go into double sessions since voters had once again turned down school bonds.

The Morans returned to their cabin for the summer. Nancy and I picked up where we'd left off, but there was a distance between us now. She began dating students from the College of St. Mary's when she turned eighteen and described those dates in her letters. I wouldn't even be sixteen for another six months.

This summer I could not swim every day as I was able to do after my accident. I had to work. So just after the Fourth of July, I got a job at the prune dryer. When trucks pulled into the dryer's unloading area, the drivers dumped each box of prunes onto a wide, slow-moving belt. The belt traveled to a vibrating grate that sifted the prunes evenly onto trays. The full trays were then stacked onto iron-framed carts with grooved wheels.

After the trays were stacked twenty-five or thirty layers high, the carts were rolled on rails into a holding area and a tag identifying the grower was attached to each load of trays. I was in charge of pushing loaded carts in and out of the drying chambers on a strict time table. The concrete chambers were 8' long by 12' wide, with a fan the size of an airplane propeller covering one eight-foot wall. The chamber's temperature was set at 120° and the fan spread the heat around and between the layers of trays. Pushing the loaded carts in and out of the bunkers was hot work, and it never let up because there were over fifty chambers in the dehydrator and drying time was staggered so that other operations wouldn't be overloaded. When I hauled a bunkerful of carts out and replaced them with a new batch, I'd roll the cooled-off carts of dried prunes down to the packing shed. Jesse ran the forklift on the day shift in the packing shed, and he would hoist up the trays and dump them on a high belt where they would once again be vibrated down into large bins. When a bin was full, Dad would wheel his forklift around the floor, lift up the filled bin, drive outside and down an alleyway to the warehouse, and stack it there. The cooperative dryer must have employed eighty people on the day shift alone— belt operators, mechanics, talleymen, stackers, separators, forklift operators, and general laborers like me.

Dad and I never talked at work. I grabbed lunch when the dryers were full, and Dad usually ate at the wheel of his forklift. The trucks never stopped arriving when the season was in full swing. They would be lined up for several blocks waiting their turn to unload. The person with the best job at the dehydrator was "Dink." Dink was 6'6" tall and worked on the exit dock stacking empty boxes. Dink got his job because he could arrange the empty boxes in very high stacks, thus saving space on the dock. After a driver had completely unloaded his prune truck, he pulled forward about fifty feet to the exit dock and Dink helped him reload with empty boxes (the boxes belonged to the coop and were all of standard size).

I lost weight from working a six-day week pushing carts of trays in and out of drying chambers. Pushing carts, however, was better than picking prunes for Mr. Grove, the coop manager, as I had done so long ago. Prune pickers were being paid seventy cents an hour in the summer of 1949. That was fifteen cents less than I'd made during the war.

I could not even go to the beach on Sundays, because I was playing first base for the Junior Legion hardball team coached by Clipper Smith. Clipper told me one day that I was a "natural-born first baseman." I relayed this news to Coach Clarence, who spent his summers pitching for the Prune Packers. Coach Clarence said, "I don't care if the King of Ethiopia says you're a natural-born first baseman, you're going to play left field for me." I told Gil about the coach's comment and it became common for one of us to say something like, "I don't care if the King of Ethiopia says Hemingway is a better writer than Fitzgerald, I say…"

The chamber of commerce kept pushing their proposal for a permanent dam at what they stubbornly called "Memorial Beach." They envisioned the creation of a deep lake four miles long for motor boating and canoeing, though they did not spell out how speedboats and canoes could co-exist on the "lake." The *Tribune* supported the chamber proposal, but had a more important axe to grind. A bill was passed by Congress that dropped the qualifying age limit for an old-age pension from sixty-five to sixty-three years. The editors were indignant. "A sixty-three-year-old person can now own an automobile, a home worth $3,500, and still draw a nice monthly income of $75," their editorial protested. The editors contended that "we should not be setting up a utopia for the old," and warned that giving them pensions "takes the responsibility off relatives."

Mr. Wood's garage was robbed on a Saturday night. The thieves got away with tools, $700 from the safe, and a 1949 Dodge. Dad and I had a good chuckle over that. We figured the thieves wouldn't get very far in one of Mr. Wood's cars. Mother called us heartless. Shortly after the burglary, Mr. Wood won a "Pontiac Best Dealer Award." The award was reportedly one of only 200 given in the entire United States. As his prize, Mr. Wood received a "huge painting of Chief Pontiac."

One of the diminutive Giacomelli brothers for whom the Frantomellis were originally named, was sentenced to sixty days in the county jail by Judge Quinn for driving with a revoked license. His license was originally revoked for operating a motor vehicle in violation of the new insurance lia-bility law. Next to this front page story an advertisement for the Healdsburg Music Store offered a "seven-day free pleasure trial" of a television set with no obligation to buy. Tomasco's drugstore was having a two-for-one Ipana toothpaste sale. Vitalis, which claimed its "60-second workout" performed miracles, was also specially priced. Lonnie's Coffee Shop advertised they were open around-the-clock "For a Steak or a Shake."

Newly purchased ballpark lights were scheduled to be turned on for the Johnny Hassenzahl memorial baseball game. Toward the end of July, the fund for Johnny's family stood at $468, not including ticket sales for the memorial baseball game. The Prune Packers were scheduled to play the San Francisco Fire Department for the benefit game, and the local artist who painted our "Vote for Monk and Chuck" signs announced that he would lead a caravan of bannered cars throughout the county to publicize the Hassenzahl game.

When the long-awaited night finally arrived, Mayor Slim Price threw the switch at the ballpark, turning on the new lights. Mayor Price also gave a welcoming address and introduced Jack Greer, representing the Pacific Coast League Oakland Oaks. Greer complimented the lighting committee and the city. State Senator F. Presley Abshire spoke briefly and Coach Art McCaffrey, who chaired the lighting committee, thanked all of the bond purchasers. The American Legion color guard and rifle team marched into the stadium and a local tenor sang the National Anthem. The Healdsburg *Tribune* reported that "a glow in the sky could be seen all the way to Windsor."

The San Francisco Firemen beat the Prune Packers 14-5 before "one of the largest crowds in history" at the Hassenzahl benefit game. Johnny was not there, so the check for $856.63 was presented to Johnny's dad before the first pitch. Johnny's father, a laborer from Windsor, cried when he accepted the check.

The Junior Oddfellows won the softball league under the new lights, but I did not play in the championship game. I only played once or twice under the lights before my right knee buckled. I tried to adjust my swing to hit a sharply breaking curveball and tore my knee ligaments worse than ever. It hurt so terribly I just lay in the dirt at home plate clutching my knee and screaming. I.I. and another teammate carried me off the field and someone ran to my house to get Jesse. This time Mother's ice packs and hot pads didn't do much good.

I was forced to quit my job at the prune dryer. Doc Robinson did not know what to do for me. I tried to rehabilitate it by swimming, but the swelling in the joint didn't go down the way it had before.

The inevitable day came when Nancy said she had another date that evening. I remember feigning nonchalance, lighting a cigarette like a tough guy in a movie. I stayed late at the beach alone, forcing myself to flutterkick with my bad leg, but the swelling refused to go down. Finally I went to see the only doctor in town who had been to orthopedic conferences—Dr. Oakleaf, the father of the Ruth Elaine. The reason my swelling would not abate was because blood was now filling the joint, so the doctor drained my knee with a hypodermic needle (causing I.I., who was with me, to nearly faint) and squirted the accumulation of bloody fluid into a pan. He encased my right leg in a hip-to-ankle cast and told me it would have to remain immobilized for a month. A week later I foolishly cut off the cast and went to work in a Geyserville apple packing plant with Gil, Charlie, and Emil.

My job at the packing shed was undemanding. After the apples were individually wrapped by women sitting at a long, high conveyor belt, they were packed in slatted boxes. I took the stacked boxes away on a hand truck and delivered them to the shipping area where they were labeled, covered and strapped with metal bands.

One day, when I had finished taking a full handcart out to be shipped, a muscular, tattooed Texan everyone called "Red" approached me.

"Hey," he said, "I hear you're a Golden Gloves champ."

"Where'd you hear that?" I asked suspiciously.

"Never mind," Red said. "I was wonderin' if you'd want to spar sometime. Where do you work out?"

I figured correctly that my buddies—who remembered my knockout by Dick Gardella—were trying to put me on the spot. "Well, I don't fight much anymore, Red," I told him, "but when I work out I like to work out with the best so I go down to Stillman's gym in San Francisco. (I'd read in the *Chronicle* Sporting Green that pro fighters all worked out at Stillman's). "If you ever happen to be at Stillman's when I am working out, I'd be happy to spar with you, but I'm not about to put on the gloves in any rinky-dink gym around here." That seemed to please Red.

"You done much fighting?" I asked.

"In the Navy," he said. "I boxed some in the Navy."

"How many fights did you win?"

"None," said Red, "but I was knocked out three times."

That startled me so much that I asked, "How does that feel, getting knocked out?"

"Jars hell out of you," Red said.

Maybe because I didn't laugh about his being knocked out, Red attached himself to me. He always sought us out at lunch time and called me "champ." "How's it goin', champ?" he would holler at me from across the plant. Red used to say that if anyone gave me any trouble he'd be "proud to fight beside me," and I would grin slyly at Gil and Charlie and Emil.

Red's friendship was about the best thing that happened to me that summer. I did pull a drowning swimmer out of the water at Del Rio one afternoon, but I had to be pushed off the raft by Gil as I stood too stunned to act. The boy was a stranger and had ventured in over his head. His father couldn't swim either and stood on the bank yelling for someone to save his son. The boy had a horribly burned back and I recoiled at the feel of his scarred skin against mine as I hauled him to safety with the cross-chest carry.

Gil and Bobby and I still went out to the brew pits on weekend evenings sometimes. Emil's girl lived in town now, and Charlie gave up frivolous pursuits when he became student body vice-president. He wrote in my yearbook, "Too bad you're still running around with the old crowd, Monk. I intend to make something of myself."

After a few beers, the three of us would head downriver to one of the dance halls at Rio Nido or Guerneville or Mirabel Park. If we didn't have the price of admission we'd stand outside listening to the music, crushing our empty beer cans, and throwing them disdainfully over our shoulders. We wore Levis, T-shirts, and MacGregor windbreakers on those summer evenings. Even when we had money to get into the dance halls, we often spent it on beer and just hung around outside. Sometimes there were fights if other Frantomellis tagged along in Billy's old Chevy. An injudicious word or glance from a city boy was enough to set off the Grantomellis.

Mirabel Park was the best of the dance halls. It featured a big indoor floor and an outdoor pavilion above the river. The pavilion was lit with strings of colored lights, and couples could walk on the beach below and still be within range of the music. When a famous big band played at Mirabel, I'd put on a white dress shirt with the Mr. "B" collar (which was wide and soft like the ones Billy Eckstine wore), my double-breasted suit, my brown suede shoes, my wine-colored tie and suspenders, and my porkpie hat. When a famous big band played at Mirabel, the audience did more listening than dancing and that suited me fine.

We saw Lionel Hampton, Harry James, and Tommy Dorsey. But the finest night of all was when Duke Ellington came to play. He had his brilliant sidemen—Ray Nance and Charlie Shavers and Johnny Hodges among them—and Al Hibbler was his vocalist. They jammed so hard that sweat streamed off The Duke and Oscar Pettiford popped a bass string during a solo. On another night, Lionel Hampton asked the crowd at two in the morning—"Are you having fun?" "Yes," we screamed, "Oh, Yes." "Then let's play all night long," he hollered, those big eyes of his gleaming.

One day toward the end of summer I walked west of town to the Miller apple packing plant where Mom sorted apples and where Coach Art was operating a hand truck—just as I had done in Geyserville. I caught the coach on a break and told him I wouldn't be coming out for football that fall. My decision was not based solely on the certainty that I'd be injured if I played. I had overheard my parents discussing the cost of my college education and knew it was going to be a hardship. So I decided to skip football and concentrate on basketball in hopes of getting a scholarship somewhere.

******

The New York Giants baseball team made preparations to hold a tryout camp at the Healdsburg ballpark. They wrote to Coach Art saying that the Giants wanted "to give some kids a chance to get started in baseball." A two-day tryout was scheduled for September 10th and 11th, and publicity was sent to every city within a two-hundred-mile radius of Healdsburg. This included San Francisco and all the other Bay Area cities. The only other California tryout camp would be near Los Angeles. Not many boys I knew planned on trying out, because they guessed that the ballpark would be mobbed by semi-pro and city league players and that they would get lost in the shuffle. We thought the Giants wanted publicity, not players—there were rumors that the team might be moving west to San Francisco soon.

After the Johnny Hassenzahl benefit game, Johnny disappeared from the news. The weekend after the benefit, a "comic" baseball game between two service clubs was played. The participating men wore skirts and used pillows and "whatnots" to catch and hit the ball, the *Tribune* said. There was a picture of Princess Margaret Rose of England on the entertainment page. The princess had just turned nineteen, and my sister Margaret pinned this picture of her namesake on her wall.

Two days before Gil left for college his dad died of a heart attack. Mr. Gilbert became a prominent citizen after the war when construction picked up. He sold his lumber yard and concentrated on building new car dealerships, the truck stop and diner, and the housing developments that were cropping up on Healdsburg's outskirts. His death was a surprise, and the Catholic Church was full for his funeral.

On the last day before school began, Bobby and I gathered some friends and drove to the coast, past the river resorts to Jenner-by-the-Sea. We ran footraces in the sand while our beer cooled in the surf and returned home by way of Santa Rosa. We went to Santa Rosa because a new drive-in restaurant had opened there; you could sit in your car and be waited on by good-looking carhops.

The high school opened with an enrollment of 456 students on September 19th. On the 23d, the *Tribune* announced that the varsity football team would play their home games under the lights at the ballpark. Coach Art was quoted as saying that he would open the season with Jere

Holbrook in the backfield. In that same issue an editorial titled "America Strikes Oil" appeared. The editorial went on to state that "America's oil worries are over. Even if petroleum reserves are exhausted within a few years, as some experts predict, this country will still have all the oil it can use for centuries to come. The answer is shale oil. The towering mountains in Colorado, Utah, Wyoming, and other states contain 30%–40% more recoverable oil than all the proven petroleum reserves in the country." The local temperature continued to be over 95°. No one was signed at the New York Giants baseball camp, an American Legion smoker featuring "The Three Eves" netted $290, and the Secretary-Manager of the Healdsburg chamber of commerce resigned, calling chamber finances "critical."

Floyd Darby, Healdsburg's most prominent attorney and a Pythian Knight, disappeared. He left his overcoat on the Golden Gate Bridge with a note pinned to it. "Sorry I must leave you," the note said, and the hand-writing was verified. Darby reportedly had tried to borrow a "large sum of money recently and was refused." A $60,000 trust fund he administered was being investigated as it appeared to be $10,000 short. Besides being a Knight of Pythias, Floyd Darby was a member of the Republican Central Committee, Lieutenant Governor of the Kiwanis Club of the California and Nevada districts, and a director of the Healdsburg Chamber of Commerce. The police department doubted the fifty-four-year-old Darby committed suicide because he withdrew $5,000 from his Santa Rosa bank three days before his disappearance. They suspected a "hoax."

Mother was annoyed because the newspaper played up Floyd's affiliation with the Knights of Pythias instead of his Kiwanis and chamber of commerce connections. Jesse was more philosophical about it. "There are bad apples in every outfit," he said. But he did point out that Floyd was seldom seen at the Knights' regular Wednesday night meetings. He and Harry Pitts and Edgar Allen Poe had talked about that around the billiard table, Jesse said.

Since I completed most of my required courses by my senior year and had been discouraged from taking fourth-year math, I indulged myself with three classes taught by coaches and a dramatics class. I had no interest in drama and took the class merely to meet some good-looking girls (Gil said girls who wanted to be actresses were generally more adventurous than other girls). The girls' P.E. instructor, Miss Petty, also taught dramatics, and the plays she chose to perform had large casts, were usually lighthearted and did not tax either audience or cast.

I also signed up for typing—taught by Coach Art's new assistant— Coach Art's social science course, and Coach Clarence's senior problems.

I worried about Mr. Vogt's physics class, not because he was a demanding instructor, but because I was as bad at science as I was at mathematics. Mr. Vogt covered up his own ineptness by being a regular fellow. He told us he once was a cab driver in Chicago and played saxophone in a ragajazz band (whatever that was). His experiments often failed when he demonstrated them in front of the class. Students sat on a platform in five ascending rows while Mr. Vogt lectured from behind a long counter filled with beakers and bottles and models. Behind him on the wall were charts of chemical elements, diagrams of physical formulas, and a very new large colored drawing of the atom, with protons and neutrons whirling around a nucleus. The drawing had a small portrait of Einstein in the lower left-hand corner. Mr. Vogt always wore his white lab coat and demonstrated an experiment for us on his counter before we all retired to the lab to try it for ourselves. His experiments rarely succeeded, and when they failed Mr. Vogt would scratch his head and mutter, "Damn it!"

After a demonstration he escorted us into the laboratory, where there were not enough Bunsen burners to go around. We teamed up in groups of three or four to try the experiment ourselves. I first hooked up with Billy Grant in junior-year chemistry. Tiger Pat and I served as Billy's assistants while he worked the experiments out of his workbook. "Get me a gram of sulfuric acid," Billy would say, and off I went. When Billy successfully completed an experiment, Tiger Pat and I recorded his conclusions in our own workbooks. Before registering for physics, I made sure Billy was enrolled in the class too.

When neither an experiment nor a lecture was scheduled by Mr. Vogt, he showed movies produced by corporations like Standard Oil or U.S. Steel. Since science classes were held during fifth period—right after lunch— many students slept during the movies. I often got a pass from Coach Art to go to the gym and put my knees under the heat lamp.

I did not know what to expect from the journalism class I had signed up for. I did know that my parents' friend, Mr. Schwietert, taught the class. Rumor had it that Mr. Schwietert encouraged young writers but did not tolerate laziness.

Music was not on my schedule at all. Mr. Finne had resigned, and a German classicist replaced him. Professor Reinling, as he liked to be called, considered himself a serious musician. He informed the *Tribune* of his impressive credentials before school even started. He said he had searched for a small school where he could teach a classic approach to orchestral music while spending most of his time composing—his primary interest.

I tried out for the tennis team, though I hadn't played since I was a freshman and was woefully out of shape. It helped that I was friendly with Stan Smith who played first singles. We originally became friends not because of my fascination with Pomo culture or because of tennis but because he lent me a sexy novel and I, in turn, lent him my secret copy of *God's Little Acre*. Now we practiced together, and I improved more quickly than I would have otherwise.

Stan's strengths lay in his left-handed slicing serve, his low, flat forehand that bounced little, and his intuition on the court. Stan was not fast, but he enjoyed fooling opponents into thinking he was a "lazy Indian," as he put it. There was no Native American Power back then, and by law Indians could not even buy liquor. But Stan was proud and saw a way to get to college through playing tennis. No one would ever call him "Chief," he told me.

I went to our football games as a spectator. Home games were being played under the new lights, and I sat in the newly purchased steel bleachers. For the first time I joined the singing when the Greyhound fight song (written by Coach Art) was played. The song was called "On to Victory."

Not playing football had its advantages. I could now ride to games away from Healdsburg in Bobby's pickup or Sky's Caddy and drink a little beer before and after the games. I seldom rode with Billy Grant, who usually transported the two cheerleaders and other girls that my mother thought were "promiscuous." For one thing, Billy's grandmother put a governor on Billy's car so that it could not travel faster than 45 miles per hour. For another thing, Billy used to get awfully drunk and, even at 45 miles per hour, he could scare you.

But on the night our team played in St. Helena, I was in Billy's car. There was a whorehouse in St. Helena near a stone bridge on the outskirts of town. The whorehouse was well known throughout the county and was discreetly referred to simply as "the stone bridge." Part of Billy's mystique was built on the fact that he was a regular patron of this whorehouse, and on the night of the game, we talked him into driving up into the yard of the house so we could see it for ourselves. We milled around outside the house after Billy parked in the yard. Soon a maid came outside to shoo us off and recognized Billy. She had been in the midst of yelling to us, "You boys go on away, you're not old enough to come in here," when she spotted Billy and grinned. "Why Billy, honey, come on in. You can come on in, Billy," she said. Even Jere Holbrook was in our car that night and when the maid's invitation embarrassed Billy so that he started to drive quickly away, Jere pitched a rock through the whorehouse window. None of us blamed Jere for his outburst because he had been ruled ineligible to play football by the North Bay League commissioner. The commissioner ruled that Jere did not complete his 1948–49 courses before he contracted meningitis, and everyone knew that the ruling was unfair. So Jere, who seldom imbibed, got uncharacteristically drunk the night of the St. Helena game.

Fifteen

A FTER NANCY MORAN AND I BROKE UP, I moped around and made a couple of bad moves. At the first student council meeting I liked the looks of the freshman class representative, who was the daughter of an Alexander Valley rancher. So before the first dance of the season I washed the family Plymouth and drove out to the rancher's place. The daughter came to the door shyly, and I asked if she would go to the dance with me. She mumbled "excuse me" and retreated inside. In a moment her father appeared. "The answer is no," he said. "You are far too old for my daughter." He reentered the house, banging the screen door behind him, and left me standing there. Too old? My God, I wasn't even sixteen yet and I knew the rancher's daughter was fourteen. As I drove away, I considered how jaded my reputation must have become.

Next, a pretty and popular girl from the drama class asked me to escort her to a Rainbow Girls installation. She had been the steady girlfriend of the boy who was last year's football fullback, the winner of the Joe Louis boxing award, and this year's starting linebacker for the Santa Rosa Junior College football team. The girl told me that she broke up with the boxer/fullback because she found me irresistible. On the way to her house after the installation, she asked me if I would like to go steady with her. I thought I understood then what Gil meant about drama girls being fast and loose. Without hesitation I removed the gold basketball I'd won as a member of last year's championship team and hung it around the girl's neck. We lasted as steadies just long enough for the girl to flash my basketball at her ex-boyfriend. She returned it to me feigning sadness, though I did not think she acted that emotion well.

After tennis practice I shot baskets in the late afternoon and evening at an outdoor court until it got too dark to see the hoop. I'd heard a college coach say that colleges played man-to-man, not zone defense; that you moved into a shot because of the man-to-man defense. You didn't plant yourself but moved and shot. So I shot and moved over and over.

Some weekend evenings I sat in the balcony of the Plaza Theatre hoping to pick up a girl, but the balcony was not all it was cracked up to be. Most of the girls had their boyfriends with them, there was a lot of coughing because of the dense cigarette smoke, and since there were no covers on the seats or rugs on the floor (because of the fire hazard) it was noisy. I never sat in the balcony on Sundays because balcony girls didn't go to the Sunday family movies. Sunday movies didn't have any sex in them. They could be violent, though, as long as the villains deserved it. I saw *Song of India* one Sunday evening with my family. The movie starred Sabu, Gail Russell, and Turhan Bey. Jesse did not comment on the picture other than to remark that it was very colorful. Mom didn't like it at all. She thought it was romanticized and that Sabu was a fake East Indian. I thought Gail Russell had a sexy, dissipated aura about her. In fact, I found Gail Russell's dark, luminous eyes infinitely sexier than Linda Darnell's cleavage in *Forever Amber* (which was promoted as being scandalously sexy and which I watched from the balcony on a Friday evening). Linda Darnell's dresses were very low-cut, and she had a beauty mark on one boob in case you didn't notice how low cut they were.

In the fall of 1949, bosoms, as Mom called them, were "in" and legs were "out." I think it was the influence of foreign movie stars who began appearing in American films. Pictures of France's Denise Darcel and Italy's Gina Lollobrigida were featured in the *Tribune*. Replacing photos of American starlets in off-the-shoulder peasant blouses and shorts, the paper printed pictures of European actresses in bikinis with their boobs hanging out. Very long, very tight skirts were "in," too, and high school girls walked with little, short steps.

The drama teacher cast me in a Thanksgiving Day play. I was given the lead role of a "typical" American husband but played the character flamboyantly. My heroes were adventurers, not typical husbands, and I did not think to base my characterization on a real person. Nor did I ask Jesse's advice on my role. It never occurred to me that he could help me in a comic characterization. I thought Mother far more "theatrical" than was my dad.

Before our North Bay League tennis matches began, Coach Worden shuffled the team around until he thought he had a winning combination. By then, Grandin and I were almost equal in competition for the second singles ranking. Instead of flipping a coin to see which one of us would play second singles or alternating us on a weekly basis, Mr. Worden put Grandin and I together as his first doubles team. This didn't make either Grandin or me happy; we both felt as if we'd been short-changed. But Grandin's father figured we'd be more valuable as a strong doubles combination than we would be fighting it out for the second singles spot each week. Stan was virtually unbeatable in our league, and the only matches that counted in league play were first and second singles and first doubles. Coach Worden no doubt figured that if Stan could win all of his matches, and if Grandin and I could win most of ours, the team should win another championship. By mid-season our team was undefeated and Grandin and I had not lost a set.

That fall my Uncle Emerson came to visit. Margaret and I were warned that Uncle Em was a little "different." "Not as bad as Cocky Lodge, mind you," Dad said, "but Emerson, too, likes to ride his bike around the suburbs of L.A. and visit with people who don't especially want to be visited with." Uncle Em seemed fine to me—he wasn't a preachy type like some of my other relatives were, and he didn't talk down to me. Unlike my father, Uncle Em had lots of grey hair, and what we used to call a granite jaw. I lent him my bike so that he could "get the feel of the territory," as he put it. This embarrassed Mother because he drew attention to himself by tipping his tweed cap to everyone as he rode around town. Uncle Emerson accompanied Mom to the Red Cross office in the afternoons, and then at three o'clock he'd bicycle up to the high school and watch the tennis team practice. He said my serve reminded him of the serve of Pancho Gonzales—whom he'd seen play in Los Angeles—and I triumphantly told Dad of his evaluation. My father commented that I shouldn't take Emerson too seriously and start getting "too big for my britches." Em flattered everyone, Jesse said. I kept quiet but Uncle Em seemed like a shrewd judge of talent to me. I thought it disloyal of Dad to criticize him.

The varsity football team was on a winning streak. After losing almost all of his preseason games, Coach Art went back to what the paper called "steamroller" football: straight ahead running behind good blocking.

Cheerleaders had to drive themselves to games or ride with friends or family. About mid-season I started riding to games regularly with Billy Grant because the cheerleaders were usually passengers in his Chevy and because Bobby Frost bought a Dodge coupe. Bobby souped up the engine, lowered the rear springs, and painted the car a metallic bottle green. His new coupe didn't have much room in it and Bobby usually had a date now that he'd bought himself a hot rod.

Billy and I were good friends by now. Since Gil had left for college, it was now Billy with whom I had long boozy, "intellectual" discussions. But his grandmother had been right to place a governor on his old Chevy sedan, the "Grantmobile," because Bill drank more than any of the rest of us. The drunker he became, the more defensive he became about his driving skills. He would deliberately drive home to the family ranch in Alexander Valley with his headlights off to prove that he was a first-class drunk driver. While other boys scrubbed and waxed their cars and tinkered with their engines, Bill's car never sounded like it was running on all cylinders, and it had grass growing up through the floor boards. Bill said that this was from all of the beer that had been spilled in his car, causing grass seeds from the ranch to sprout. Billy was my best friend for many years, and my parents became admirers of his grandmother, whom Bill called "Battling Minerva." Long after Bill had left Healdsburg, Jesse and Mom used to drive out to the small old Powell ranch and bring Minerva Powell to town to do her shopping.

Billy was cursed with some sort of neurological disorder that from time to time caused a skin rash—like poison oak rash—to break out all over his body. It caused him great discomfort and humiliation. He was never able to participate in sports for very long before parents complained about their children coming in contact with him, and most proper girls avoided him as if he had leprosy. Many saw Powell Grant as the natural debauched culmination of an aristocratic line; Billy Grant just seemed like a cruel joke. Trying, no doubt, to fill his brother's shoes after he graduated, he fought doggedly when provoked and was seldom knocked off his feet. But he fought with a sort of weariness. As long as I knew him, I never heard Billy complain.

My parents loved Billy. Jesse provoked imitations of local townspeople from him, and Mother thought him a good influence on me because of his intelligence—he made the honor role every semester—and because of his even-temperedness, if not for his temperateness. After our class graduated, Bill got into some serious trouble for trespassing and attempted burglary. Mother intervened (she was foreman of the county grand jury by then) to have him sentenced to college rather than to jail. Bill eventually graduated from San Francisco State while I was sporadically attending college and apprenticing as an actor there. We roomed together and worked as actors in San Francisco and Hollywood before he drank himself to death. Mother pugnaciously defended his death from alcoholism by citing the incredible emotional and physical pain he suffered over the years. But that all happened later. In high school, Billy and I were just drinking buddies.

He always seemed to be available to drink with and to go places with when other boys were not. There was always room for one more body in the Grantmobile. And it was in the Grantmobile—on the way back from a football game—that I got together with the other Nancie.

The only thing that Nancy Moran and Nancie Rich had in common was that both were Roman Catholics. Other than that, they were as different as night and day. Nancie Rich was one of three cheerleaders—the others being Babs, and a third girl who went to games with her parents. On this particular night some eight or ten of us were stuffed into Billy's sedan on the way home from a game. We drank G.B. and there was some groping and squeezing and squealing going on in the back seat along with the drinking. At some point I asked Nancie to go steady with me and she said "Yes," even though we'd never even dated each other—or talked to each other much for that matter.

I hardly even knew Nancie. She was a year behind me in school, and I knew her brother and her father better than I did her. I played sports with her brother, Bill Jr., who was known around high school as "The Heap" (the real "Heap" was a comic book monster who looked and smelled like a walking swamp). One inspection day, Coach Art almost fainted when Bill, Jr. opened his gym locker, and he was known as "The Heap" ever after. Nancie's dad tended bar at Vic 'n' Sis 'Nuf Sed saloon and played Dixieland piano.

Nancie's nickname was "The Body." Mom didn't approve of Nancie and Babs and some other local girls because they smoked in public and cruised around together and stood insolently (Mom said "provocatively") in front of Tomasco's drugstore, which was right across the street from the Red Cross office. None of them belonged to the Rainbow Girls or the Sunshine Girls and none of them ever made the honor roll.

When I woke up the morning after the game, I remembered asking Nancie to go steady. I wondered if I couldn't get out of it somehow. Then I thought maybe she wouldn't remember it and I would be off the hook. But when I got to school, there was Nancie with my gold basketball around her neck.

I figured that if I ignored the situation and Nancie too, maybe it would just go away. I didn't even know Nancie. After several days of walking the other way whenever I saw her, Nancie cornered me and asked if we were going steady or not? We agreed that we ought to at least talk about it, and I said I would try to borrow my folks' car.

There was no guarantee I could do that. Jesse was very jealous of the car because it had been expensive, and I knew what Mother's reaction would be if I told her I wanted to use the Plymouth to park somewhere and discuss going steady with Catholic, provocative, and probably promiscuous Nancie Rich. Mother believed Catholic girls were "looser" than other girls because they could confess their sins once a week to a priest and then go out and sin all they wanted to until the next weekend. Nancy Moran somehow escaped this judgment because she was a rich Catholic girl. Poor Catholic girls were the worst sinners of all and Nancie Rich, as Mother used to put it, "flaunted her body" as well.

Somehow I got up the courage to ask anyway. Mother headed for the garage, and Jesse followed to calm her down. He eventually gave his permission, but told me to be careful. He also said Mother would get over the shock, but she never did. I found out that Nancie's folks weren't too hot about me either. But we agreed to try going steady for awhile and see if it worked out.

Adlai Stevenson was in the midst of a "friendly divorce" at the time, which Mother did not approve of either. Harry Bridges' perjury trial—for claiming he wasn't a Communist—was underway in San Francisco. Max Reinling abruptly resigned as the high school music instructor, saying, "There must be a heaven somewhere, because it sure is hell down here." Professor Reinling was replaced by Reuben O. Linger. Mr. Linger prided himself on being from the South, but he was vague about the exact location. Soon he managed to purchase enough new uniforms and instruments to outfit a forty-piece marching band, though he had only twenty music students. To fill out Mr. Linger's new band, he cajoled old band members like Tiger Pat and me into coming out of retirement. He cajoled us by promising to excuse us from Mr. Vogt's physics class. Mr. Linger also recruited band members by telling them he could quickly instruct them with new methods he learned at Stanford University. He tantalized prospects by displaying flashy red silk uniforms with black capes and caps that they would get to wear in parades.

"Netters Trounce Tomales," the sports page of the *Tribune* announced. It was cold and windy in Tomales Bay the day we played; Grandin and I did not remove our sweatsuits in our 6-1, 6-0 win.

We studied short stories in Mrs. Long's senior English class. I liked "The Most Dangerous Game," though Mrs. Long dismissed the story as the weakest in the entire anthology. She extolled the virtues of "Paul's Case" and the genius of Willa Cather, and I became very bored. So I handicapped horses in class. I wasn't really handicapping but only figuring out my imaginary winnings and losses from the horses I'd bet on in the previous day's *Chronicle*.

250

My attraction to horse racing began the previous summer, when a group of us went to the county fair in Santa Rosa. I won $7.50 at the races and began to take a serious interest in horse racing. In the evenings I sat on my porch and handicapped horses running at Bay Meadows or Golden Gate fields, betting a thousand dollars here and two thousand there. Then, when our *Chronicle* arrived in early morning, I slipped out the Sporting Green and stashed it among my books. I checked my bets in Mrs. Long's first period class. Mrs. Long was as angry as I ever saw her when she yanked the Sporting Green out from under my anthology of short stories where I tried to hide it. I was sent to Mr. Christensen's office, and Mother was summoned to the school.

Mother annoyed Mr. Christensen by not taking my gambling habit seriously. "But it wasn't real money," she kept saying.

Mr. Christensen argued, "That's not the point. A gambling habit is an evil thing."

"I only play horse racing as I would play a game—like monopoly—using imaginary money. If I had any real money I would put it in the Bank of America, not gamble it away," I said. I would not normally have been that outspoken in front of Mr. Christensen, but I took courage that Mother seemed to be on my side. I might have gotten away with that argument, but I added that Mrs. Long's class bored me. I doubt that anyone had ever been that sacrilegious before.

Mr. Christensen just shook his head sadly as if I were a hopeless case and slapped me with five demerits. My standing with Mrs. Long was ruined. She was not a forgiving woman, and if she had designated a section in class called the "other side of the tracks" as Miss Shanahan had, I would have been sentenced there.

Journalism class was another matter. Mr. Schwietert allowed his students great latitude in developing their own individual styles of writing. The *Red 'n' Black*, the high school newspaper, began to show variety and individuality. Stan Smith wrote a weekly tennis column completely in jive language, and Mr. Schweitert did not edit a word of it.

As Thanksgiving approached, the *Tribune* noted that, against all odds, the HHS football team had won the league championship. "High School Netmen Capture Another Tennis Crown" was a smaller headline, and the "undefeated doubles team of Worden and Manley" was mentioned. Healdsburg's first basketball tournament, which would open the season, was in the final planning stages. The article said that "seasoned vets" Morse, Tillis, Anthony, and Manley were expected to "lead" the team.

On Thanksgiving Day, Mr. Linger led the Healdsburg High School marching band in their colorful new uniforms down West Street as part of National Kids' Day parade. The parade drew eight hundred local boys and girls. Spectators observed that, though the band numbered forty caped marchers and was led by a high-stepping, gold-baton-pumping, red-and-black-shakoed Mr. Linger himself, the music emanating from the ranks of musicians seemed surprisingly thin. That afternoon, the alumni football team coached by Two-Yard Art Ruonavaara, Coach Clarence's brother, defeated the high school league champs coached by Coach Art. The game was low scoring, but Two-Yard, who played fullback as well as coached the alumni, ground out more yardage by himself than the entire high school varsity was able to manage.

The high school dramatics class presented two public performances of the holiday comedy, *Our Famous Forefathers*. On the day school was dismissed for Thanksgiving vacation the play was previewed at a student assembly. The program said the play was about a "typical American couple." At the beginning of the first act I was discovered at the breakfast table reading the morning paper and smoking a pipe. My wife, played by one of the "promiscuous" girls who hung out in front of the drugstore, entered in an apron and asked, "Darling?" My face was hidden by the paper, and when I lowered it to reply ("lovingly," the stage directions said), "Yes, dear?" the student body laughed and hooted so loudly and so long that we could not continue with our dialogue for over five minutes. After the play Miss Petty thanked the audience and announced that, as a Christmas treat, the Drama class would stage Charles Dickens' *A Christmas Carol*.

******

On the Friday night after Thanksgiving Mr. Linger was cut and bruised when his car struck a concrete bridge abutment near Windsor. Fog was blamed for the crash.

The average height of our varsity basketball team in 1949 was 6' 2". It was a tall team for that time, and the town and the school expected another championship. We were issued slick new uniforms: white silk warmups with black trim, and zippers at the ankles. Beneath the flashy warmups we wore black silk trunks with either white or black jerseys, depending on whether we were playing at home or away. We each bought a pair of white Converse high-top "Chuck Taylor All-Stars," and to add a final touch of class, we purchased trench coats to sport on the road. Being cool was very important; we intended to dazzle our opponents with finesse and style.

On the weekend of December 10th, the first Healdsburg High School Invitational Basketball Tournament was played. Coach Art invited several large schools from other leagues. Though we played well, we lost to Ukiah by a point, 37-36, and finished with the consolation trophy. The crowds for the tournament were tremendous—people were standing ten-deep in every corner of the gym.

The *Tribune* article reported that I appeared as "the embittered Scrooge" in *A Christmas Carol*. I must have been awful. I recall posturing while trying to look embittered, miserly, and mean, and saying, "Bah, humbug" loudly whenever I forgot my lines. But audiences loved the play. Our old Owl Patrol promoter played Marley's Ghost and Bobby Frost was Fezziwig.

There was always a burst of activities before school let out for the Christmas holidays. The American Legion held their annual Christmas party for children, and Fathers' Night was celebrated at a high school dinner meeting. After dinner R.O. Linger conducted the high school orchestra in "Victory Overture" and "Cossack Dance," a trio of girls sang "Stardust," and Bobby Frost and I sang a duet of "Silent Night." The tumbling team staged a demonstration, and a film sponsored by the Santa Rosa Tuberculosis and Health Association was shown by Mr. Vogt.

The Healdsburg police announced that despite the holiday they would continue their investigation into Floyd Darby's disappearance. The Warren Richardson's home was featured in *Sunset* magazine, and *The Girl From Jones Beach* was a special holiday film at the Plaza Theatre. The movie starred Ronald Reagan and Virginia Mayo; the teaser proclaimed: "They met at low tide and by high tide they were love tied."

Healdsburg teenagers traditionally skipped town on New Year's Eve to attend the community dance in Geyserville. The reason everyone went to Geyserville was that it was easy to be served liquor and there were no police in that small town. A pretty good band was always booked, and if you didn't take along a date there would always be the Geyserville and Cloverdale girls to check out. Our belief was that these small town girls who mostly lived on farms were easy to make out with because they couldn't withstand a sophisticated Healdsburg boy's pitch. Liquor flowed freely and fights were common.

The Geyserville American Legion Hall, where the dance was held, was a large ballroom that occupied the entire second story of an old building that housed the Rex Grocery, the Rex Cafe, and the Rex Bar at ground level. There was also a five-room hotel at the building's rear. The Rex Grocery, Cafe, and Bar were the only businesses in Geyserville unless you counted two service stations and a couple of junkyard/auto repair lots. Not many strangers stopped in Geyserville unless they ran out of gas or their cars broke down. In a sense, it was a little like an old Western town, with one main street and railroad tracks running along next to it. Outlying ranchers and their hired hands came to town occasionally for supplies, a bite to eat, and a few drinks. The sidewalks were several feet above the street to accommodate wagon loading. But on New Year's Eve it seemed like everyone who lived in northern Sonoma County descended on Geyserville for the dancing, drinking, and fighting.

A narrow flight of stairs between the cafe and bar led up to the hall, and it was difficult to get in or out of the dance because of the people jamming the stairs and the hall. The Rex Bar was packed wall to wall, and many patrons took their drinks outside on the sidewalks. Though extra bartenders were always hired for the occasion, they had neither the time nor the inclination to check drinkers' identification. Drink orders were usually hollered out from behind several rows of patrons, so teenagers never had trouble getting served. Bartenders worked so quickly that they hardly looked up from the bottle wells, simply handing drinks to those nearest the bar, asking them to "Pass this back, will ya?" On this New Year's Eve some boys put through a call to Bombay, India, on the Rex Bar's phone. Powell Grant was on a cargo ship bound for the Far East and had told someone the name of a famous Bombay hotel where he intended to stay. Powell was not registered at the hotel, and the boys billed the Rex for the call without anyone's paying the slightest attention to them.

Nancie and I went to the dance with Billy Grant. A friend of Nancie's had reluctantly agreed to be Billy's date, with the understanding that Nancie and I would pull Billy off her if he started to get drunk and amorous. Nancie and I bought a couple of drinks at the bar and then struggled our way up the stairs to the dance hall, leaving Billy and his date in the bar.

Once in awhile I elbowed my way down to the bar to buy a couple of beers and to check on Billy, but the evening seemed to be going smoothly. Then Tiger Pat rushed up with news that Billy was fighting in the parking lot. He told me the name of Billy's opponent and ventured that "Billy is getting the shit kicked out of him."

I raced down the stairs and across the street with Pat, intending to break up the fight. I didn't want any part of the big Geyserville boy with whom

Billy was tangling, but the drinks I'd had and the sight of Billy's bloody, pummeled face caused me to lose natural reason. The fight had attracted a crowd, who were cheering for the Geyserville boy. So I stepped in and said something that I hoped sounded authoritative like, "What's going on here?" To which the Geyserville boy replied, pointing to Billy, "The son of a bitch tore my shirt."

In what was probably a combination of liquid courage and an attempt to show solidarity with Bill, I asked, "Like this?" and proceeded to finish the shirt-tearing job. I ripped that big boy's shirt right down to the waist, causing buttons to pop and the crowd to murmur ominously. The boy balled up his right fist to smack me.

I balled up my own fist, and suddenly a voice piped up from the crowd. "Don't hit him, Champ, it ain't fair," the voice shouted, and Red came shoving his way through the crowd toward us. "My God, Champ, you'll kill him," Red said to me, and then faced the bigger boy. "Jesus Christ," Red said to the other boy, "He's a golden gloves boxing champion. You want to get yourself killed?" Then grabbing me by the arm he warned me sternly, "Those fists are lethal weapons, and the police could arrest you for hitting that poor boy."

Everyone stood dumbstruck—including the boy, who, had he thought it over, knew very well that I was no golden gloves champ. Red escorted me out of the crowd before anyone had time to react, while muttering, "Jesus, Champ, it's a good thing I was around. I sure wouldn't want you to get in trouble. C'mon, lemme buy you a beer so you can cool off." I was so grateful that I bought the beers.

On New Year's Day, my friends and I played the annual Second Street All-Star Touch Football Game in the street in front of our house. A special restriction was placed on our game that year. Mr. Schuman, who lived across the street from us, had bought one of Healdsburg's first television sets, and the phone company had obligingly strung wires from the telephone pole on our side of the street across the street to Mr. Schuman's rooftop. We had to try to keep our punts and passes away from his wires because, when they were jiggled, Mr. Schuman's TV reception jiggled. We were not always successful in avoiding the wires, and when an errant pass or punt tangled with them, Mr. Schuman would come out on his front porch and cuss us out. My inclination was to provoke Mr. Schuman into greater anger by deliberately aiming our aerial game at his TV cables, but Dad had taken to going over to watch games on television and, now that I had certain automobile privileges, I didn't want to rock the boat.

After our street game, we'd all sprawl about the dining room to listen to the East-West game on the radio. Mom would supply us with lemonade (no Cokes at home, they were "bad for the teeth") and sandwiches. Jesse probably went across the street as much for the peace and quiet as for the television picture because in those days every televised game looked like it was being played in a heavy snowstorm. Our family never did own a television set while we lived in Healdsburg. Mom didn't buy one until she moved away and then she only watched the news. We all believed that the good shows were still on the radio and that radio forced a person to use his or her imagination, just like books.

Though I went out with Nancie on most weekend nights—usually after a basketball game—Billy and I developed a semi-regular Saturday routine that winter. We went on what we called our "Saturday afternoon stinkos." Saturday was the day Billy brought eggs from the ranch into town to sell. He had regular customers and most of the egg money was his to keep, so he was usually fairly flush on Saturdays. Billy would drive to my house about noon, and after visiting for a while with my folks, he and I would go off to sell his eggs. When we had the egg money, I bought beer at Flossie's and we headed out around the mountain to Del Rio. It was the same routine that Gil and I had followed the year before. It was usually raining, and after marking the river's height we'd settle back in the Grantmobile with our G.B. The rain beat on the roof, the windows got all fogged up from our breath, and we felt cut off from the world. We talked about everything—girls and games and grades. The afternoons were full of boozy camaraderie and we always went on our stinkos alone.

Around four or five o'clock, I'd call Mom and ask if I could ride out to Billy's ranch for dinner. If my mother acquiesced I would call Nancie with an excuse, and Billy and I would drive out to Alexander Valley.

The Powell ranch was a poor ranch by Healdsburg standards: only ten acres of prunes, a broken-down barn with one cow and some chickens, and the ancient ranch house. Like me, Billy slept on a drafty screened porch and the only things to commend the Powell house was a living room filled with overstuffed, comfortable furniture and the hardbound editions of classics that covered the walls. Mrs. Powell was a proud woman and very old, at least she seemed so to me. While Powell had referred to her as "Battling Minerva," Billy affectionately called her "Minnie," and she let him get away with it. One would not have known that Minerva Powell was descended from aristocrats except for her bearing and her knowledge; she wore plain cotton dresses, spoke plainly, and did not suffer fools gladly. I do not think that Mrs. Powell liked me particularly, but she liked my parents. I was careful not to venture any great opinions about the world or literature in her presence. I knew that Billy had invited Cash Watson to dinner one night and Cash, attempting to impress Mrs. Powell, had said that his favorite writer was "Sir Francis Draken." Cash had never been invited back again.

I liked listening to Mrs. Powell talk about books, but it was her cooking that lured me out to the ranch. Mrs. Powell would already be in the kitchen when we skidded into the driveway. She usually had a caustic remark to make about the lateness of our arrival and the need for promptness in milking the cow. Billy changed quickly then into his old boots and a red baseball cap he wore—for no reason I could discover. Grabbing the metal milking bucket from the back porch, we'd trudge out to the barn. Again, for no discernible reason other than it seemed to be a sort of ritual, Billy would punch the cow once or twice sharply in the ribs. Then he would squat on a stool while I stood by, always fascinated by the procedure. Bill often offered to teach me the art of milking, but I was never enthusiastic about learning, and in any event, we always arrived too late for a lesson. Billy disliked the farm and, unlike other country-bred boys, had no wish to continue on there after high school. As it turned out, though, loyalty to Minnie kept Billy on the old ranch for a couple of years after his graduation.

When the bucket was filled, we slogged back to the house and Billy changed again. We washed up and then gathered around what had once been a fine oak dinner table. My favorite meal at Mrs. Powell's was homemade corned beef hash, hot homemade bread, home-churned butter, and a big glass of the warm milk that Bill had just pumped out of the cow. Sometimes Mrs. Powell cooked a roast or baked a chicken. Billy and I were usually too lazy and comfortable after one of Minnie's Saturday dinners to go out and look for any excitement. Billy built a fire in the small living room fireplace, and after the dishes were done, we sat around and talked about books. After a couple of hours, Bill drove me home at a steady forty-five miles an hour.

Mrs. Powell always treated Powell and Billy with a sort of loving scorn. She used to accuse Powell of being worthless and of running around with common hoodlums. If he were around, she would say things like, "Mr. Powell Delano Grant is no doubt too haughty to join us in the parlor." Powell, with his flashing smile, replied that they had no common ground for discussion since Battling Minerva refused to read Sartre or Nietzsche. She treated Bill more gently, but unfailingly greeted him at the door after a late night by saying plainly, "Billy, you're drunk!" To which Bill, just as unfailingly, would reply, "No shit."

Our basketball team won several games by slim margins. We had more form than substance. We patterned our style of play after the Blue and Golds, a semi-pro team from Oakland. The Blue and Golds played in the American Athletic Union league and represented Blue and Gold beer, which was produced locally. They were a loose, stylish, mercurial team that featured a forward named Don Barksdale and a shooting guard by the name of Davage Minor. We thought they were the essence of cool. Charlie Morse, the ex-Frostomelli, played the forward spot on my side of the court and was not playing physical basketball—frequently he did not bother to follow his shots—and was certainly not replacing "The Blond Bomber." Our other forward, John Tillis, was distracted by off-the-court problems.

Smooth, curly-haired John had recently been forbidden to participate in extracurricular activities because his parents had joined the Pentecostal Church. They cut John off from dating and playing the trumpet and he was afraid his days as a basketball player were also numbered. John's and Charlie's attention seemed to wander on the court, and the team suffered from it. I was not without blame: I carefully shielded my knees and avoided physical contact under the basket as much as Charlie and John did.

Mom and Dad regularly attended home games. They were always squeezed tightly in the bleachers, right in front of I.I.'s mom and dad. Mr. Anthony, a real estate man and an old athlete himself, had a face as red as an apple. I.I. once showed me his father's block sweater—an old-fashioned white pullover with a red "H" on it like you would see in college movies with Jeannie Crain. Whenever I.I. scored two points, Mr. Anthony yelled, "That's my boy!" Whenever I scored two points, Mr. Anthony pounded Jesse on the back and screamed, "That's your boy!" Jesse suffered the pounding good-naturedly and always feigned stiffness the day after a home game.

There was no jocularity between Mother and me regarding Nancie Rich. Mother regularly reported to me that Nancie—as seen through the large window of Mother's storefront office—was smoking a cigarette, or wearing an unusually tight sweater and skirt, or hanging out with some other girl of "bad reputation." In reply I had learned enough Shakespeare to quote from *Othello*: "Reputation is an idle and most false impression; oft got without merit and oft lost without deserving." But it did little good. Nancie was never invited to our house, and Mother never wasted any opportunity to criticize her. It was Mother's habit, after raking Nancie over the coals, to say something like, "Well, I suppose you really can't blame her. After all, her father is a bartender." Bill, Sr., her father, had at least become friendly enough to greet me gruffly on the street, though he still considered me a college-bound boy who would probably walk away from Nancie after graduation. For our part, my friends and I had come to admire Mr. Rich for his honky-tonk piano playing. He looked and sounded a lot like Hoagy Carmichael.

On the local political scene, Healdsburg promoters licked their chops at news that the Air Force intended to build their own military academy. The promoters thought the old Fulton Air Base near Windsor would be a fine location for this new "West Point of the Air," and *Tribune* editors agreed, "This area would be a good place for the finest young manhood in the country to come to." The chamber of commerce announced that it had scored a major coup by persuading the Yakima Bears to hold their spring training in Healdsburg. The Bears were a Washington farm team for the Pacific Coast League San Francisco Seals, and would play at the ballpark from March 25th through April 15th. Less encouraging to local tub-thumpers was the Sonoma County Board of Supervisors' vote to hold up the Memorial Dam proposal for six months.

I went to see Alan Ladd in *The Great Gatsby* at the Plaza Theatre. The advertisement for the movie pictured Alan Ladd slugging Barry Sullivan, who played Tom Buchanan. The picture caption said: "A Great Guy, But Stay Out Of His Way!" The movie was terrible. I saw *Four Feathers* at about the same time. It was an English movie based on a Kipling story about India and was authentic and adventurous. When *City Across the River*, the sequel to *The Amboy Dukes*, played at the Plaza, the plot and the characters seemed juvenile.

My basketball game came alive toward the end of the season. But my improvement came at the same time everyone else's game tailed off badly. Suddenly I was the high-point man in several games; I had stopped being careful and was playing with abandon: diving for loose balls and battling for rebounds. The season came down to our game against Cloverdale late in February.

Both Healdsburg and Cloverdale were undefeated on the rainy Friday night Ralph bussed our team twenty miles north for the game. Spectators were already arriving when he pulled the bus under the overhanging trees in front of the auditorium. Playing in a foreign gym was always a disadvantage—especially early in a game. Besides the hostile crowd, you always had to deal with an unfamiliar court: the spring of the floor's surface, the flexibility of the backboard and the basket rim, the intensity of the lighting, all were factors that worked to a home team's advantage. The Healdsburg gym seemed compact and tight because the bleachers unfolded to within two feet of the black out-of-bounds lines. Cloverdale's multi-purpose room that doubled as their gym was built to emphasize space and light, and their bleachers sat well back from the sideline benches.

Our varsity's custom was to sit in the stands and cheer on our light-weight team until halftime. Then we went to the locker room to put on our uniforms. The North Bay League hired coaches from other leagues to referee our basketball games. The theory was that these referees were neutral since they did not have a stake in the game's outcome, yet were competent officials. The referee that night in Cloverdale was the Petaluma baseball coach who picked up extra money for working the game. Those of us who had played baseball against his team called him "the Nutscratcher." We called him that because when hitting fungos and grounders to his players during warmups, he unconsciously scratched his crotch and said things like, "Let's get two on this one" or "Peg it home, Johnny" or "Come on, Bud, dig it out of the dirt."

We criticized the Nutscratcher's refereeing during the first half of the "B" game that night, but our shouted comments were meant to encourage our lightweight team. Referees knew that players "talked it up" and figured jeers and hoots came with the territory. But when our varsity took the floor, the Nutscratcher asked who our captain was. Coach Art used a rotating-captain system and it happened to be my turn that night. When I indicated that I was the captain, the Nutscratcher said to me with an evil glint in his eye, "I hope you can play as well as you can yell." Then he proceeded to ensure we lost the game.

Their center was a fine player and neither of our centers could cover him alone, but if they even breathed on him they were called for fouls. So they gave the giant center extra room, and he scored almost at will. Somehow we stayed with Cloverdale point for point until the end of the fourth quarter. None of us had ever fouled out of a game before, but the Nutscratcher, becoming desperate, quickly got rid of Charlie and I.I. on non-existent fouls.

The *Tribune* concluded its story on the game by saying: "With one minute remaining, Dave Manley tied the score at 29 and this thrilling play brought the packed house to its feet. He fouled out on the next play." There wasn't anyone near me when the Nutscratcher called me for a fifth foul, and in anger I slammed the ball to the floor, causing it to sail high up toward the gym's metal rafters. The Nutscratcher then added a technical foul, which gave Cloverdale two free throws. We lost the game 34-31, and Healdsburg fans were so enraged that the Nutscratcher had to be escorted out of the gym and to his car by a band of Cloverdale rooters. The Cloverdale principal made the mistake of gloating and an "unknown fan," according to the *Tribune*, decked him. The "unknown fan" was Bobby Frost.

When we returned to school on Monday, we were lectured by Bud Christensen for "unsportsmanlike conduct" and for inflaming the fans. Coach Clarence warned us that he would brook no criticism of the Nutscratcher, an old colleague and a man of the utmost integrity who would never stoop to partisanship or maliciousness. I got no consolation from Jesse. He dismissed my complaints by saying that injustices are a part of life. Mother was sympathetic but thought a game was something unworthy of real anger.

A week later we played Sonoma for a share of the league championship. Whoever won would finish in a tie with Cloverdale. We had beaten Sonoma during our preseason tournament and should have handled them easily. We met them in our own gym, but the steam had gone out of our team. The *Tribune* said that I "stripped the net from all angles," and it really did seem as if I could not miss that night. I scored more than half of our team's 38 points, but it was not enough. We lost in the final few minutes, 42-38. Though that game probably won me an all-league spot, as a team we were depressed about the season. The townspeople were not pleased with us either because the school's string of four consecutive championships. We were too flashy and without fire they thought—and that was true.

Sixteen

EVERYTHING SEEMED ANTI-CLIMACTIC after we lost the basketball championship. I should have looked forward to baseball season, but I couldn't get excited about playing left field. Instead of joining in pickup games and shagging flies to get ready for the season, I found myself at my old haunts shooting baskets.

The town was ready to forget and move on to baseball. There was no doubt about that. Season tickets for the Yakima Bears spring training games went on sale for $3 and were eagerly snapped up. The Prune Packers announced they planned a tough spring schedule against out-of-town teams like Crown Machine Works of Santa Rosa.

Meanwhile, two hundred Windsor landowners met at the Windsor Grange to oppose the "West Point of the Air." Warren Richardson led the opposition, saying that agricultural land should be preserved, and blamed the Santa Rosa and Healdsburg chambers of commerce for promoting the academy idea. One sarcastic rancher asked how the Santa Rosa Chamber of Commerce would like it if ranchers got together and proposed selling the downtown business district to the federal government. The landowners noted that 2,000 people would have be displaced by the "West Point of the Air."

At another public meeting, Mr. Gibbs asked Mother to describe the activities of the Red Cross Home Services Committee. Mother was quoted as saying, "Home Services is a social welfare program for members of the armed forces, for veterans, and for families of both groups, and includes such specific functions as counseling in family and personal problems, reference services, financial assistance, and assistance in applying for government benefits." She noted that aid was not given unless no other welfare agency in the community was able to lend a hand, because that would be a duplication of services. In conclusion, Mother said Red Cross Home

Services also represented the Travelers' Aid Society and assisted displaced persons "who have moved to this area."

Mother made this speech in public, but in fact she often didn't insist that people prove they were veterans or were displaced. If they looked hungry she helped them one way or another. Mother did not fight with her superiors over charitable expenditures as Grandfather had done so long ago in the Godaviri River delta. She told board members what they wanted to hear and then stretched the rules to help society's undesirables and outcasts. A *Tribune* editorial that followed Mother's presentation urged "folks to support Red Cross fund-raising."

That particular *Tribune* front issue was full of interesting news: One headline read: "Local Man Gets Stay of Execution." The story reported that "Powell Grant of Healdsburg was brought before Judge Edward Quinn on charges of drunk driving and sentenced to seventy-five days in the county jail or a fine of $150. He was arrested on Saturday night and was given a stay of execution until March 6th." Another article said: "Healdsburg High School Play a Big Success. *That Face Is Familiar*, a hilarious farce with gay situations and clever lines was well attended. Audiences were kept in stitches by Lucille Peterson as the Duchess of Warwick. Mirth was added by the appearance of Richard Eddington, known by all as Dave Manley, a New York stage actor."

The paper also reported that public funding of summer band concerts would be placed on the ballot in the upcoming elections, that many young locals were getting married in Reno, that a new 800-seat modern movie theater with no balcony was going to "rise on North Street" and that Villa Chanticleer's promised reopening would occur "within ninety days." A "lush resort" was pledged with a "rodeo" highlighting opening ceremonies.

Our varsity baseball season opened. Opposing teams seemed to feature hard-throwing pitchers with tight, snapping curves in 1950. I did not regain my form at the plate. The fact that I had damaged my knee swinging at a curve probably had something to do with it, but I worried about being beaned by one of those hard-throwers too.

We traveled to Petaluma to face the Nutscratcher's team and his pitching ace, Bones Walker. Bones shut us out 6-0, but that wasn't the highlight of the game. With the score 4-0 and Bones sailing along, Russ, our shortstop, hit a clean single to left field. Russ tried to stretch his single into a double and the umpire called him safe at second after Russ's headlong slide. The Nutscratcher protested the call, and in spite of howls from our bench Coach Clarence allowed the Nutscratcher to prevail. Russ left the field, head drooping—our only scoring threat wiped out by our own coach. Then in the final inning, with a Petaluma player on second base, their star hitter cranked a single into left field off our pitcher. I fielded the ball on one hop and threw cleanly to home. Our catcher was waiting for the ball, straddling the plate, and tagged out the runner by a good two feet. But the umpire called their runner safe. Now it was Coach Clarence's turn to protest. The umpire refused to change his ruling, and so Coach Clarence appealed to the Nutscratcher to nullify the bad call. After all, his team was ahead 5-0 and Bones had something like fifteen strikeouts. The Nutscratcher looked Clarence dead in the eye and said, "It looked like a good call to me." We did not rub it in. We figured it was a painful lesson Coach Clarence learned about his friend. But we never forgave him either, because we figured he should have stood up for us.

When the announcement came that Villa Chanticleer was finally going to reopen as a "lush resort," some Frantomellis drove up to take a look at it. While they were on top of Fitch Mountain, poking around the construction site, they came on an overgrown dirt road that led to a wooded plateau. This grassy shelf in a grove of oak trees had a magnificent view of Healdsburg, the river, and the coastal mountains. At night, the distant lights of Healdsburg sparkled and it was very dark and very quiet.

Before long, news of this discovery spread around the high school, and boys began to park there with their girls. Before much longer, the spot was christened "Pecker Point." The name was a misnomer because if a boy was planning on seriously making out he would never have taken a girl to Pecker Point—it was far too crowded. There was room in the grove for perhaps fifteen cars, and on weekends lovers were usually unable to jam their way in after 11:00 P.M. Pecker Point was more of spot to do some necking, listen to the car radio, drink a few beers, and mingle with occupants of other cars. Most of us had steady girlfriends now, and Pecker Point was a good place to both be with your girl and drink a few beers with your buddies. You never looked into another car's windows when you walked around to talk with some buddies; that was an unspoken rule. If a couple were "going all the way," they didn't come to the Point, but parked in the maze of winter-closed prune or apple dryers, in Oak Mound Cemetery, or even at the brew pits, which were pretty much abandoned now.

When we wanted to be alone, Nancie and I parked a little farther down the mountain among the horse barns at Bellvue Villa. One black night, the watchman shined his long flashlight through the Plymouth's windshield, catching Nancie with her blouse off. So we hunted for other private places, but usually made a trip to Pecker Point for at least a few beers and a little talk with other couples. And sometimes we got lucky and the place would be deserted. Then with the car radio playing late night jazz, the rain pounding on the roof if it was winter, and the windows all steamed up so we couldn't see outside, Pecker Point was a wonderfully romantic spot. You could always hear another car approaching—revving hard to climb the steep dirt road. This warning gave couples time to straighten out their clothes. Nancie would not "go all the way" with me, so we spent more time at the Point than some couples. When spring arrived there was nothing finer than sitting in the warm Plymouth, drinking beer, necking, and listening to Jimmy Lyon's jazz program from San Francisco while the town's lights danced across the windshield.

Nancie was a proud girl, and I think that rankled Mom more than anything else. She was also smart enough to know that people had already prejudged her, and that nothing short of a plea to be forgiven for things she hadn't done would satisfy her critics. She would not grovel, and instead of pretending false modesty she flaunted her sexuality. I did not realize until much later that I was attracted to Nancie because she was more scornful of adult's judgments than anyone I had ever met. And she was more stoic than my mother in the face of their condemnation. It was far more difficult for a girl than a boy to be a rebel because girls had much more to lose in terms of reputation, and the likelihood that any future-conscious boy would marry them was slim. Parents drummed into their sons the horrible thought that an evening's passion with one of the "gang girls" could lead to a lifetime of regret, to say nothing of the unwanted child. In fairness, it was not entirely the adults who spread rumors about rebellious girls. Rejected boys and boys who had been unsuccessful in their attempts to "put the make" on certain girls lied about them out of anger and to assure their own reputations. Much as I heaped abuse on Nancie's brother for his lack of hygiene, he always defended Nancie as well as he could, and so did her folks.

Mom and I finally had a serious fight over Nancie. We had been out late the night before and Mother came out on my porch to talk to me about it. In spite of my quote from *Othello*, she continued to pass on nasty tidbits of gossip about Nancie and her group of friends. I don't remember what the scandal was on this particular morning, but Mom wound up by saying that Nancie was the type of girl that probably would have sex with a boy so he would marry her. If she thought I was going to refute that accusation by claiming contrary firsthand knowledge, she was wrong. And I told her so.

I also told her while she was talking about Nancie behind her back, Nancie was in Windsor at the Hassenzahl home with her friends. They regularly took Johnny for rides on Saturdays to visit his friends—who had stopped going to see him, now that the novelty of his injury had worn off. Johnny's wife had lost no time in abandoning Johnny either, taking their small child with her. I asked Mother what the Red Cross had done for Johnny lately. For the first time in our lives, Mom slapped me. She fled to the garage and I apologized after the atmosphere between Jesse, Margaret, and me became too charged to be bearable. Dad never intervened in my quarrels with Mom over Nancie, but he never said anything against her either. He even let me buy a "necker knob" to affix to the steering wheel of our car. The clear purpose of the knob was to be able to steer the car with one hand, leaving the other arm free to put around a girlfriend.

It was too bad that Mother was obsessed with Nancie, because otherwise she was happier with my activities than she'd been during my junior year. Bobby's and my singing duo grew into a quartet, and we practiced regularly on my porch. We tried for a jazzy sound with broad harmony like the Four Freshmen, who were just becoming popular. We called ourselves "The Pastels," and at the spring concert we performed several "old time favorites" according to the *Tribune*.

I bought a portable phonograph for my overcrowded porch and began to collect jazz records on the new '33 unbreakable vinyl discs. Long-playing records had just been introduced and most of the time I had to travel to Santa Rosa to order them. I bought Miles Davis, Thelonius Monk, and Charlie Parker. Mother thought my music was a phase I was going through and didn't complain when I turned up the volume. Margaret closed her door tightly, though, and Jesse groaned loudly. Sometimes he referred to me sarcastically as "a real cool cat."

Powell Grant's mother paid his fine, and he immediately shipped out. Two new Healdsburg policemen began arresting drinking minors without letting them off with warnings any more, so only youths whose judgment was seriously clouded ventured downtown on weekend nights.

It was other drugs that were becoming the focus of community fears. Anti-drug propaganda was rampant in the papers and in movies. *Reefer Madness* played at the Plaza Theatre and, while we all laughed at the film, parents took its message very seriously. The San Francisco *Chronicle* ran several stories on the drug menace in the city. The only thing my friends and I knew about drugs—especially cocaine and heroin—was that a lot of musicians used them and they often died in poverty and despair. But there was widespread fear that drugs might work their way up Highway 101 from San Francisco and capture Healdsburg's youth.

In March the commander of the Bureau of Special Services dealing with narcotics and vice in San Francisco addressed the Healdsburg Kiwanis Club on the subject of marijuana. According to the *Tribune*, he said that "marijuana is no different from most other narcotics in that its effects are entirely of a destructive nature, and therefore it cannot be used as a sedative." Because "the effects of marijuana produce criminal tendencies in the user," the commander advised his listeners to contact the police if they spotted anyone with cigarettes rolled in brown paper and sealed at both ends or if they should discover any strange or unusual plant.

Ralph Sandborn entered the race for city constable. Ralph was pictured in the paper wearing a double-breasted, pinstripe suit and snap brim hat and looking just like George Raft. The baseball varsity lost to Santa Rosa 13-3, and to Petaluma 3-1 on consecutive days. Mother was elected president of the fourteenth district of PTA. Her subordinate officers were from San Rafael, Mill Valley, and San Francisco. She got a lifetime membership pin (which she always treasured) and was named as a delegate to the National Congress of PTA.

******

I used to collect songs about April. Mostly they were melancholy songs like "Lost April," "April, Give Me One More Day," "I'll Remember April." But April in Sonoma County was the usually the finest month of the year. Heavy rains were replaced by showers, and the fields were resplendent with wildflowers. Birds and squirrels and deer appeared on the hillsides, and the grass turned a deep, bright green. The Russian River ran clear and deep, and you could see why the chamber of commerce wanted to create a permanent lake at Merryland. Mother and Jesse resumed their Sunday drives—to Knight's and Alexander valleys to picnic among the lupines Mother loved and to the coast at China Beach or Goat Rock. Mother and Margaret strolled along the sand collecting seashells, and Jesse hunted driftwood, especially balsa wood buoys, to carve. I usually avoided these spring outings, but this year I went several times, climbing the coast rocks and looking out to sea, imagining myself captain of the occasionally glimpsed freighter on the horizon.

Spring was a season of concerts and plays and fairs, of golf tournaments and track meets and baseball. The Yakima Bears arrived in town, and the players, most of whom were not much older than we were, dated local girls.

The paper said, "Everyone knows that traveling athletes, like traveling actors, are only after what they can get, and then they will move on." But some girls believed the players' promises and were heartbroken when spring training ended. The girls had put on airs parading around town with their Bears, and when their players left, no local boy would have anything to do with them. In later years, when touring in a play, I sometimes wound up with a local girl and remembered the *Tribune*'s warning about actors and athletes.

In April the paper reported that James Roosevelt, candidate for governor, would "speak here on Monday at 2:00 P.M." "Jimmy," as the editors called him, would speak "from his sound truck tractor, which will be stationed in the vicinity of the Plaza." In the same edition, the paper announced that Jere Holbrook won a cash award of $100 for placing first in Sonoma County's Mental Hygiene Clinic poster and essay contest.

Most Lytton Home students never left the grounds except to be bussed to and from Healdsburg schools. The home was lovely, with its stately presidio-like buildings, rolling hills and lakes and lawns, but most of its residents had never experienced the pleasure of wandering unchaperoneed through downtown Healdsburg, let alone making a trip to the Pacific Ocean.

Townspeople seldom visited Lytton Home, except to attend the Salvation Army's annual Easter Sunrise Service, but I went there often to play pickup basketball games. Lytton possessed the only other wooden gym floor in the area and, even after our disappointing season ended, I kept playing wherever I could. On spring Saturdays my parents sometimes gave me the car and a note authorizing me to take a couple of Lytton boys for a ride. I dressed in the old Lytton locker room, and we scrimmaged all morning. In the afternoon, I would drive two or three boys to the coast, trying to spread the rides around so that all the boys I played with got a chance to go.

They were always fascinated with a jutting headland called Death Rock. Scores of fishermen and sightseers had been swept suddenly off this rock by waves that seemed to come from nowhere, and warning signs were posted around its perimeter. The signs displayed an up-to-date count of the victims, whose bodies had never been recovered. Geologists thought there was an underwater cave at Death Rock and that the bodies of the drowned had been jammed into it by the undertow. They thought the concavity of the cave contributed to the sudden tidal waves. This was all speculation, of course, which added to the mystery of Death Rock. No geologist was brave enough to dive down and try to find the cave. We ate the lunches Mother packed for us and watched the fishing boats come home, curling their way around the long jetty at the harbor's entrance.

Sometimes we would buy salt water taffy before we started back. My Lytton Home friends were not good at expressing gratitude for these outings. I cannot even explain how I knew that they were grateful because sometimes I thought the trips left them more depressed than they had been before.

Miss Petty decided that our class was more serious about dramatics than were her previous classes, so she chose *Jane Eyre* as the year's final play. Two girls would alternate as Jane, I was cast as Rochester, and according to the paper, "night rehearsals are now in progress so that this production will be successful." Our cast had become serious about dramatics because most of us saw Laurence Olivier in *Hamlet* as members of Mrs. Long's senior English class. The Santa Rosa theatre where *Hamlet* played for a "very limited time" presented the film as an artistic service to the community, not for profit. We were stunned by the film's stark beauty, by the acting of Olivier, and by the play's realism. Shakespeare did not seem dated or mannered in this production. Olivier's athleticism was almost as dazzling as Errol Flynn's. Jean Simmons' fragile Ophelia captivated us. We had never seen anything like *Hamlet*, and all other films seemed trivial beside it. Even Mrs. Long, whose own interpretation of the play differed considerably from Olivier's, was moved. So we all worked hard on *Jane Eyre*.

The Plaza Theatre advertised Danny Kaye as "the general with an army of beautiful babes" in *The Inspector General*. At one Wednesday night performance, JC Penney's presented a spring fashion parade onstage using local models. The annual Future Farmers of America fair was scheduled for the last weekend of April: opening ceremonies would be held at the Legion Hall at 1 P.M. Friday and the fair would conclude with a dance at the same hall on Saturday night. The Healdsburg Chamber of Commerce was searching for a Queen ("fifteen to twenty years old") to ride on the City of Healdsburg float in the Santa Rosa Rose Parade. Reuben Linger announced that martial airs including "The Marines' Hymn," "The Thunderer" and "American Patrol" would be included in the annual high school band concert repertoire. The Federated Church choir under the direction of Smith Robinson was "making a name up and down the land."

Spring sales were promoted by local stores: Rosenbergs placed a large ad in the *Tribune* to publicize their new Stetson Seaview hat, which the store was selling for $5. Safeway had halibut steaks on sale for $.52 a pound, marked down from $.65, and pork roasts were on sale for $.48 a pound. Mother's best dish, besides curry, was her pork roast, which she cooked with hunks of garlic pressed into it.

Honor students were listed in the paper at the end of April; Margaret made the list at the elementary school. Jere Holbrook made the high school list, but Billy Grant did not. I was doing poorly in school myself. I lost interest after the basketball season and at the same time wondered how I could arrange at least a partial scholarship to college. I knew my parents had put college money aside for me, but I also knew they hoped I would become a doctor or a teacher. I wanted to decide about what to do with my life. I knew no college would recruit me to play basketball—Healdsburg was played in a small, rural league. I would have to get letters from my coaches and convince some small college to take a chance on me. In the meantime, I practiced at the grammar school and at Lytton Home and worried and didn't study.

In May, the chamber of commerce voted to abandon plans for the 1950 Harvest Festival, citing insufficient interest by city businessmen. The Summer Events Committee announced it would sponsor a smoker at the American Legion Hall to raise funds for the summer band concerts. The city council was furious because the county board of supervisors awarded Santa Rosa $561,000 to build a Veterans' Memorial Building, leaving only $65,000 for other projects. The supervisor who represented Healdsburg cast the only dissenting vote. The dissenter said the Healdsburg Chamber of Commerce's Memorial Beach plan would put the funds to better use, but the other supervisors pointed out that the beach could not be used as an auditorium to serve the entire county. A small story noted that "Congressman Richard Nixon, who is a candidate for U.S. Senator, will be in Healdsburg this afternoon at 3:00 P.M. He will be stationed at the south side of the Plaza, where he will give a talk and answer questions."

Young Man With a Horn, starring Kirk Douglas and Doris Day, played at the Plaza Theatre. The film purportedly was a biography of Bix Beiderbecke, but Douglas didn't look anything like poor, wasted Bix. The film's music didn't even include Bix's great song, "I Can't Get Started With You." Our high school concert featured a trumpet solo by Stan Smith and a coronet solo by Tiger Pat. Pat had learned to play the coronet during the times he was excused from Mr. Vogt's physics class. Lucille Peterson contributed a vocal solo, and our quartet sang "The Whiffenpoof Song." After the concert, Reuben Linger resigned from the faculty.

The Pastels were invited to compete in an amateur hour held at a out-of-town movie theatre. We lost in the finals to a seven-year-old spoon player. The newspaper reported, but did not comment on, our production of *Jane Eyre*. Our audiences were not enthusiastic either, and I doubt Miss Petty produced any more dramas.

Undaunted by the county's refusal to create a Memorial Lake at Merryland, the chamber of commerce continued trying to put Healdsburg "on the map." Toward the end of May, local merchants gave $150 to Plaza Theatre manager Kenneth Dennis to "underwrite the expenses of a promotion." The promotion involved a donated Cadillac with banners attached to it traveling to Phoenix, Arizona, and back to Healdsburg. The purpose of the trip was "to publicize the city of Healdsburg and its resources and at the same time to exploit a motion picture, *The Baron of Arizona*, which will be shown here shortly. Accompanying Dennis will be well-known rodeo rider 'Nevada' Carson, a direct descendent of Kit Carson. On the way to Phoenix, they will contact radio stations, schools, and businessmen's groups. On reaching San Rafael, the two men will meet members of the Russian River Riders, who will supply horses for the men to return to Healdsburg." The release concluded by saying that the trip was to be part of a $3,000 contest for the best publicity of the picture.

On the first day of June 1950, Richard Nixon spoke to a "small group of local citizens," and the chamber-of-commerce-sponsored Arizona trip was postponed. A chamber spokesman reported that Hollywood—overcome by the chamber's and theatre manager's idea—had called and asked them to postpone their trip until September. The trip would then be used to promote *Pony Express*, another film. The chamber enthusiastically endorsed Hollywood's scheme, though the summer season would be over when the new trip came off so Healdsburg would not benefit from it. But as I discovered when I went off to the magic kingdom, most small town folks thought Hollywood was the most powerful place on earth—if it was considered earthly at all.

The Junior-Senior Prom was held on the first weekend of June. It was the custom to eat at a fancy restaurant before the dance, and Bobby Frost and I made reservations for ourselves and our dates at a resort west of Santa Rosa. I remember kicking Bobby under the table when he asked, "What is the fil-let mig-non?" Bobby did not remain forever ignorant of the finer things in life. After graduation he took over the family hop ranch, and when the bottom fell out of the hop market he planted vineyards. Before he turned thirty-five Bobby sold the ranch and retired. But on the night of our

Junior-Senior prom, we were both unsophisticated boys. We chose a remote restaurant so we would not be known. We were naive enough to think that our suits and our dates' formal gowns would not give us away and that we would be able to order drinks with our dinner. But when we ordered them, the waiter asked for identification. Since I was too embarrassed to produce my forged DeMolay card, we stopped in Windsor on the way back to Healdsburg, bought a bottle of bourbon and some Seven-Up, and had cocktails in the Plymouth.

If I remember few details about dinner and the dance itself, it is because Nancie surrendered her virginity to me that night in a lonely parking spot. We would never have thought of disrobing entirely in those days and so it was an awkward act of love—awash in petticoats and shirt tails. The process was so sudden and just as suddenly it was over. But we were flushed with joy, and I was so grateful that I promised eternal fidelity to her—even if we had to wait to marry until I had graduated from college.

Shortly after the prom, we seniors were allowed to skip a day of school on what was called Senior Cut Day. After gathering on the football field the seniors would be driven in three buses to Dillon's Beach for a day of swimming, hot-dog roasting, soda pop drinking, and good clean fun. Then the class would bus home in the late afternoon. Some of us argued that it wasn't a "cut" day if we were being chaperoned by teachers, and Mr. Christensen finally agreed that if some "rowdy" students did not want to join the rest of the class, they could go their own way for the day. So Bobby and I and Billy Grant and Tiger Pat and Sky Richardson left the night before and camped at a remote beach with several cases of beer.

We reminisced and vowed everlasting friendship no matter where our futures might take us. The next day Bobby could not resist buzzing Dillon's Beach just once in his Chevy hot rod. Other than that small act of defiance, we kept well away from the sanctioned party.

"Dress-up Day" was the next traditional event that the seniors were allowed. Young men and women of the graduating class came to school dressed in zany outfits, and classes were not taken seriously on that day. Most girls costumed themselves in their fathers' clothes—often World War II uniforms—or in demure harem outfits, or as clowns. Though the faculty allowed us to dress up, they did not allow us to dress down. Strict dress codes were enforced—especially for the "young women," who were not allowed to wear shorts or swimming suits. Most of the boys didn't dress up with much imagination. They came to school as athletes, truck drivers, soldiers, or mill workers. Many boys took seriously the notion that they had become "young men" overnight. And in fact most of them were only three weeks away from having to earn a living. Very few boys and hardly any girls were college-bound.

My friends and I hatched a special Dress-up Day scenario. There was a large vacant lot across from the school that had recently been put up for sale, and we planned to camp on it as if we were migratory workers with no place else to go. Each of us—Bobby, Billy, Tiger Pat, Sky, Satchel Jack, and I—created a separate identity. Then we gathered all the equipment we would need for our "set" and moved it onto the lot in the dead of night before Dress-up Day. We erected a large, ragged tent to house us and strung clotheslines out to an outhouse made of wooden, slatted dehydrator trays. Bobby brought in his battered flatbed farm truck, and we decorated it with foxtails, mudflaps, and a sign that said, "For Sale. $450."

We rose before dawn and assumed our identities. Billy was the family patriarch, a World War II vet from Oklahoma who'd fallen on hard times. He wore tattered khakis and one of the Army Air Force mechanic Art's old caps that I lent him. Fair-headed Satchel Jack was the pregnant mother in a gingham dress, kerchief, and pillow strapped around his middle. The rest of us were their family. Tiger Pat and I were twins who dressed in faded work clothes and rope belts. Sky, a fat brother, wore huge overalls stuffed with padding so that he looked like a big, blue balloon with a straw hat. Bobby was the youngest brother—a half-witted guitar player.

We strung some clothes on the clothesline and, as dawn broke, Ralph Sandborn discovered us while walking to his custodian's job. He stopped, flabbergasted, and hollered to us threateningly: "Hey! Get out of there, you Okies! That's school property. You can't camp there. I'll call the police on you. Get out of that lot!" Ralph was too far away to tell we were not real and too timid to tackle us by himself, so he hurried toward the main buildings. We ignored him and busied ourselves cooking breakfast on our outdoor campfire. All of us spoke the Okie dialect fluently, and we had spent so much time on our costumes that unless you came up very close to us, you could not tell we weren't for real.

When the morning schoolbuses rolled by, we all waved from our campfire. Very few of our classmates waved back.

The faculty, by and large, were not amused. I do not think they knew whether we were serious or not about our homeless family, and that made them uncomfortable. They did not like students stirring up controversy or being "smart alecks." With few exceptions, they did not encourage originality at all. Vice-principal Osborne and Mrs. Long decided that Jack's impersonation of a pregnant woman was inappropriate and made him remove his pillow. When we grieved over our Mother's miscarriage, Mr. Osborne became even angrier. He accused us of ridiculing poor people.

Seventeen

T HE DAY I DECIDED TO BECOME AN ACTOR, I called Mother from college
to tell her. I said I was giving up my small athletic scholarship to
accept an even smaller drama scholarship, and Mother hung up on
me. Jesse called me back in a flash to tell me he was behind me.

But in the beginning, when I was first considering colleges, my main
concern was finding one with a good basketball program. Shortly after
Dress-up Day, Mother, Jesse, and I visited College of the Pacific in the San
Joaquin delta. I was armed with letters from my coaches and felt hopeful,
if not confident. But my confidence waned as we wound through the delta
on our way to California's Central Valley.

When we reached the college, my nerve was all but gone. C.O.P., as it
was commonly called, was a tranquil college set in the country north of
Stockton. It resembled an eastern school with its brick architecture and ivy
crawling over the buildings. It was very green because its sunken lawns
were watered by artesian springs.

C.O.P. was then a private liberal arts college administered by the
Methodist church, but the first two years of study were administered by
Stockton College, the adjoining junior college. Freshmen students were
housed, fed, and attended classes on the C.O.P. campus, however, if they
were enrolled there. The only exception to C.O.P.'s class participation for
freshmen and sophomores were its sports teams. Athletes played their first
two years for Stockton College before they were eligible to play for C.O.P.

In the afternoon, after a morning tour of the campus, I left my parents
sitting in the college gardens and walked to the athletic department offices.
I presented my letters to a graduate assistant who leafed through them—
rather amusedly I thought—and told me, "Our basketball scholarships were
filled long ago." I was about to leave when Van Sweet, the tall coach,

ducked his head and entered the office. Van verified the assistant's claim that no scholarships were available, but read my letters without laughing, and when he finished, said to me, "You're big for sixteen." We shook hands and I was walking out of the gym when he stopped me. He sounded as if he were as surprised as I was when he said, "Maybe we can help you out with some tuition. It wouldn't be much."

It wasn't much, but it salvaged my pride. I became a sort of special project for Van, and I disappointed him immensely the day I quit. But that was in the future. "I'll see you in September," was all Van said to me that day in May. When I rejoined my parents in the garden, Jesse grinned at my news. Mother was less enthusiastic, wondering whether my knees would hold up and whether basketball would interfere with my studies.

My sister Margaret was also preparing to graduate, along with seventy-eight classmates, from the elementary school. Margaret's friends filled her room while planning wardrobes and parties. The Pastels were singing at three upcoming events as well as at graduation, so our group filled my porch with music. Then suddenly it seemed as if I would not graduate at all. Billy, Bobby, and I had all grown goatees and Mr. Christensen had ordered us to shave them off before graduation. One week before the ceremony I had not complied and was sent home from school with a final, written ultimatum. What happened between my father and me that afternoon is clearly etched in my memory.

First I informed Mother that the principal refused to budge and so I wouldn't be graduating. I told her it didn't matter because I had other plans.

Mother didn't stick around to hear my plans, but went straight out and into the garage. I knew she would sit crying, waiting for me to come out and apologize and say I'd changed my mind. Or, better yet, for me to come out minus my goatee.

Jesse was due home at any time and I knew there was no use trying to hide from him, so I went out and sat on the back stoop. I thought Jesse might even side with me since there was a principle involved. Probably not, though. He and Margaret would give me the silent treatment until I broke down and went out and apologized to Mother. But I promised myself I wasn't going to do that.

Mother began crying loudly, but I wasn't going to give in this time. There wasn't any rule that said you couldn't graduate from high school if you had a goatee.

Besides, I had an ace up my sleeve that might just bring Jesse around to my way of thinking. I'd miss the big graduation party, of course. I'd miss playing in the summer softball league, and, most of all, I knew I'd miss playing college basketball. But you had to fight for what was right. Wasn't that what my mother and father had taught me?

Finally I heard the front door open and close, and I knew Jesse was going into the bedroom to hang up his hat. None of the teachers, except Jesse, wore hats any more and it always puzzled me that no one ever made fun of him for it.

When he came outside I saw he was still wearing his shiny slacks and his old sport coat. He hadn't even taken the time to change into his gardening clothes. Mother was crying very loudly.

He walked about halfway out to the garage and stopped, as if weighing something in his mind. My mother must have heard him standing out there on the gravel walkway, because her crying dropped to a steady sobbing.

Finally he looked at me and said, "I don't guess I have to ask you why your mother's in there crying. I see you've still got that fuzz on your face."

That stung me. It was a pretty good goatee, and with a little black shoe polish on it, it didn't look like fuzz at all. "They made their final decision. You might as well know it. They're not going to let me graduate unless I shave it off, and I'm not about to do that. There's no law that says you have to be clean-shaved to graduate. They're picking on me because I won't conform. Besides, I don't care. I've got other, better plans."

Jesse looked heaven-ward. "I'm sure you have," he said.

"I have...I..."

"Hold your horses," Jesse said. "Just hold your horses. Let's forget about your plans for a minute and talk about your—uh—goatee. What's so important about it?"

"Aw, Dad, it's not just the goatee; it's the principle of the thing. Don't you see that?"

"That's not what I mean. I mean, why a goatee? Why not a nose ring or green hair if you want to be different?"

"You miss the whole point, Dad," I said. "I didn't grow this thing just to be different or rebellious. Do you remember telling me about Pompeii Williams?"

Jesse heaved a sigh and shook his head. He must have figured he was in for a longer session than he had originally thought because he came over and sat next to me on the stoop. "Now what has Pompeii Williams got to do with it?" he asked.

"Well, remember how you said he was your best friend in school when you were growing up in Kansas? And how all the other kids used to yell at you when they saw you together—'Nigger and a White! Nigger and a White!' Remember you told me how big he was and how much you admired him for never whipping the white kids, but just being proud to be who he was and content in himself and proud of his race?"

"Yes, but I never said Pompeii was very bright either."

"I know, but it's his race I'm talking about. The reason they won't let me graduate is pure racial prejudice, I know it. Bob and Billy and I grew our goatees because we listen to jazz and all the great musicians have them. Dizzy and Charlie Parker and Thelonius Monk. What's wrong with that?"

"Well," Jesse said, "I've known Bud Christiensen for a long time and, to tell you the truth, I don't believe he knows Thelonius Monk from Theodore Roosevelt or Dizzy Gillespie from Dizzy Dean. I just think he feels that if he lets you and Billy and Bob wear your goatees to graduation, he'll open the door for stranger things than a little facial hair at commencements. You've got to draw the line somewhere. Even Pompeii shaved off his whiskers and put on his Sunday suit for church—albeit the suit was way too small for him." He smiled faintly at the remembrance of it.

"Actually," I conceded the point, "Billy and Bob shaved off their goatees yesterday."

"Did they now?" Jesse didn't seem surprised. "Well, sometimes discretion is the better part of valor. After all, they've got all summer to grow them back if they want to."

"The important thing isn't the goatee, Dad. To tell you the truth, I'd probably shave mine off too if I didn't have this plan. I'm excited about it and I think you'll understand. It's the chance of a lifetime, and if I go ahead with it I won't need to graduate."

"Don't tell me," Jesse said, "you're going to start pulling green chain tomorrow at the sawmill and work your way up to a forklift operator's job."

"Seriously, Dad," I was getting pumped up now. "You remember Earl Colcutt, don't you?"

"Earl? Sure I remember Earl. He worked himself up out of a bad situation at home and was making something out of himself last I heard. What about Earl?"

"Aw, come on, Dad, he went to sea. He fixed it so Powell Grant could ship out too."

"I know that, Dave," Jesse said quietly.

"Powell came by the school today between trips. He said Earl has got his third mate's papers and is going to be a permanent mate on the Pacific Far East Line."

There wasn't any response from Jesse.

"Listen, Dad, Powell said I could go back with him to San Francisco, and he'd get me into the maritime school at the Sailors' Union of the Pacific like Earl did for him. I could start lifeboat school right away, he said."

"So that's the plan, eh?"

"I thought you'd be happy, Dad. You always wanted to go to sea. You told me so yourself."

Jesse sighed. Sometimes he could seem very old and very tired. "No, Dave, I never said that. What I said was that at one time I wanted to run away to sea. I also wanted to run away and be a gypsy or a tragic actor once. Mostly, I guess, I just wanted to run away. I guess there's a time in every boy's life when he wants to do that. Tell me, Dave, are you scared?"

That surprised me. "Scared? No, of course I'm not scared. Of graduation, you mean? Why should I be scared?"

"No, I don't mean of graduation. I mean of what comes after graduation. Because I'd understand that—if you were scared."

"What have I got to be scared about? I've got the scholarship. I've been accepted. I just don't want to go to college, that's all. I've always wanted to go to sea—to see the world—to do all the things you wanted to do and never did."

"Listen, Dave, what I wanted most of all was to get away from that damn farm in Kansas. Any way I could. And the best and most permanent way I knew how to do that was to get an education."

I guess Jesse thought he might be getting a little hard on me, which wasn't his way; or maybe he was just being thoughtful, remembering. Anyway, he continued in a milder tone, "When I wanted to go off to sea it was because an old sailor used to come to visit with the farmer and get drunk. He didn't have any money and drank the farmer's whisky and he lived in a boarding house in town and swamped out the saloon. The gypsies used to camp by the creek and they were dirty and uncouth, ignorant folks who taught their children to steal. When I decided I wanted to be an actor, I'd seen a troupe in town drumming up business for their travelling show. They were all pretty down-at-the-heel too. Of course, I didn't realize all this clearly until I'd gotten an education and could see it all in perspective."

"But you wanted to be an artist. You told me that. After you finished college, you wanted to be an artist." Looking at Jesse in his old teaching clothes, his glasses and his balding head, he looked less like an artist than anyone I'd ever seen.

"Yes, son, yes, I always wanted to be an artist. And I'll tell you the truth, it almost broke my heart when I chose to give it up. But all those years of walking five miles to school on muddy or dusty country roads just got to me somehow. I wasn't prepared to walk the streets of New York peddling my drawings with holes in my shoes and no raincoat. I figured I'd done enough suffering for an education and I wasn't going to suffer any more for my art."

"Are you telling me you were scared?"

"No, son, I was scared sure enough about going to college, but I wasn't scared when I made my decision to become a teacher and not an artist. That was a hard, but conscious choice. And it was education that gave me the freedom to make that choice."

"So you think I ought to graduate." It was a statement, not a question.

"What'll it cost you besides your goatee?" Jesse asked. "You can always go to sea afterward. But I think you should try college too. Who knows, maybe you'll learn enough to be a sea captain, or a fine actor, or a writer who's a gypsy of sorts."

"Not an artist?" I asked, and smiled for the first time. Jesse and I both knew that I had about as much talent as an artist as Margaret Truman did as an opera singer.

"No, no, I think you can scratch that career right now," Jesse said, smiling too.

"Well, OK," I said, "I'll go ahead and graduate, but I won't promise anything after that."

"What about the scholarship?"

"Well, I might try college for a semester—see how I like it. How does that sound?"

"Sounds like a wise decision to me."

"Choice," I said.

"Right. Choice."

Jesse and I sat silently on the stoop for a few more minutes. June was a wonderful month in Healdsburg. The late afternoon sun was still warm as it descended in the west; it made you lazy enough to take a nap. Suddenly, as if taken by the same thought, we both realized that the sobbing from the garage had stopped.

"I forgot all about Mom. Do you want me to go get her?"

"No, I'll fetch her," Jesse said, standing up. "I can probably explain things more quickly and maybe we can help her get supper on time. That'll give her a boost. Why don't you go set the table. If we hurry, maybe she won't put the chops in the pressure cooker."

I started to go inside, then stopped and watched my father head out to the garage. Jesse bent over and picked a flower before he opened the door.

With that settled, there was nothing left but to face our final week of activities before Saturday's graduation ceremony. The *Sotoyomans* we had ordered were delivered and we spent a lot of time getting teachers and other students to sign them. I only remember three inscriptions: Nancie took up a page telling me she loved me; Mrs. Long, who never signed student annuals but could not refuse in 1950 because we had dedicated the book to her, wrote brief messages for other seniors, but in mine just signed "Irene Long"; and Coach Art scrawled—next to a picture of himself with a whistle around his neck—"Wish you had one more year."

On Tuesday the Class of '50 were guests of the Kiwanis Club at a luncheon at the American Legion Hall. On Wednesday we had a Senior Breakfast at the golf course clubhouse. On Friday afternoon we all returned to school for the long-awaited awards assembly for seniors.

In a special graduation issue, the *Tribune* carried a picture of the Class of '50 on its front page and listed all the awards. By any calculation, Gloria Pedroncelli (of the Pedroncelli wine family) scored a clean sweep. She received a $100 scholarship to San Jose State College, a Bank of America Certificate of Excellence in social science, and another Bank of America award for general excellence in the liberal arts. Our other class valedictorian received a *Reader's Digest* subscription, and the senior who had introduced the Key Club to the high school was awarded a plaque for being the outstanding senior student-citizen by the Kiwanis Club. In a mild surprise, the Greyhound trophy, which recognized athletic ability, citizenship, and sportsmanship, was awarded to Wally Wood. Stan Smith, who should have won the Greyhound trophy, accepted the championship tennis trophy. In another surprise, Bill "The Heap" Rich, Nancie's brother, won a scholarship to St. Mary's College. The irony that Bill's attendance at St. Mary's would make him eligible to court Nancy Moran was not lost on me.

Very few of my classmates planned on any further education. In the graduation issue, the *Tribune* editors recommended that graduates stay closer to home and not leave for "greener pastures."

Graduation night itself was anticlimactic. The gymnasium was crowded and hot, and many people had to stand in the aisles. My partner for the processional was the only married girl in our class and worked part-time in the principal's office. I suspected this was prearranged so that I wouldn't pull some stunt in revenge for having had to shave off my goatee. The valedictory speeches, coached by Mrs. Long for content and by

Miss Petty for dramatic effect, were dull. Our quartet sang "Were You There When They Crucified My Lord?" which seems a strange choice in retrospect. There was no organized class party afterward. Eighty-nine of us marched out of the gym and went our separate ways.

My friends and our girlfriends went out to Sky Richardson's ranch for a swimming pool party that lasted until dawn. Bobby and Tiger Pat were there. Billy Grant was invited, but since Powell was in town he went off somewhere with the remnants of the Frantomellis. When the sun came up, Nancie and I drove in to Lonnie's Coffee Shop for breakfast. The cafe was full of boozy graduates. I drove Nancie home and went home myself, parking the Plymouth carefully in the garage, and that was the end of it.

******

That summer Gil and I pulled green chain in a planing mill far out on Mill Creek. The Heap, Satchel Jack St. Martin, and one of the Giacomelli twins made up the rest of our crew on the swing shift. Gil and I spent afternoons at the beach, and as often as not went to work at 4:30 P.M. in our wet swimming trunks. After our shift ended at midnight, we sat in Gil's car and talked until three or four in the morning. Toward summer's end, I ran into Nancy Moran at a band concert, and we went off downriver to Mirabel Park. We made a date to meet in September at San Francisco's Kezar Stadium when College of Pacific played St. Mary's. The next day I broke up with Nancie Rich over the phone. It hurts me now more than it did then when I record that she pleaded with me not to hang up on her because she was alone and crying in a phone booth and could not face stepping outside of it to walk home.

The Korean War began to claim local boys' lives. Some of my classmates began to be killed in action and were tallied up in the *Tribune*. The transfer student to whom I lost the student body presidency was killed when his bomber was shot down. Bubby, who upset Brucc Holbrook in the boxing show, died at the Cho Sin reservoir. Rita Rose's brother was blinded by mortar fire. Before the year was out, Gil, Bobby, and Tiger Pat would all be in the Army.

Ralph Sandborn realized his dream of becoming Fitch Mountain's constable when the incumbent quit the job. Floyd Darby was found in Buffalo, New York. He had been missing for thirteen months, and authorities said he was too ill to be brought back to stand trial for grand theft since he recently underwent cancer surgery. It was revealed that Darby absconded with more than $51,000 from a trust fund he had managed and was using the alias of Rex Baggett. He was traced to a hospital through his letters and telephone calls to Bay Area friends.

Jesse wrote to Bill several weeks after I went away to college. The letter said, in part, "David is going to college in Stockton and seems to be enjoying his work a great deal. I hope the present enthusiasm continues throughout the year. He is very young to be in college, but he seems to be quite well adjusted to the new mode of living. Going to college now isn't what it used to be 'when you and I were young, Maggie.'"

I am not sure what my father meant, but I was not a distinguished college student. After several years of academic life I decided that the proper study of acting was real people, and for that a Greyhound bus station was as good a laboratory as a college campus. I played a succession of athletic leads like Stanley Kowalski, Charlie Castle, and Liliom in and around San Francisco after I'd left C.O.P. and San Francisco State College. Jesse had been right about Mother coming to terms with my choice of a career, and they always drove down from Healdsburg to attend my performances. But Jesse seemed about as excited over my dramatic characterizations as he had over my basketball prowess.

Then one spring, in Berkeley, I played the part of a drug addict in a production of *A Hatful of Rain*. Handsome Johnny was a weak young man, made out to be a hero by his wife, brother, and especially by his father. They made every imaginable excuse for his morphine addiction. In the end, Johnny admits that he is less than he appears to be, that he is above all afraid, and he asks for help. The role was very difficult for me. It was easy enough to build a strong, confident character, but hard to orchestrate his disintegration. The Berkeley theater was tiny and cramped, and the audience was practically forced to become a member of our stage family. Mom and Dad dutifully drove down to the East Bay to attend a performance one Saturday night, and after the play Jesse seemed subdued. Then he hugged me—a gesture I was so unprepared for that I could not even respond. He collected himself and said only, "That was damn good."

The Berkeley theater owner and three others, including myself, opened a summer stock theater at Bridge Bay Resort on Lake Shasta the following summer. Mom and Dad passed through to see me for a day on their way to the Willamette Valley in Oregon. It was the first real vacation they had ever taken, and they were very happy. Two weeks after their visit I was sitting in my cabin blocking a play I was scheduled to direct, when one of my partners came to the door with the bad news. Jesse and Mother had stopped on their way home from Oregon at a friend's farm. The farmer was baling hay and Jesse, perhaps remembering his youth in Kansas, pitched in to help. Those who were there say that Dad suddenly stood up straight, turned to face my mother, smiled a radiant smile, and fell dead of a heart attack.

I took a day off from rehearsals and drove to Healdsburg for my father's funeral. St. Paul's was packed and Jesse's friends spilled out into the street. Mr. Kent spoke simply, and the little choir sang that gentle hymn, "The King of Love My Shepherd Is, Whose Goodness Faileth Never…"

I drove north again. In those days I still believed that the show must go on, no matter what. So did Mother, for she wrote to Bill and Ide in August, 1958: "We are getting along well. Jess left everything in good order. We went down to the Chapel of the Chimes last week and arranged for the urn to be put in the velvety green of the Garden of Memory. Somehow it seemed a more natural place for Jess—under the sky, with the gurgling fountain, the breeze lifting the branches of the trees overhead, the fog, sun and rain coming down. I arranged to be next to him."

The typing in this paragraph was erratic, the words misspelled. But Mother's concluding paragraph was typed clearly: "Only three weeks until school starts—four for Margaret. It will really be good to get back into the routine. Even though my evenings will be a bit bleak until I get used to it— I don't want to get used to it immediately. A good person should be missed! But it won't depress me—be sure of that!"

At the close of the summer stock season I left for Hollywood. I took with me Jesse's pocket watch, his penknife, and his high-muckety-muck ring from the Knights of Pythias.

Shirley and the kids, Nicholas and Sarah.